# TABLE OF CONTENTS

# QUICK GUIDE TRADES FOR RESIDENTIAL, BUILDING & GENERAL CONTRACTORS

## STATE AND LOCAL LICENSURE REQUIREMENTS

https://floridaconstructionschool.teachable.com/p/florida-construction-ce

www.myfloridalicense.com/dbpr/pro/division/servicesthatrequirealicense_construction.html

*To View Videos*
https://floridaconstructionschool.teachable.com/p/florida-construction-ce

## CONTRACTORS

A Contractor is someone who demolishes, subtracts from, builds or improves any building or structure for compensation. Examples of compensation are cash, goods, services, etc. Essentially, if you pay someone to construct a building or a structure, make structural alterations to load bearing walls, or perform services such as plumbing or air conditioning work, that person has to have a state contractors' license.

These items are offered as examples of services you do need to hire a person with a Florida license and services you do not need to hire a person with a Florida license. The list is not all inclusive. If you have specific questions, please contact the department at 850.487.1395 or review the rules for the profession at www.myfloridalicense.com. You should also check with your county or city to learn whether or not a local business tax receipt or certificate of competency is required for services that do not require a state license. Please visit our Unlicensed Activity page to learn more about how you can help us combat Unlicensed Activity.

| *Needs a License* | *Does not need a license* |
|---|---|
| Build a carport or sunroom for compensation. | Install a driveway or install pavers/tile walkways regardless of compensation. |
| Construct a roof for compensation. | Install awnings that do not become a fixed part of the structure regardless of compensation. |
| Install a dishwasher (requires connecting to drinking water) or replace a hot-water heater for compensation. | Add a water filter onto a faucet regardless of compensation. |
| Install a central air-conditioning unit for compensation (requires structural work and wiring). | Insert a plug-in A/C window unit regardless of compensation. |
| Clean central air and heat ducts for compensation (requires partial disassembly of the system, such as removal of air grills). | Change an A/C filter or cleaning ducts that do not require removal of the air grills regardless of compensation. |
| Repair or replace swimming pool pumps for compensation. | Clean swimming pools. |
| Install an above-ground pool regardless of compensation. | |
| Perform plumbing work or irrigation installation that requires the contractor to connect lines to potable (drinking) water for compensation. | Install or repair irrigation systems that have a backflow preventer connected to a potable (drinking) water supply regardless of compensation. |
| Build a barn, metal building, or detached garage for compensation. | Install prefabricated tool shed less than 250 square feet in size regardless of compensation. The shed may be up to 400 square feet if it bears the insignia of approval from the Department of Community Affairs. |
| Remodel a home that requires alteration or replacement of a load-bearing wall for compensation. | Paint; install cabinets, wood or tile flooring, and insulation regardless of compensation. |
| Installation or replacement of drywall if the contract also includes work on the load bearing part of the wall, plumbing, electrical, or air conditioning work. | Installation or replacement of drywall if the contract does not include other work on the load bearing part of the wall or any plumbing, electrical, or air conditioning work. |

## SCOPE OF CONTRACTOR LICENSE

There are three categories of licenses in Florida for all-around builders and then there are 'specialty licenses' for narrow categories like pool contractors, roofing contractors, etc.

A **General Contractor license** allows building construction that is unlimited as to the type and size of the construction project.

A **Building Contractor licensee** is one whose services are limited to the construction of commercial buildings and single dwelling or multiple dwelling residential buildings. These buildings cannot exceed 3 stories in height. A building contractor may also construct the accessory use structures in connection with these buildings. An accessory use structure would be a garage, guesthouse, garden shed, or other outbuilding.

This license also allows remodeling, repair, or improvements of any building – If the services do not affect the structural elements of the building.

A **Residential Contractor licensee** is one whose services are limited to the construction, remodeling, repair, or improvement of 1 family, 2 family, or 3 family residences, which are not more than 2 stories in height. It also covers the accessory use structures in connection with these buildings. An accessory use structure would be a garage, guesthouse, garden shed, or other outbuilding.

## JOB COMPLETION SCHEDULES

*See Job completion schedules in Guide to Accounting*

| Task Name | Start | End | Duration (days) |
|---|---|---|---|
| Start date | 9/21/2014 | 9/30/2014 | 9 |
| Demo Prep | 10/1/2014 | 10/6/2014 | 5 |
| Demolition | 10/6/2014 | 10/24/2014 | 18 |
| Excavation | 10/25/2014 | 10/29/2014 | 4 |
| Concrete | 11/1/2014 | 11/13/2014 | 12 |
| Pre backfill | 11/13/2014 | 11/15/2014 | 2 |
| Framing | 10/25/2014 | 12/5/2014 | 41 |
| Roof | 11/19/2014 | 12/10/2014 | 21 |
| Plumbing | 10/29/2014 | 12/9/2014 | 41 |
| Windows | 11/22/2014 | 12/15/2014 | 23 |
| HVAC | 11/29/2014 | 12/20/2014 | 21 |
| Electrical | 12/10/2014 | 12/22/2014 | 12 |
| A/V | 12/10/2014 | 12/15/2014 | 5 |
| House wrap | 12/27/2014 | 12/30/2014 | 3 |
| Insulation | 12/3/2014 | 12/21/2014 | 18 |
| Drywall | 1/3/2015 | 1/23/2015 | 20 |
| Exterior stone | 1/3/2015 | 1/17/2015 | 14 |
| Exterior case work | 1/4/2015 | 1/13/2015 | 9 |
| Laundry/furnace room flooring | 2/16/2015 | 3/11/2015 | 23 |
| Hardwoods | 1/19/2015 | 3/10/2015 | 50 |
| Tile | 2/3/2015 | 2/14/2015 | 11 |

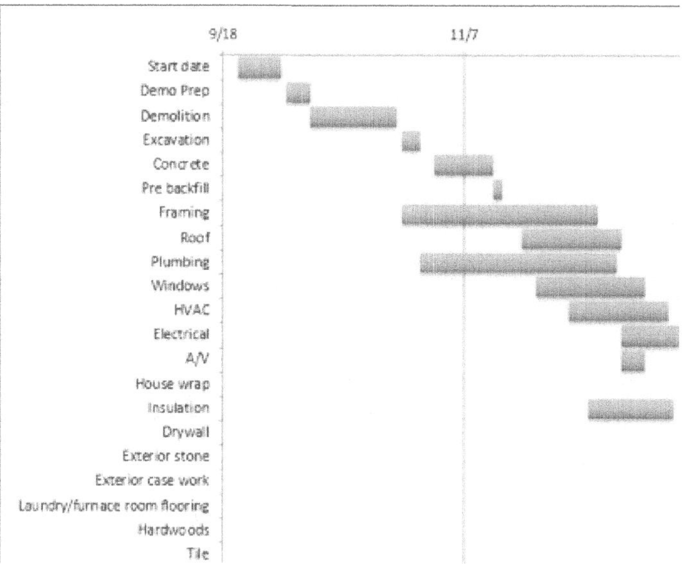


The draw schedule is a detailed payment plan for a construction project. If a bank is financing the project, the draw schedule determines when the bank will disburse funds to you and the contractor.

The goal is to make progress payments to the contractor as work is completed. You don't want to pay for materials that have not been delivered or work that is not complete. It's not your job to provide working capital for the contractor. (If you are an owner-builder, the draw schedule will determine when the bank releases money to you to pay for materials and subcontractors.)

Draw schedules are typically proposed by the contractor and may be further negotiated between the contractor, the bank, and yourself. If a bank is involved, they may want to use their own standardized draw schedule. But in any case, the bank's appraiser will make sure the draw schedule is reasonable based on his knowledge of construction costs. If you are paying cash, you will need to do your own independent estimate (or hire an estimator or appraiser to review the draw schedule), or trust that the contractor's proposed payment schedule it is reasonable.

The number of payments in the draw schedule will depend on the size of the project and the preferences of the builder or bank. A draw schedule of five to seven payments is common for a new house.

Most draw schedules link payments with milestones in the project, such as completion of the foundation and completion of the rough framing. Sometimes, the draws are more generally based on the percent complete of the total job. In either case, the payment should be roughly equal to the value of the work completed. These line-item values have been determined by the owner or builder in their detailed estimate, and are summarized in budget breakdown called a schedule of values. This cost breakdown will also become your project budget. If you are working with a lender, contact them first to see if they have a specific format to follow.

## SCHEDULE OF VALUES

To avoid conflicts over payment, it's important that the draw schedule closely reflect the actual value of work completed. The schedule of values can be highly detailed or pretty basic, depending on the type and size of project and the financing arrangements. In either case, a good draw schedule is based on an accurate, detailed estimate, and the resulting schedule of values:

See FLA XTRA 2 9 JOB COMP SCHED New Home Schedule of Values.

Sample Schedule of Values for a 2000 sq. ft. Custom Home

| | Cost | % of total |
|---|---|---|
| Plans and specs | $2,000 | 1 |
| Permits, fees, inspections | 4,000 | 2 |
| Impact fee | 3,000 | 1.5 |
| Clear lot, rough grade | 1,500 | 1 |
| Survey | 1,000 | 0.5 |
| Water hookup and fees | 3000 | 1.5 |
| Sewer hookup and fees | 3000 | 1.5 |
| Well, pump, hookup, and water treatment | NA | |
| Septic system and hookup | NA | |
| Excavation and backfill | 4,000 | 2 |
| Foundation and flatwork | 12,000 | 6 |
| Rough Framing | 31,000 | 15 |
| Windows | 6,000 | 3 |
| Exterior doors and hardware | 2,000 | 1 |
| Roofing | 5,000 | 2.5 |
| Siding and ext. trim | 10,000 | 5 |
| Gutters and downspouts | 1,000 | 0.5 |
| Plumbing rough-in | 9,000 | 4.5 |
| Electrical rough-in | 8,000 | 4 |
| HVAC | 8,000 | 4 |
| Insulation | 3,000 | 1.5 |
| Drywall | 10,000 | 5 |
| Stairs | 3,000 | 1.5 |
| Interior trim | 7,000 | 3.5 |

| | | |
|---|---|---|
| Interior doors | 2,000 | 1 |
| Painting interior/exterior | 7,000 | 3.5 |
| Cabinets and countertops | 12,000 | 6 |
| Appliances | NA | |
| Lighting Fixtures | 2,000 | 1 |
| Plumbing Fixtures | 4,000 | 2 |
| Floor coverings: wood, tile, carpet, vinyl | 12,000 | 6 |
| Garage doors and opener | 2,000 | 1 |
| Porch, wood deck, or patio | 5,500 | 3 |
| Driveway and walkways | 6,000 | 3 |
| Landscaping | 6,000 | 3 |
| Other | 5,000 | 2.5 |
| TOTAL CONSTRUCTION COST | $200,000 | |

Note: Add $30,000 to $40,000 (15% to 20%) for contractor's overhead and profit, plus an additional $6,000 (3%) for construction financing, and an additional 5% for sales and marketing, if purchased from a developer.

The sample above is based on a typical, small custom home. The numbers, of course, will vary enormously, depending on a wide variety of factors, including the size and quality of the home, the materials selected, and the location. But the numbers in this sample are typical for an average new home, and will give you a sense of where the money goes, and where you may be able to cut if your house comes in over budget and you need to make cuts.

If the estimate was done by you, the owner, the numbers will represent your actual cost for materials and labor. If your contractor does the estimate, these numbers will be as much as 20% to 25% higher, accounting for the contractor's overhead and profit.

## THE PAYMENT SCHEDULE

Banks distribute money for a project in several payments as the work progresses. While procedures vary a bit from lender to lender, all follow the general principal that the bank does not want to pay for work that has not been completed. (Nor should you if you are funding the project with your own cash!)

A typical draw schedule for a new home has five to seven payments, but some may disburse money as frequently as once a week. Most draw schedules link payments to the "substantial completion" of a phase of work such as the foundation or rough framing. Some correspond more generally to the percent of completion of the entire project, a more difficult number to track, leaving greater room for disagreement. A bank draw schedule is generally more complex than a cash job. Compare the draw schedule in Fannie Mae's model Construction Loan Agreement to the samples below from owner-financed projects.

| | | |
|---|---|---|
| Sample Draw Schedule: Small Remodeling Project | | |
| (owner-financed) | | |
| | Work Completed | Amount |
| Draw 1 | Demolition | 3,000 |
| Draw 2 | Framing, wiring and plumbing rough-in, insulation. | $6,000 |
| Draw 3 | Drywall, windows, cabinets. | 6,000 |
| Draw 4 | Patch exterior, painting, flooring, fixtures, cleanup. | 5,000 |

| Sample Draw Schedule: Custom Home or Addition(owner financed) | | |
|---|---|---|
| | Work Completed | Amount |
| Draw 1 Foundation | Plans and specifications, permits, excavation, footings, foundation. | $37,500 (15%) |
| Draw 2 Rough Framing | Wall and roof framed and sheathed. Subflooring, interior partitions. | $37,500 (15%) |
| Draw 3 Dry In | Asphalt shingle roofing, wood siding, windows, exterior doors. | $37,500 (15%) |
| Draw 4 Rough In | Rough HVAC, electrical, plumbing. Set tubs and shower. Insulation. Flatwork. | $30,000 (12%) |
| Draw 5 Trim Out | Drywall, interior doors, cabinets, countertops, interior trim, finish flooring. | $50,000 (20%) |
| Draw Substantial. Completion | Exterior trim, gutters, water and sewer hookups, finish plumbing and electric, carpeting, garage doors. | $45,000 (18%) |
| Draw 7 Retainage | Substantial Completion | $12,500 (5%) |

**Payment for work completed.** The contractor, naturally, is in a rush to get paid for work completed and would like to be a little ahead to have some working capital. You and the bank, on the other hand, only want to pay for materials delivered and work completed. It's not your job, or the bank's, to provide the contractor with working capital. However, some jobs do require more money than normal upfront, for example, to for costly special-order items such as SIPs (structural insulated panels).

Simply put, the contractor is afraid of not getting paid for work completed or materials he has purchased and the owner (and bank) is afraid of paying ahead of time for work that may never be done or done incorrectly.

A good draw schedule strikes a reasonable balance between the builder's need to get paid on time and the owner's and bank's need to pay only for work completed. The key is to have a payment plan that based on an accurate budget, fair to all parties, and easy to follow. In that case, there should be few problems with payments.

**Front-loading.** Some builders like to front-load the payment schedule to improve their cash flow and to act as a buffer in case, for any reason, the owner withholds the final check. They may ask for a large down payment, or simply fatten the early draws to stay ahead of their expenses. Another ploy is to link payments to the beginning, not the completion, of a phase of work. This is risky for you since many things can be started without any being completed.

For example, if $20,000 is due at the start of Rough-In, it doesn't mean that the siding has been installed even though it was paid for in the previous draw. This benefits the contractor, but can leave the owner far ahead on payments. Banks will not approved this type of payment schedule and neither should you if you are paying cash.

## DISBURSING THE FUNDS

The most common approach is to make payments contingent on substantial completion of key phases of construction, such as the foundation or rough frame. Banks send an inspector to approve each payment and charge an inspection fee of $50 to $100. If no bank is involved, you (or your construction manager) will want to stop by to confirm that the reported progress is being made.

"Substantial completion" means that the payment request if valid even if a few 2x4s are missing from an otherwise complete frame. The contractor should not request a payment before it is due, and you should not nitpick a few loose ends. An exception is the final check, which should not be released until everything is complete and correct.

**Title companies.** Some bankers use a title company to conduct the inspections and disperse funds. This adds more fees and delays payments, so discuss the pros and cons of this procedure with your lender, as you may be able to opt out of using a title company and handle the disbursements yourself.

**Lien wavers.** Assuming the inspection passes, the proper documentation is supplied, and the general contractor signs a lien waver, the funds will be wired to the builder's account, minus the 5% to 10% held back for retainage. The bank may require other lien wavers, for example, from key subcontractors, or the largest supplier, before the last check is released. Even without a lender involved, you will want to get lien wavers from the general contractor and main suppliers, at least before cutting the final check.

**Change orders.** It is in the best interests of all parties to keep the work on schedule, pass all inspections, and avoid changes to the plan. Some banks will not pay for change orders, which can be a good thing as it motivates the builder to make sure nothing essential is left out of his bid. If the owners decide to add a $3,000 jetted tub or to upgrade from carpet to hardwood floors, they will have to come up with the cash out of pocket.

**Final payment.** Generally, progress payments are made directly from the lender to the contractor, while the final check is made jointly payable to the owner and contractor after all work is complete and certificate of occupancy (CO) has been issued. The joint check, requiring both endorsements to cash, gives you, the owner, some leverage to get the contractor to take care of any punch list items, or other loose ends before handing over the final check.

**Conflicts over payment.** While most projects with a reputable builder proceed pretty smoothly, occasionally bad things happen. A contractor can skip town or go bankrupt, a sub can show up drunk or not at all, an innovative building system may not work out as planned, or the new super-duper paint specified for the project peeled off the new wood siding for some reason.

## CONTRACTS

Contracts are agreements made between two or more parties that are legally binding. Bid invitations and RFPs are not contracts, according to the AIA. Some contracts may be or oral, but this is rarely advisable. The typical language used in contracts is a boilerplate. When contracts are unclear, the judgment will be against the party who created it

### *Contract Requirements:*

- Offer & acceptance
- Consideration (payment)
- Competent parties & legal purpose

### *Typical Key Sections:*

- Agreement
- General conditions
- Special conditions
- Technical specifications
- Drawings

Failure to comply with a contract is a breach. There are different types of breaches, which may be material or immaterial. Liquidated or stated damages will appear in the contract, and any financial loss is considered a damage.

The contract is considered accepted once it is signed. The contract will outline the method of payment such as progress payments, which are partial payments made after certain phases of work. The engineer or architect determines when the job is finished. Retainage is money withheld from these payments until the project is finished and is used to make sure the project is done while protecting the owner from liens.

Contracts terms, conditions and services are the responsibility of the contract manager who must enforce them. The contract manager acts as a liaison between the organization and the contract provider. Other responsibilities include:

- Monitor the progress of the contractor

- Make sure that payments are promptly made
- Periodically inspect the goods and services
- Hold meetings with the contractor
- Keep records of exchanges with the contractor
- Inform the contractor of dissatisfaction in writing
- Use appropriate methods to collect feedback
- Resolve issues
- Involve senior management when necessary

Contract managers may have to manage changes and make sure that they follow the conditions of the contract. All information involving the construction is kept in the Contract Management File.

Contract administration is the act of determining how well the contract activities meet the requirements. It requires working closely with the contractor until job ends with payment, termination, or contract resolution. Responsibilities include:

- Inform the contractor that work should begin
- Monitor construction activities
- Review all necessary reports
- Provide documentation that accepts deliverables
- Oversee spending
- Validate and approve invoices
- Make renewals or amendments when necessary
- Confirm that work is complete
- Complete closeout activities

Contract administration duties and degree of involvement will vary with different contracts. They must understand the contract documents well enough to communicate clearly on the subject, and they must understand the accounting process. Legal resources should be consulted with questions or problematic behavior from suppliers.

The contract administration process begins with post award orientation that establishes clear communication between the contractor and administrator. A pre meeting with involved officials should be done before the orientation to establish the specific responsibilities.

### CMP

Contract Management Plans (CMP) outline how contracts will be managed, and they are the responsibility of contract managers. They are no required, but they are encouraged. A CMP is considered a living document that needs to be reviewed periodically. A CMP will establish the following:

- Methods to monitor contractor work
- The party who will oversee the approve contractor work
- The processes to request, modify or approve work
- Establish audits and inspections
- Determine the financial audits to be used
- Methods to approve contractor payments

- Hoe to manage documents and records

Single contracts are traditionally used in the construction industry. They provide a clear relationship, but the owner has less control over the day-to-day activities. Multiple contracts involve separate contracts for different aspects of the project and may be required in certain projects. Coordinating multiple contracts is the job of the contract manager.

### *AIA*

The guidelines of the AIA are typically used in contracts. Conditions that the AIA and the AGC recommend are: General Provisions; the Stop Work Procedures and Owner Responsibility; Claims Procedures and Architect Responsibility; Shop Drawing Procedures and Contractor Responsibility; Subcontractor Responsibility; Work Procedure Changes; Owner or Separate Contractor Construction; Timing and Extensions; Protection of Property and Safety of People; Procedures for Completion and Payment; Bond and Insurance Descriptions; Laws, Tests, and inspections; Work Correction; and Terminating/Suspending Contracts.

The AIA provides many standards forms and contract documents, such as:

- AIA A101 – is used in lump sum contracts between two parties.
- AIA A102 – is used to establish Guaranteed Maximum Price Contracts.
- AIA A103 – is used in contracts like cost plus that do not have GMP.
- AIA A107 – is used in any situation with a small, inexpensive project.
- AIA A132-2009 – is used to establish the cost of work along with Exhibit A.
- AIA A133-2009 – includes a GMP amendment.
- AIA A134-2009 – is used in basic payments such as Cost of Work Plus Fee.
- AIA A401 – is used after contracts are awarded and include the form, schedules, conditions, and scope of work. Payments, and project conditions.

### *EJCDC*

The EJCDC and the AGC include the following articles in their recommendations: Preliminary Matters; Definitions; Bonds and Insurance; Intent, Reuse, and Amendment of Contract Documents; Land Availability and Physical Subsurface Conditions; Insurance and Bonds; Contractor and Owner Responsibilities; Engineer Status; Work Changes; Price Changes; Time Changes; Contractor Payment and Completion Procedures; Inspections and Tests; Disputation Resolution; Defective Work Removal, Correction, or Acceptance; Work Suspension/Termination.

The EJCDC also provides the standard contract documents:

- C-700 – outlines the general conditions of the contract.
- C-550 – called the Notice to Proceed, it establishes the date and time.
- C-610 – acts as a Performance Bond.
- C-615 – acts as the Payment Bond.
- C-620 – called the Contractor's Application for Payment, the form establishes the schedule of values and the quantity and work amount.
- C-940 – the Work Change Directive addresses changes to the project.
- •C-941 – the Change Order establishes time and place.

### *CSI*

The Construction Specifications Institute (CSI) provides the most commonly used organizational manual, the MasterFormat.

It provides a list of numbers and titles that help organize the information. The format begins with divisions that are then broken down into three-digit section numbers. This departs from Unicode, which uses functional elements to arrange information.

### *Divisions are:*

- 0 – Requirements for Contract and Procurement
- 1 – General Requirements
- 2 – Site Work
- 3 – Concrete
- 4 – Masonry
- 5 – Metal
- 6 – Plastic/Wood
- 7 – Thermal Moisture Protection
- 8 – Windows and Doors
- 9 – Finishes
- 10 – Specialties
- 11 – Equipment
- 12 – Furnishing
- 13 – Special Construction
- 14 – Conveying System
- 15 – Mechanics
- 16 - Electrical

### *The first division is divided into 10 sections:*

- 01 00 00 – General Requirements
- 01 10 00 – Summary
- 01 20 00 – Price and Payment Procedures
- 01 30 00 – Administrative Requirements
- 01 40 00 – Quality Requirements
- 01 50 00 – Temporary Facilities and Controls
- 01 60 00 – Product Requirements
- 01 70 00 – Execution and Closeout
- 01 80 00 – Performance Requirements
- 01 90 00 – Life Cycle Activities

The National CAD Standards (NCS) classifies the data on electronic building design, and uses V5 as of this publication. The Uniform Drawing System (UDS) it uses includes the following: Schedules, Drawing Set Organization, Sheet Organization, Drafting Conventions, Symbols, Terms and Abbreviations, Notations, Code Conventions.

### *Negotiations*

In contract negotiations, the most preferred position (MPP) and least preferred position (LPP) for both parties should be identified. Most negotiations begin with the MPP. Negotiation plans typically include the following steps:

- Identify and rank objectives.

- Collect documentation to support the perspective.
- Assess and research the opposing position.
- Decide on a strategy style.
- Find a place with a comfortable atmosphere to negotiate.

### *There are different negotiation strategies to choose from:*

- Competitive negotiation attempts to win at any cost.
- Collaboration negotiation attempts to satisfy interests of each party.
- Accommodating negotiation attempts to create goodwill and maintain the relationship at any cost.
- Compromise negotiation attempts to find compromises that satisfy the interests of all involved.

The proposal analysis should be based on pre0negotiation exchanges that provide clarification and address requirements. Fact finding exchanges occur in non-competitive negotiations before negotiations. When negotiations are competitive, it is necessary to understand clarifications to attain awards.

In cases where documentation is necessary, the written exchange is necessary. Technical projects may require exchanges to be done face-to-face.

### *Terms to remember:*

- **Indemnification:** This identified party is not held responsible if there are third party damages.
- **Warranties/Guarantees:** The obligation of the contractor to replace or repair defects.
- **Lump sum contract:** Called a fixed price contract, it outlines a lump sum and is a risk if the details and specifications are not accurate. It is the best contract for projects that are well defined. In this contract, the owner may wait to pay for materials until they are used.
- **Unit price contract/cost plus contract:** This is a useful contract when the plans and specifications are not available and the scope is uncertain. The payment is based on labor, materials, and it includes a small markup that may or may not include the GMP.
- **Guaranteed Maximum Price Contract:** the construction manager promises not go over a specific amount, and no fees are charged with a risk.
- **Design/build:** This contract establishes a single contractor for the entire project.
- **Turnkey:** called the EPC (engineer, produce, construct), it includes the contractor who is responsible for the land and financing, but in other ways, it is similar to the design build.
- **Change orders:** These order changes made to the contract after the project begins and must be signed by the owner and the contractor, and typically involve addition, revision, or deletion.
- **Consequential change:** the owner requires a change knowing that it will alter the cost.
- **Construction change** directive: used before a change order is negotiated, the document is issued by the architect and allows construction to continue.

Drawings that the owner provides the contractor at close out that are created from change order modifications are As-built drawings.

## PROJECT DELIVERY METHODS/CYCLES

Project delivery systems are contractual agreements that define relationships between the individuals involved in the project. The three commonly used are Traditional System, Design/Build, and Construction management.

**DBB (Design/Bid/Build) –** a traditional system that starts with planning ⊠ design (where the engineers use analysis to establish the scope, schedule, and budget) ⊠ final design (drawings/specifications) ⊠ construction ⊠ completed project is evaluated. It is also called a DAB (Design/Award/Build).

The architect is chosen first and works with the owner to choose the contractor who works as the general contractor while the architect acts as the owner but there is no contractual relationship between the two.

**DB (Design/Build) and DBOM (Design/Build/Operate/Maintain)** – are cycles that add phases or use multiple contractors. It is also called an EPC. Each phase must be completed before a new one begins. The DB is the least complicated for owners because it has one procurement source.

**Fast track** – A DAB variation causes the award and construction phase before the project design. While faster, there is an increased risk of problems.

**Bridging** – a combination of DB and DBB uses an architect to create a preliminary design that is completed by design build entities.

**Construction management** – A construction manager (CM) is designated the owner's agent, but the other agents (contractors, architects, etc. are contracted by the owner.

Shell projects involve building the core components of a structure. Other items such as doors, electrical fitting, etc. are completed in a separate project.

Large projects may choose the multiple prime contractors for different aspects of the project. The owner is responsible for the coordinating, control, and scheduling of the project.

**Functional studies** used goals to determine the needs of users, regardless of the opportunities or limitations. The project manager is responsible for the communicating the needs of the user.

The site is determined using site studies, which uses the constraints and opportunities to understand if a site has the necessary functions. There are necessary technical and environmental studies. Technical studies examine the soil, water, geotechnical investigations, traffic, zones, etc. Environmental studies require adhering to the National Environmental Policy (NEPA) and state laws while also evaluating neighborhood impact.

**Commissioning** provides quality assurance for construction and installation. The commission should begin before the predesign phase and continue throughout the entire project. Although expensive, the commissioning process can save money over time.

### *Commissioning phases are*

- **Pre-design** – The owner and contractor define the parameters.
- **Design** – Outline the design and the systems that are going to be installed.
- **Construction** – Construction is observed after the submittals and manuals are reviewed and the functional performance test plans are written.
- **Occupancy/operation** – also called acceptance/post acceptance, the phase uses the functional performance test plans to verify the systems, equipment, and controls are operational and make corrections as necessary. Contractors do performance testing. The commissioning report is completed afterwards, and building operation staff are trained. A handover will go smoothly when there is a review. At the post acceptance stage, the Operation and Maintenance staff are responsible for making sure that the systems are functioning, alter systems as uses change, keep the facility history, and document all changes. Seasonal performance testing may be done at this phase.

The phases of retrocommissioning are planning, investigation, implementation, and hand-off.

Commissioning requires team communication and cooperation. Since holistic design may not be observed, commissioning will involve the different stakeholders in the process to reduce confusion. The commissioning lead verifies that building meets owner requirements. The process needs to change to meet the goals of the owner, and contract wording may need to be altered in commissioning.

## QUALITY MANAGEMENT:

- **Quality control** – requires taking measurements, inspection process, testing, products or processes to ensure that specifications are met. The objective of these assignments is to document installation and testing to prevent duplication and establish responsibilities.
- **Quality assurance** – a process that makes sure the requirements meet the stakeholder's needs. It includes design, production, development, documentation, and services.

Quality management plans outline design change procedures, which includes the sign-off documentation and quality requirements. It includes a procedure for personnel member to check drawings, calculations, and specifications. The process of quality management includes: 1) setting standards, 2) scheduling inspections, 3) managing rework that is necessary. Constructability reviews are used to make sure that construction principles are sound and engineering practices. Design validation is used to make sure that the project meets the requirements.

The design manager may perform assurance work in in-house systems, which is overseen by the project manager. In any QA or QC program, the contractor must be able to describe the responsibilities and activities along with the measures taken. It is necessary for the contractor to submit a procedures manual.

An Operation and Maintenance Manual (O&M) outlines the procedures for operation, maintenance, and repair for all equipment. It includes all of the data from the manufacturer.

### *Total Quality Management*

Total Quality Management involves all organizational processes, and it can be used in any sector. Management requires sampling, which is choosing a sample to represent the whole. The samples used are random sampling or probability sampling, which reduces the risk of bias by choosing elementary units.

Statistical Process Controls (SPC) are typically done before the random sampling. Tracking variances of critical tolerances identifies processes that need to be corrected. Control charts plot the project measurements using two different scales. The charts find out if variations are small, normal, or large, which helps determine the actions that should be taken. The charts have the borders upper control limits (UCL) and lower control limits (LCL). These limits are 3 standard deviations from the mean (+or -). The center line on the chart is the average value. Plot points that fall within the UCL and LCL range are in the control limits. Processes are out of control if they fall outside the range. The data discovered will determine which type of chart is used. Types of charts include: XbarR, P, C, and U.

The option to replace control charting is pre-control. Data is assigned the code green, yellow, or red. The purpose is to prevent units from losing conformity rather than detecting it. There is a risk of over control along with less power detection. This option does not work with a wide range of applications.

Phil Crosby established the zero defects standard. The standard is criticized for being extreme and impractical.

### *Six Sigma vs. Lean*

Six Sigma is focused on eliminating waste and tools and demands data driven decisions. It streamlines processes with quality tools and problem solving. Six Sigma is focused on the cultural infrastructure. Lean, on the other hand, focuses more on cutting waste based on the flow of value and eliminating steps in the process. Lean requires examining the project in entirety to increase value, while Six Sigma places focus on quality and is more statistical. The two methods work well together.

### Scorecard Balance

The balanced scorecard scores activities and offers an overview of the entire business performance. Human issues and financial outcomes are used for scorecards. The 4 processes necessary for score cards are:

- Create operational goals based on visions.
- Share the vision and connect it with performance.
- Complete business planning.
- Adjust strategy based on feedback.

### SWOT

The environment can be monitored using SWOT analysis:

- **Strength** – internal factors of the organization that are beneficial attributes, such as well-trained employees.
- **Weaknesses** – internal factors of the organization that are harmful, such as a low budget.
- **Opportunities** – external factors that are beneficial to the organization, such as tax incentives.
- **Threats** – external factors that are harmful to the organization, such as growing competition.

### MBO

Management by Objectives occur when all parties understand, agree upon, and work towards goals and objectives. This uses SMART (Specific, Measurable, Achievable, and Realistic) goals. Each level of organization creates its own objectives, and managers are able to connect the organizational objectives with their own.

### MBE

Management by Exceptions focuses on exceptions such as breaches. Exceptions are indicators of problems. The same value is placed on all actions, but key actions need to be identified to improve optimization.

### ISO 9001: 2008:

International management practice standards are outlined in ISO 9000 standards. ISO 9001: 2008 is a standard is applicable for all organization types. It provides the basic outline for quality systems but does not explain how they should be implemented.

The quality control systems used for the military or government are USACE, NAVFAC, AFCESA, and NASA. Guidelines for the state and city are FTA Quality Assurance and Quality Control Guidelines.

## ORGANIZATION

The project management team needs to be carefully organized and includes a project manager. The construction manager plans, oversees, and manages the project. This role may be combined with the project manager.

Project management may be split into two teams or groups. The engineering and specifications team creates the design and specification while the field site management team oversees the construction.

The organization and operations will vary according to each project, but there are three basic techniques:

- **Separation** – different organizations play different roles
- **Integration** – a joint venture or single venture has different organizations under one command
- **Mixed** – the integration varies at separate levels of the organization

It is important to not that the original structure and organization can change and has a high chance of being altered after work begins.

- **Construction Project manager** – is responsible for preparing budgets, working capital, and calculating cash flow management. The manager is also responsible for coordinating the schedule with the budget, hiring and overseeing subcontractors, creating the execution strategy, confirming change orders, and contacting owners and designers. The manager also develops the estimate with the Superintendent.
- **Owner/builder** – keeps a number of employees to handle numerous projects and shares interests with contractor. The builder is focused on the final costs of the project.
- **Contractor** – is in charge of the method, procedures, techniques, and sequences of a project and the necessary means.

Design professionals possess seals that are necessary for the project. These seals are applied to documents that local government officials require. Engineers and architects may place seals on drawings, reports, specifications, plans, etc. Surveyors that perform assignments must be qualified by the state.

- **Superintendent** – supervises the foreman and coordinates the activities with and schedules of the workforce. The superintendent also coordinates with the subcontractors.
- **Crew leader** – oversees and directs the crew as the structure is being built.
- **Field engineer/project engineer** – acts as an assistant to the superintendent to handle engineering problems.
- **Planning and scheduling engineer** – gathers field material delivery information and uses it to develop future schedules.
- **Cost engineer** – gathers field data to create forecasts for costs.
- **Estimator** – finds the contractor's overhead.

### *Specialized work:*

- **Acoustical tile setter** - puts together the tile suspension system and places the tiles on the ceiling and walls.
- **Bricklayer** – installs bricks, structural tiles, and blocks.
- **Insulator** – places insulation in walls and ceilings and around pipes and boilers.
- **Stonemason** – works with natural cut stone, limestone, and fieldstone to construct walls.
- **Carpenter** – raises wood and concrete framework and install windows and doors if they are manufactured.
- **Boilermaker** – uses structural steel for tanks, vats, boilers, and pressure vessels.
- **Cement mason** – is responsible for the screed and trowel of concrete surfaces that are exposed.
- **Electrician** – responsible for installing junction boxes, wires, and conduits.
- **Communications electrician** – install equipment necessary for low power data communications and electronic communication equipment.
- **Drywaller** – connects the wallboard to the framework.
- **Taper** – is used to seal the joints between wallboards.
- **Fireproofer** – is responsible for placing fire proofing material.
- **Floor covering installer** – responsible for installing floor coverings such as carpet.
- **Elevator operator** – configures and installs escalators and elevators.
- **Glazier** – is responsible for the installation of pane glass, mirrors, and plastic.
- **Instrumentation fitter** – prop pressure and flow instrument, tubing and valves.
- **Lather** – is responsible for the installation of board laths: wood, rock, or metal.
- **Paperhanger** – hangs wallpaper.
- **Painter** – puts paint and other finishes on construction surfaces.
- **Pipefitter** – installs metal pipes that are welded or bolted.

- **Pile driver –** drives piles made of concrete, steel, or permanent wood.
- **Plumber –** responsible for the installation of sanitary, waste water, and domestic water pipes as well as pluming fixtures.
- **Plasterer –** plasters the walls and ceilings.
- **Rigger –** is responsible for putting together concrete slings and cranes for lifting.
- **Millwright –** puts together equipment and rotating machines.
- **Operator –** operates equipment.
- **Mechanic –** keeps equipment in repair.

## READING PLANS

Blueprints are two-dimensional plans that explain the specifications for construction. Most are made computer aided design (CAD). The site or plot plan is the page of the blueprint that shows the boundaries of buildings. The horizontal display is a plan view. The vertical display is the elevation view that only shows one side of the project. A feature is shown in the section view, which is the cut-through. The elevation page shows the external view.

In architectural blueprints, the scale is inches for feet. The scale typically used is ¼ inch. This equals ¼ inch to represent each foot.

In the engineering scale, multiples of 10 are used, typically with metric measurements or feet and decimals. When the building is being laid out, the measurements begin at the benchmark.

- **General plans –** provide information about material, size, and building structure maintenance.
- **Fabrication drawings –** shop drawings that include the size, shape, material, and any structural attachments and connections.
- C**onstruction drawings –** provide orthographic views.
- **Detail drawings –** include details on the sections and details.
- **Window schedule –** the blueprint section that includes the window brands and model numbers. Window dimensions should be provided as W x L.

*There are basic elements of a blueprint:*

- **Site plan –** this is the plot plan
- **Elevations –** these are shown on the front, back, left, and right.
- **Foundation plan –** pinpoints the placement of steel and the footings.
- **Floor plan –** there is one for each level.
- **Roof plan –** includes the framing of the roof.
- **Electrical plan –** shows where the switches, services, etc. are located.
- **HVAC and plumbing**

Elevations, sections, room finishes, window schedules, and door schedules are found in architectural drawings. Floor plans may be included in architectural drawings. They offer the location of details and sections. Walls, doors, fireplaces, stairways, floor finishes, mechanical equipment, and built in cabinets are also found in floor plans.

The lines of construction drawings differ in width and pattern, not color.

- **Property line –** heavy with long dashes that alternate with two short dashes.
- **Border line –** placed at the drawing's edge.
- **Object line –** heavy line that is unbroken.
- **Hidden line –** medium line that uses short dashes.

- **Dimension/extension lines –** thin lines used to show the direction and extent of dimensions.
- **Callouts –** indicate where doors, windows, plumbing, and electrical schedules are placed.
- **Schedules –** defines which windows, etc. are placed in the building.

Dimension lines are the length of the measured distance. Extension lines are perpendicular to dimension lines and specify features. Break lines indicate that object continues past what is shown. The sectional view is created by section cutting lines.

- ¼ scale – 3 ½ inches = 14 feet.
- **Builder's level or dumpy level** – measures horizontal levels.
- Leveling rod – shows the difference between to points.
- When laying out a square building, the diagonals will be square.

### *Styles:*

- **Hopper –** window hinged at the bottom.
- **Raised panel door –** a door that s comprised of rails and stiles.
- **Right hand door –** door that opens outward and has hinges on the right side.

Plans must comply with the appropriate building codes. For example, kitchens should be designed to be at least 7 feet x 7 feet and have a 36-inch clearance in the passage to adhere to the IBC.

### *Preparation*

Before construction begins, the jobsite needs to be prepared, and union regulations need to be considered. When a job site does not have a union affiliation, it is an open shop. A dry shack must be provided so that the employees have a place to eat and change. A jobsite layout plan will determine where the dry shack and other facilities are placed as well as the area for material storage and the movement and handling of the storage material. Typically, the lowest paid employee is the one responsible for transporting material at the jobsite. All layout problems and contract reviews should be addressed at the preconstruction meeting. This is also an opportunity for the employees to meet each other.

### *Buildings are classified according to their occupancy:*

- **Assembly –** A-1 (performance arts and motion pictures), A-2 (food/drink), A-3 (recreation, amusement, worship), A-4 (sporting events and indoor activities), A-5 (outdoor functions)
- **Business –** B: has occupancy of 50 or fewer. Space that has fewer than 750 square feet is B occupancy.
- **Educational –** E: used in buildings that contain 6 or more people or children over the age of 2 ½. Religious structures that hold over 100 people are A-3.
- **Factory and industry –** F-1 (moderate hazard occupancy), F-2 (low hazard occupancy), F-3 (has populations of low density): used in structures that house processing, assembly, manufacturing, etc.
- **Hazards –** H-1, H-2, H-3, H-4, H-5: H-2 through H-4 are allowed in F and S occupancy groups. Fire areas in all buildings need to be kept apart.
- **Institutions –** I-1, I-2, I-3
- **Mercantile –** M: used to sell and store merchandise.
- **Residential –** R-1 (includes transient units), R-2 (includes multiple units of permanent occupancy), R-3 (under Section 101.2) R-4
- **Storage –** S-1, S-2
- **Utility/Misc –** U: includes agriculture buildings, barns and garages.
- **Daycare –** D

### *Types of Construction*

- **Frame –** (VA or VB types) are structures with combustible roofs, exterior walls, or floors. The may also include noncombustible exterior walls with floors and roofs that are combustible.
- **Jointed masonry –** (IIIA or IIIB types) have exterior walls of fire resistant masonry with at least 1 hour rating along with combustible doors and roofs. Different types of masonry can be used. Steel requires protection, and heavy timber requires longer than average beams.
- **Light noncombustible –** (IIB) the exterior walls are made of light metal and noncombustible materials in the roofs and floors.
- **Masonry noncombustible –** (IIA) the exterior walls are noncombustible masonry and the noncombustible or slow burning roofs and floors.
- **Modified fire resistive –** (IB) exterior load bearing walls are noncombustible and nonbearing walls uses combustible or slow burning materials.
- **Fire resistive**

The IBC and Insurance Services Office (ISO) define construction types. Most contractors adhere to the IBC. Materials that are noncombustible fall under types I and II. Materials that are noncombustible will pass the ASTM Test Method E136 and cannot burn, ignite, release gas, or combust.

Material that is limited combustible does not comply with the NFPA definition of noncombustible. They do not go over the value of Btu of 3,500 a pound. Wood that is treated with fire retardant is used in nonbearing walls must have a rating of 2 hours.

Construction type III is the type used in exterior walls that are noncombustible and interior elements that are made of anything. Type IV, called heavy timber construction, has exterior walls of noncombustible material and interior spaces of laminated or solid wood that lacks concealed spaces. VA is the type used to in apartment building design, and VB is used in commercial structures that are one story.

Height is a factor in types. Buildings that are type I are typically taller, which is why they require fire protection. A indicates that the materials are fire resistant or coated, while B indicates that the materials are not protected. All building types may require cement siding based on wind exposure.

## BUILDING DESIGN

### *Egress*

In areas where it may not be possible to evacuate during a fire, areas of refuge are necessary. The IBC requires that buildings have at least two means of regress. Egress doors should be at least 80 inches high and 32 inches wide. Most egress doors will swing outward and be able to handle a load of at least 50 people. Door that do not swing must comply with IBC section 1008.1.2 #6. The hardware for a fire door needs an unlatching force that is no more than 15 pounds.

Egress openings should be at least 20 inches wide and 24 inches high. Windows on the ground floor must be 5 square feet, and windows on higher stories must be 5.7 square feet at least. Windows must not be more than 44 inches from the floor when they are possible methods of egress.

Basement rooms require emergency exits to the outside when they are 4 stories deeper or more, according to the IBC.

## ENERGY EFFICIENT STRUCTURES

Each state will have its own standards for energy efficiency. There are, however, federal standards that must be considered when building:

- **US Department of Energy's Building Energy Codes Program (BECP) –** collaborates with federal, state, and local agencies as well as national code organizations to improve efficiency in both the residential and commercial building by assisting in code creation and enforcement.

- **Energy Conservation and Protection Act (ECPA)** – requires every state to have a building code established that meets the requirements outlined in Standard 90.1-1999 ASNI/ASHRAE/IESNA.
- **ASHRAE 90.1** – typically applies to commercial and other nonresidential structures.
- **Model Energy Code (MEC)** – also called the International Energy Conservation Code, it usually is applied to residential structures in most states.
- **International Residential Code (IRC)** – applies in certain states that are not guided by the MEC for residential structures.
- **NFPA** – includes energy codes for residential and nonresidential structures that mirror ASHRAE 90.1 and 90.2.

The US Green Building Code (USGBC) developed the Leadership in Energy and Environmental Design (LEED) in 2000. LEED is a system of green building certification that establishes the design, construction, maintenance, and operations for operators and owners. Most LEED buildings are known to save 25% to 30% in energy. LEED buildings that are gold and platinum certified will save 50% of energy.

### *Forms used:*

- A101-2007 SP: owner and contractor negotiate the sum
- A201-2007 SP: the contract's general conditions are explained
- A401-2007 SP: outlines terms between the contractor and subcontractor
- B101-2007 SP: outlines terms between the architect and owner
- B214-2012: the standard LEED certification form for architects
- C407-2007:contract between the consultant and the architect

### *Terms to remember:*

- **Brownfield** – sites that have, or may have, pollutants, contaminants, or other hazardous substances.
- **Swale** – naturally filters pollutants.
- **Blackwater** – water that must be processed before reuse.
- **Greywater** – water that does not need to be processed before reuse, such as showers and sinks.
- **VOC (volatile organic compound)** – compounds that give off vapors at room temperature such as paint, composites, and carpets.

Each square foot of a construction project generates 4 pounds of waste.

### *Verifying Measures*

The formal process for determining how much functional energy is saved with automated systems is measurement and verification (M&V). This process measures with data trends, utility bills, and system diagnostics to verify different variables and assumptions determine the savings, which is compared to the energy conservation analysis.

- **Solar Reflectance Index** – determines how well a material reflects solar heat.

### *U factors and R values*

Understanding both thermal transmittance (U factor) and thermal resistance (R factor) values is essential to energy efficiency. The effects of framing and insulation of solid objects such as walls and roofs on the interior and exterior is the domain of the U factor, which is the level of heat transfer. (Batt is the term for precut insulation that is used between framings Windows and nearby frames are measured with a U factor, which is normally between 0.25 and 1.25 and measured in Btu/h·ft$^2$·°F. Lower U factors are preferred.

The R factor is the U factor's reciprocal and determines resistance based on how fast heat is conducted by the surface. It is not the best energy performance indicator, although most codes provide for an R factor adjustment. When using the R factor, higher is better.

### *Energy Features*
### *Terms to remember:*

- **OVE (optimum value engineering)** – reduces wood by identifying where it will be the most useful.
- **SIP (Structural Insulted Panels)** – panels made of oriented strand board or plywood.
- **OSB (oriented strand board)** – 4 to 8 inch board that has laminated sheets over foam.
- **ICF (insulating concrete form)** – a form for concrete reinforced with steel, the ICF is typically made of two foam board layers that have been extruded.

A thermal envelope that is designed well will reduce water vapor migration. The construction method and ventilation system chosen will determine if the vapor should towards the outside or towards the inside. When creating a thermal envelope, it is essential that the insulation and sealing be done correctly. Sealing air leaks will greatly increase energy costs. On the other hand, adequate ventilation is necessary to prevent air moisture infiltration. The balance can be found with the use of (ERV) energy recovery ventilators and (HRV) heat recovery ventilators.

Sloped ceilings need 1 ½ inches of free opening space between the insulation and sheathing to allow the movement of air. The side of a wall or ceiling that is too warm can use the installation of a vapor retarder.

## ACCESSIBILITY

The ICC has established standards for building accessibility and usability. The floors and walkways have basic standards. The surface of all flooring must not have any opening that will allow a sphere larger than ½ inch. When floor has a ¼ to ½ surface level, a bevel slope change cannot be made over 1:2. The greatest slope of a floor space that is clear is 1:48.

When creating a circular turning space, the knee to toe clearance must be at least 60 inches. Elements that are 9 inches off the floor require a 25 inch knee clearance according to the ANSI.

Objects may protrude 4 inches in the circular path when they have edges between 27 and 80 inches high. Handrails may protrude into the path by 4 ½ inches. A guardrail or another barrier is necessary for a vertical clearance below 80 inches. The height above the floor may not be more than 27 inches.

When floor space is unobstructed but has a parallel approach to an element, the element height must not be over 48 inches, and the low point must be at least 15 inches off the floor. Elevator buttons need to be no more than 48 inches from the floor.

Accessibility demands providing the safe routes, which are free from turn styles, revolving doors, and revolving gates. The hallways need to have a 36 inch width cleared for access. The exception to this rule is providing a 32 inch hallway width when the length is no more than 24 inches.

Accessible doorways are at least 32 inches wide, and the opening must remain clear. The threshold needs to be ½ inch high when it is offered. Operational parts of the door need to be 34 inches away from the floor; this includes pulls, latches, door handles, etc. Doors that are interior and hinged, folding, or sliding should have a maximum opening force of 5 pounds. Fire doors need to follow the lowest opening force to be accessible, and the IBC demands that rating of fire doors be the same as the structure assembly.

Ramps are walkways with slopes that are more than 1:20.

Ramps and landings that are wheelchair accessible must not have a slope over 1:12.

For exterior ramps, the clear width must be at least 36 inches.

The ramp runs must be between the handrails and maintain a 36-inch width.

When outdoor ramps change directions, the turnabout needs to be 60 x 60 inches.

A cross slope of ramps and landings must be 1:48 to keep water from accumulating.

Each ramp requires a landing that is the same width as the ramp run and at least 60 inches long, and the ramp rises that are over 6 inches require handrails.

Curb ramps must be at least 36 inches wide. The landings need to be the same width, which does not include flared sides. The length must also be 36 inches.

Elevator buttons need to be easily pressed and require a diameter of at least ¾ of an inch. The control buttons for emergencies need to be positioned so that their center lines are at least 35 inches from the floor, on the bottom panel. The lighting in elevator landing sills, platforms, landings, and car controls and thresholds need to be at least 5 feet candles.

The elements such as parking lots also require accessibility. When there are more than 60 spaces, at least 3 must be accessible. Van parking spaces must have a minimum width of 132 inches, and the overhead clearance must be 98 inches both in and out. Signs that say van accessible must be placed 60 inches over the lot. Parking spaces that are handicap accessible must have a width of 96 inches, and the access aisle needs to be at least 60 inches. Slopes in these spaces may be no more than 1:48, and slopes for aisle access must be no more than 1:48.

The handrails need gripping surfaces when over ramp surfaces, walking surfaces, and stair nosings. The top should be 34 to 38 inches from above the surfaces, and there needs to be a clearance of at least 1 ½ inches. When handrails have a circular cross section, they require an outer diameter between 1 ¼ to 2 inches. Cross sections that are not circular and are 2 ¼ inches demand an outer diameter between 4 and 6 ¼ inches. Distance ramp handrails should extend 12 inches over the landing, horizontally.

Plumbing is also affected by accessibility. For example, water fountain spouts must not be more than 36 inches from the floor.

Water closets must have at least 60 inches of clearance when measured from the side wall, perpendicularly. When measured from the rear wall, perpendicularly, the clearance need to be 56 inches. The distance from the sidewall to the centerline must be between 16 and 18 inches. The seat in a water closet may only be between 17 and 19 inches high. Grab bars in the rear wall need to be 36 inches long. Fixed side grab bars, on the other hand, must be at least 42 inches long and extend 54 inches from the rear wall.

Doors in toilet areas should be at least 42 inches from the toilet for handicap accessibility. The rim of the toilet cannot be over 34 inches from the floor once it is finished. The grab bars that have circular cross sections require an outer diameter between 1 ¼ inch and 2 inches. The hand space between the completed wall and inner grab bar must be 1 ½ inches. All grab bars must support at least 250 pounds, and the tops should be 33 to 36 inches from the floor.

### *Misc.*

- According to NFPA 72 smoke detectors must audibly notify residents, and the IBC requires that they have stand by power.
- The symbol for Enter and Proceed must be a circle when it is a raised tactile surface of a function key, according to the ANSI.
- Type A dwelling sink rims must be no more than 34 inches above the floor.

### *Stormwater*

Stormwater discharge must be considered before the project begins. Sediment is a main source of water pollution. If more than 5 acres are being used, a National Pollutant Discharge Elimination System (NPDES) is necessary.

## MECHANICS OF CONSTRUCTION

There are four types of construction according to the International Building Code:

- **I and II** – materials used are noncombustible.

- **III –** the exterior is noncombustible, and the interior adheres to the local building code.
- **IV –** uses heavy timber (HT). The exterior is noncombustible, but the interior has laminated wood that has no concealed space.
- **V –** any material that adheres to code is used.

The designation of A indicates that the structure is rated fire resistant. The designation of B indicates that the structure is not rated as fire resistant.

### *Construction Strength and Loading*

Mechanics is a physical science that examines the bodies at rest or in motion when they are under the action of different forces. The study of mechanics includes the fields: stability, vibrations, engineering performance, stability and strength of structures and machines.

- **Statics –** the study that focuses on the description of forces and how they affect equilibrium.
- **Equilibrium –** occurs when the sum of all forces is zero.
- **Force –** the connection between two bodies that equals a pull or push.
- **Particle –** an object that has mass but a negligible size.
- **Newton's First Law of Motion –** particles at rest stay at rest and particles moving in a straight line will continue to do so, unless they are subject to unbalanced forces.
- **Newton's Second Law of Motion –** the product of mass and acceleration of a particle are the same as the net force.
- **Newton's Third Law of Motion –** When two particles have the same force on each other when they interact and they are the same in magnitude, this causes movement in the equal and opposite direction.
- **Dynamics –** the study of bodies in motion and forces that cause the motion.
- **Kinetics –** the study of motion alone but can relate back to the forces.
- **Vector quantity –** includes direction and magnitude in the quantity.
- **Centrifugal force –** explains inertia in rotation. It includes inertial or fictitious force in reference to a non inertial frame and corresponds with centripetal force.
- **Friction –** force opposing the motions or tendencies of bodies that are in contact.
- **Triangle law of vectors –** the sum of two vectors will represent the third of a triangle. If a quadrilateral has two sides that are parallel, the opposite sides will be equal and the angles will be congruent.

Force has different definitions and measurements. It causes change or work and the equation for force is F=ma (mass x acceleration). There are measurement for the English system and the International Systems of Units (SI)

Force (SI) – 1N (Newton) = force necessary to accelerate 1kg (kilogram) at a rate of m/s2 (1 meter per second squared).

Force (English) – A slug equals the mass that a pound of force can accelerate at 1ft/s2. A pound mass is the mass a pound of force can accelerate at the rate of 32ft/s2.

### *Stability and Strength*

The strength and stability of a structural design is determined by the structural analysis. The strength is its ability withstand loads based on the elements of the system's structure. A stable structure system, however, means that it can safely transfer loads to the ground. The analysis is consulted to determine the cause of structure failure. It needs to include the strengths and weaknesses of the following components: walls, columns, connectors, beams, roofs, and braces. Volumes limits should also be included.

### *Methods of structural analysis:*

- **Mathematical model –** typically used with large projects
- **Scaled model –** are the preferred method of analysis

- **Actual structure** – used when other structures like it will be created

Strength tests may be static or dynamic. Static tests, called isometric tests, applies tension to fixed, unmoving resistance. Dynamic or isotonic tests, however, move a single or multiple parts against resistance.

In most states, a registered engineer provides an opinion on the structural integrity of a building after an inspection. This is not a guarantee, however.

### *Loads*

Restrained dimensional changes such as occupants, possessions, building materials, movement, and the environment create loads. Loads are typically considered variable. Some variable loads, however, are the considered permanent when there are few variations. Certain loads are static, which means that they slowly increase and the effects are usually negligible. Loads that are part of the structure (floors, walls, roofs, etc.) are dead loads, these include the weight of formwork and concrete. Live loads are the weigh of occupancy such as furniture. Environmental loads such as snow, rain, wind, etc. are not part of live loads. Loads cause structural failure when the material holding the load reaches its limit.

- **Vibratory loads** – are always in motion
- **Shock load** – the load values shift with time
- **Axial load** – force moves past the centroid and continues in a perpendicular movement down the plane to create a structure that bears weight evenly.
- **Eccentric load** – is perpendicular but does not move through the centroid. The focus is a supporting wall or column.
- **Torsional load** – creates a twisting force because the center is offset from the shear center.

It is important to note that the shift between eccentric and axial loads may cause the collapse when not part of the design.

### *Design Elements:*

**Posts/columns** – transfer the load to the foundation from the floor or roof, typically using axial force.

**Beam** – called sill and girder depending on the region, must resist shear and bending in design because the load is horizontal to columns from the roofs and floors.

**Truss** – an element with one or more triangular units

**Common truss** – called a pitched truss, is typically used to construct roofs.

**Parallel chord truss** – called a flat truss, may be used in flooring because it has top and bottom chords that are parallel.

**Floor truss** – can reach more unsupported spans because larger trusses are needed for larger spans.

**Fink truss** – a truss that has a W bracing and is triangular in shape.

**Panel points** – the intersecting points between the chords and web members in a truss.

**Mezzanine** – the floor between two main floors and should not be more than 1/3 of the portion of the room.

Connections between elements are roller (resists vertical force), fixed (resists moments), and pin (resists horizontal and vertical force).

**Exterior walls** – the enclosing wall that may or may not be load bearing and typically has a slope of 60 degrees or more. All exterior walls must be weather resistant.

**Wall covering** – materials that are placed on the wall for insulation, weather resistance, or appeal. (Exterior wall covering that is plywood does not require sheathing.)

**Wall envelope –** system of wall components that offer protection from the environment

**Veneer –** a facing that offers protection, insulation, and decoration.

### *Seismic Design*

The American Society of Civil Engineers (ASCE) outlines seismic provisions in Standard 7-05, Minimum Design Loads for Buildings and Other Structures. There are three systems in the Uniform Building Code (UBC) when it comes to seismic design: bearing wall, building frame, and moment resisting.

Bearing walls are called sheer walls. They are vertical load carrying and can be found in exterior and interior locations. There purpose is to resist lateral forces while they do not typically have space frames to carry vertical loads, they might support roof and floor vertical loads with columns. Bearing walls remain on continuous footings that are twice the width of the shearing wall.

Building frames support vertical loads using three-dimensional space frames. They resist lateral force with braced frames or sheer walls. A one-story house requires at most a brace that is 25 feet from the center. Moment resisting frames are often comprised of steel, masonry, or concrete. They are complete frames that carry vertical loads and possibly lateral forces as well. These systems may be combined when specific rules are followed.

Wall panels that are designed to only carry wind load are curtain wall panels. In construction, curtain walls that are sandwiched, have air space between the insulation and outer wall. In masonry, they are exterior wall that do not support the different stories.

### *Other structures:*

When creating temporary structures (used for fewer than 180 days), it is necessary to follow local fire code. Structures larger than 120 sq/ft require building permits, and anything 100 sq/ft or more requires the greatest exit access.

Walkways require two fire-barrier wall separations, with a rating not fewer than two hours, from the interior. The barriers should extend 10 ft above the roof or any connected buildings and 10 ft below the walkway. They also need to extend 10 ft to the side of the walkway. There should be openings with sprinklers or devices that have a fire protection rating of ¾ hr according to NFPA 13, and IBC requires that the door and windows have ¾ hour protective.

Marquis height must not exceed three feet when it is 2/3 between the property line and curb. When it is less than 2/3, the maximum height is nine feet. Marquis must be sloped to offer the appropriate drainage.

Fabric awnings may be placed over public property, but any rigidity needs to be fewer than 7 ft 6 in from the grade while the entire awning drop should be fewer than 7 ft. The frame should not extend further than 2/3 between the property line and curb.

- The edge a construction load must be within 1 foot of the of the joist end's bearing surface.
- The most weight that a bundle of steel joists can hoist is 1,000 pounds.
- A ceiling joist's end requires a wood frame or bearing of 1 ½ inches or a masonry bearing of 3 inches.

## SOIL AND FLUIDITY

Every project must have a thorough understanding of soil mechanics, which studies how the masses of soil, water, and air respond to loads. Soil engineering is necessary for tunneling, foundation engineering, retaining wall design, dam design, etc. because it allows you to predict how the water and air move through the soil. Rock mechanics, how rocks and masses respond to forces, is also necessary to understand before constructing a structure.

Before any construction can begin, it is important to assess groundwater. If ground water comes within 5 feet of the bottom floor, it is necessary to conduct a subsurface investigation of the soil. The costs of the excavation and foundation are affected by groundwater levels as is the soil bearing capacity. Dampproofing is necessary when the groundwater comes within 6 inches of the bottom floor. When retarders are used to dampproof foundations, they should be at least 6 inches.

The ability of fluid to travel through soil is permeability, and it is measured in units of velocity. Compressibility, on the other hand, describes how stress affects the change in soil volume. The level of shear stress that causes shear failure is shear strength. The indices that are used to classify and gauge the engineer properties of soil are the Atterberg Limits. The limits discovered are the plastic, liquid, and shrinkage limits.

Pore pressure is not likely to change when the soil is coarse grained such as gravel, sand, or non-plastic silt because they are pervious against changes in stress.

It is difficult to determine the shear strength of fine-grained soil such as plastic silts and clays. Their void ratios are typically higher and the permeability lower, which affects the particle interaction. Lower shear strength typically comes with a void ratio that is high.

When the soil is shrink-swell, also called expansive, it can change in volume by 30% or more, which causes lifting. The following are indications that the soil is expansive:

- 10% or more of the particles pass through a 75 mm or No. 200 sieve.
- 10% or more of the particles are under 5 micrometers.
- •There is a PI (plasticity) index of 15 or more.

The less moisture there is in clay soil, the stronger the soil is. When conducting tests, soil samples are necessary. They should be undisturbed for shear testing. Consolidation testing is necessary when there are fine grains in the sediment. Consolidation occurs when the water in the soil depletes and is not replaced by more water or air. This typically occurs when the load is static.

The soil needs to be stable and compact or there will be settlement problems. Soil needs to extend at least 50% from the footing base to the influence depth. The type of foundation used will alter influence depth due to the stress they place on the soil. The compaction necessary for concrete footings is 90%.

### *Reports and Classification*

Soil requires surface evaluation and subsurface investigation. Surface evaluations discover landscaping and drainage requirements. Subsurface investigation establishes the foundation needs and costs. The best, but most expensive method of testing subsurface soil is test pit. The test that discovers the soil's optimal capability for compaction relative to its content of moisture and dry density is a proctor test.

In situ testing is necessary for foundation materials that are coarse-grained. To estimate the friction angle of sand and find relative density with empirical calculations, the SPT test (ASTM D-1586 (1984)) is used. In Europe, the CPT (ASTM D 3441-79 (1986a)) test is another option, and it is gaining popularity in the United States. Nuclear compaction testing is used to determine the density, water content, and soil aggregate. The benefit of this test is that it can be done on site.

The rate of the flow of water through saturated soil is measured using the coefficient of permeability. The quality of the strength of soil below the pavement is measured using the California Bearing Ratio (CBR). To discover the in situ dry density, the core cutter test is used.

To find wetlands and intermittent streams, the US Geological Survey has topographic maps. Water tables will provide the level of water underground. The Department of Agriculture will also provide soil maps with aerial photographs and soil types.

The classification system for soil and rocks ranks them according to their stability. They rank in order of stability from A (cohesive), B (cohesive/non cohesive), C (unstable like sand), D.

### *Soil Classification:*

- **Granular** – more than 85% gravel and sand and less than 15% clay and silt.
- **Cohesive** – has plasticity, which means the soil molds between the hands at .3 cm in diameter and remains stable while the tensile strength can hold a 5 cm section while held out at an end.

- **Granular cohesionless –** does not have plasticity and contains less than 15% clay and silt. Soil that is cohesionless is not likely to adhere to itself.

Soil swell or bulking occurs when the soil increases in volume after being moved or disturbed. This will depend on the type of soil. Compact soil with sand and gravel will swell 12%. Sandy soil requires a wellpoint system when dewatering is necessary.

### *Grading and Excavation*

Foundations need to meet the specified pounds per square foot (PSF) in their bearing capacity before being placed. The PFS is not important if there is a structural analysis that the design meets. When a layer of soil has a lower bearing value and another does not, the load should be determined using the lower value.

Residual forces can change the soil's configuration in excavation, and this can lead to cave ins. OSHA requires that excavation be safe and precautions taken to prevent cave-ins. Additionally, it is important not to excavate too close to the adjoining property. Legally, steps must be taken to ensure that neighboring property is not affected in the event of a cave in or settlement. If the soil is at risk, artificial means must be used to prevent encroachment on existing structures. These include shoring or needling. Lateral support is done when both the land supported and the supporting land are on the same plane. The support is sub-adjacent when the supporting land is below the supported land.

In trench excavations, the excavations are deeper than their width. The width, however, is 15 feet at most. When trenches are deeper than 4 feet, ladders, stairways, and other methods of lateral travel should be provided, and lateral travel should be limited to 25 feet. At this depth, the oxygen levels should also be tested.

The greatest risk with excavation is sidewall cave-ins. The three methods of support to prevent cave ins are slurry walls, steel soldier piles, and interlocking steel sheet piling. Five-foot banks are stable slopes that can be used to protect employees from cave-ins. Slurry walls are useful in wet, problematic soil sites and are a mixture of benonite and water. Kickouts occur when the crossbeam fails or is released accidentally.

The soil properties at the excavation site affect the angle of the slope. The slope equation used in excavation requires understanding the top, bottom, vertical, and height. It is:

H/3 x {A + B + square root(AxB)}

The slopes of angles at excavation need to be no more than 1 vertical to 1 ½ horizontal. If an excavation is below 20 feet in type C soil, the slope may not be higher than 1 ½ horizontal to 1 vertical.

The tools and equipment necessary for excavation depend on the following key factors: price, materials, volume that needs to be removed, conditions, time, and haul distance. When the excavation is 6 feet or more, barriers, such as guardrails, fences, etc., should placed to protect the employees.

The designs for support systems and shields must be kept in writing, along with the engineer's name and the tabulated data. Shields are called trench boxes, and excavations should not occur more than 2 feet below shields.

### *Formula to estimate material in excavation:*

L x W x D/27

### *Points to Remember:*

- Footings will help the soil with the load by distributing the weight of the structure.
- Haunch boards are used to mold footing sides.
- The pressure soil is able to resist can be estimated by using a hand penetrometer and calibrating it to tons/sq ft.
- Coarse and granular soils have greater capacity than fine soils such as silt and clay.
- Clay that is firm has a bearing strength of 1,600 psf.
- Sedimentary rock has a bearing strength of 20,000 psf.

- The bearing capacity of soil increases with compacting.
- Sand has a bearing strength of 6,000 psf when it is dense.
- Sandy gravel has a foundation pressure of 3,000 psf at most.
- Clay has particles less than .002 mm in diameter, and breaking it into smaller pieces can create visible fissures.

### *Excavation for Piping*

Light utility bulldozing equipment is useful for landscaping and other excavation projects. Bulldozers typically travel at 1 ½ to 4 miles per hour. Before using a bulldozer, the load factor must be established, and the formula to determine this is:

Loose volume/bank volume or

Bank volume/bank volume + swell factor

The load will be lost if the operator does not lift, tilt, and angle the blade in an appropriate manner. Additionally, the blade needs to be even with the blade dump area. When moving soil long distances, the U shaped blade is better. A complete U blade holds more material than the semi U blade, and an angled blade will better reach side cast material than a straight blade. When using a scraper in muddy soil that is self-loading, a dozer needs to push the blocks to the bowl's back.

A tape measure is used to find horizontal distance. When a slope is downhill, it is a negative grade. When a slope is at a 45° angle, it is at 100%.

When using a trench box for support, the center of it needs to be installed no more than 5 feet over the pipe. Soft soil requires the use of a backhoe when a trench is installed. If compaction is necessary, puddling is the simplest method. In narrow spaces, it is not possible to add water and wet the space. In trenches that are wide with no cross-lines, a sheepsfoot roller is the best option for vibratory compaction.

## MASONRY AND CONCRETE

Cement and concrete are different, but cement is an ingredient used to make concrete, which also includes sand, stones/gravel, and water. Concrete is unique because it is in a plastic state when it arrives at the site. A cubic foot of concrete weighs approximately 150 pounds. Temperature can affect how concrete sets up once it is placed. Temperature sensors can be used to identify the surface temperature. The higher the temperature, the concrete gets stiffer than it does at a lower temperature. When curing concrete, the water needs to be free from salts, which can cause corrosion and cracking. It is possible to increase thermal resistance by using concrete insulation. Insulated concrete forms (ICFs) are specialized concrete that places insulation sheets between the concrete.

### *Most projects include the use of Portland Cement.*

### *Portland Cement Types:*

- I – Basic Portland cement.
- II – Cement that is sulfate resistant.
- III – an early strength 28 day cement.
- IV – used in areas that need a low heat of hydration.
- V – used in areas that need high sulfate resistance.

While Portland cement hardens, it undergoes hydration. Too much water will cause a high slump and reduce the strength. After 7 days, type III cement will be at 60 – 70% of its full strength.

When using structural concrete, the following needs to be documented:

- The reinforcement's strength or grade
- The reinforcements, anchors, and structural elements' location and size

- Stages and ages at which concrete is used as well as its compressive strength
- Dimensional change provisions
- The length and location of lap splices along with anchorage length's reinforcement. (Lap is the most common type of rebar splice.)
- Pre-stressing force location and magnitude
- Welded splices and mechanical reinforcement location and type
- Post-tensioning tendons' stressing sequence
- When positioning, the least concrete compressive strength
- Isolation joint details and contraction location

The process of mixing water begins with placing 10% of the water into a drum before adding dry materials. Concrete that is ready mixed requires 300 revolutions in a drum, which is the equivalent of 90 minutes.

Wetter concrete increases the slump, which should be 3 to 4 inches in most moderate concretes. Vibrating the concrete mixture is done to remove air from it. When concrete is tested, it falls under the standards of the American Society for Testing and Materials (ASTM).

Choices must be made based on the highest resistance. This includes the greatest minimum strength necessary and the lowest water-to-cement ratio. The water-cement ratio needs to be .40 to .50.

It is important to cure concrete to keep the moisture and temperature range at satisfactory levels. If the concrete becomes too dry, the cement will not react like it is meant to and the concrete will weaken. Fog spraying will prevent water evaporation in curing.

The aggregate will affect the quality of concrete. They typically make up 60 to 80% of the concrete volume, and the project will determine the aggregate used, which will range from fine to coarse. In the world of construction, pebbles are not considered aggregates. When creating cement walls, the aggregate must be ¾ of an inch or smaller.

Concrete that is not reinforced need support to handle tension, although it can easily resist compressive stress. Measuring concrete's compressive strength is typically requires knowing the pounds per square in (psi). Measuring the necessary force for concrete to break a cylinder as it hardens inside will determine the psi. An alternative measure is penetration.

When new concrete is mixed correctly, it is called quantity yield. ASTM Specification C94 outlines how to calculate ready mix concrete's volume. Specifically, divide the total weight of a fresh concrete batch by the average weight per cubic foot (outlined in the ASTM C138) to discover the volume. This requires the testing of three samples from three loads.

The split cylinder test will help establish concrete's tensile strength, and it is found in ASTM C 496. The tensile strength will typically be a small percentage of compressive strength (10% to 15%). Before testing, the cylinders need to be held at 60 to 80 degrees for at least 48 hours.

Corrosion is the reaction of metal and other material to the environment that causes the metal to deteriorate. The most common corrosion in steel is rust. Using the proper water-to-cement ratio will help prevent rust along with calcium nitrate, a corrosion inhibitor. Additionally, epoxy coating and stainless steel can prevent metal corrosion. Concrete can be altered with admixtures included before or during the mixing of concrete. Typical admixtures include water reducers, air-entertaining agents, accelerators, and retarders. Additions such as fine sand and fly ash will help reduce bleeding in concrete.

Prestressed concrete uses prestressing tendons to improve tensile reinforcement. The tendons are high tensile steel rods or cables that balance stresses. It is typical to use prestressed concrete anchors to handle seismic events or other factors that alter dynamic or cyclic loading. A prestressed concrete joist that is shaped like a keystone has a span up to 36 feet.

Post-tensioning is used to reinforced concrete or prestressed concrete after the concrete is placed. This is done by stretching and mechanically fastening tendons through conduits. When the process is done before concrete is placed, it is pre-tensioning.

In concrete floors, tendons are used to create tension. The post-tensioning tendons require sheaths, typically made of high density polyethylene that allow the movement of the cables. These tendons are pulled once the concrete is 75% hardened. A hydraulic jack is used to stress the steel after the necessary hardening of the concrete.

Anyone who leads post tension operations must have 5 years experience at least. When post tensioning is done in formwork, installation drawings are needed. The edge needs to be marked so that the center of the tendon will be placed.

- Before installation, the sheath should be cut back no more than an inch.
- A tail of 12 inches is necessary when both sides of the tendon are stressed.
- In beams, the tendon bundles need to be spaced 1 ½ inches away from each other.
- ½ inch tendons should not be bundled in more than 5.
- Bundles with tendons that are .6 inches should have no more than 4 in a bundle.
- The smallest bar used to support post-tensioning is #4.
- Small or medium block-out openings require at least a 6-inch clearance.
- The final pull of the 2 stroke pull requires 60% of the full stroke jack to be calculated beforehand.
- Water caps need to be installed fewer than 24 hours after stressing but not more than 96 hours after.
- Grouting stress pockets must not include the additive chlorine.
- Cables are typically 7 wire strands that have ½ inch diameters.
- A force of 80% is necessary when installing the end anchor when back stressing the cable barrier.

The durability and workability of concrete need to be understood. The factors that influence both include: temperature, amount and type of cement used, ratio of water to cement, wind, ratio of sand to aggregate, and chemical admixtures. To discover how workable a concrete mix is, conduct a slump test, which measures consistency. This test needs to be in an established tolerance or range from a target slump and requires tamping each layer with a rod 25 times.

Durability uses either a prescriptive or performance approach. The prescriptive approach requires specifying materials, methods of construction, and proportions using the fundamental practices and principles. The performance approach requires identifying functional requirements (changes, strength, volume, etc.) and developing the best mix based on information from concrete producers.

Hot weather conditions, according to ACI 305, include wind speed, high ambient temperature, low relative humidity, solar radiation, and high concrete temperature. Retardant is added to concrete used in high temperatures. Cold weather conditions, according to ACI 306, are average temperatures under 40°F (5°C), which lasts for three days consecutively. During this time, the temperature will not rise above 50°F (10°C) for more than 12 hours. Calcium chloride is added to concrete used in cold weather.

- **Shrinkage** – is caused by too much water in the mix. It takes place over years at a decreasing rate. The average shrinkage the first 90 days is 60% and 80% after a full year. Water can cause the volume to return to close to the original size.
- **Creep** – deformation that occurs over time. Increasing the load will increase the rate of creep.
- **Fatigue** – causes fracture as the loading fluctuates. Fatigue is defined as the material strength that remains after 200,000 loading cycles.
- **Blisters** – bumps on concrete surface that are both small and hollow; this is the greatest risk of air-entrained concrete.

Air entrained concrete includes air in the mixture, which increases the workability, and it is useful in exterior slabs as well as driveways and sidewalks. The volume of air is typically 4% to 7%.

Thin concrete slabs need to be poured when the temperature is at least 60 degrees, and it should not be delivered when the temperature is 90 degrees or more. When concrete is being pumped, the aggregate should be rounded and presoaked 70% to 80% to make the process easier. It is necessary to ensure that the concrete will not be exposed to freezes within 5 days of being deposited when used in a foundation.

Concrete joints are commonly used in construction when there are designed breaks in the concrete. The three types of concrete joints used in construction are, isolation (allows joint to both contract and expand), expansion (allows vertical and horizontal movement), and contraction. The spacing between joints needs to be 24 to 36 times the concrete thickness at most. The joints must be sawcut between 4 and 12 hours, and they need to be cut ¼ of the slab's depth. Water stops prevent fluid from traveling through the joints, and the most effective stops are made of PVC.

## SURVEYING

The survey places markers to guide and provide boundaries for the project. Surveys need to be completed before starting construction on the foundation. Survey markers and benchmarks are part of the survey. Benchmarks are points of elevation, and monuments are markers that create the boundaries of the lot. Backsights are reads that look back across the progress line.

The survey equation is:

Benchmark + Backsight = Instrument height

In surveys, 120 degrees is the equivalent of 2 minutes.

Placing drawings are done after the survey, they are necessary for the placement of reinforced steel and to show provide the fabrication details.

### *Foundations*

Foundations support most structures. Constructing a foundation requires understanding the settlement, bearing capacity, and the ground's movement. Discovering the ultimate bearing capacity is the finding the maximum pressure (theoretically) that the soil is able to support without failing. The ultimate bearing capacity that is divided by a specified safety factor is the allowable bearing capacity. If the bearing capacity is low, raft, mat, or floating foundations are necessary. Foundation walls require a psi of 3,000 when there is the potential for weathering.

It is possible to prescriptively design or engineer foundations in compliance with code. The In areas where the ground is prone to freezing, T-shaped foundations are used. In areas where freezing is not common, the slab on grade may be implemented. They are typically monolithic and have a thicker exterior edge. If the frost-protected method is implemented in heated structures, it requires the insulation be two stiff sheets of polystyrene insulation.

### *Foundations and Support:*

- **Underpinning –** support that extends the foundation to a new bearing stratum.
- **Bearing pile –** a foundation pile that is dependant on material strength and the cross section.
- **Sheet pile –** foundation pile that handles horizontal pressure, not vertical, and holds soft soil above the bedrock.
- **Pile cap –** reinforced concrete that is piled over pile groups to share the load.
- **Wood pile –** the foundation pile that is lightweight with a life expectancy that is uncertain underwater and creates skin friction.
- **Shell type Cast in place pile –** a shell/casing that is made of steel is placed in the ground and filled with concrete.
- **Cofferdam –** a temporary structure that can be used in wet soil or below water. It is water tight, made by sheet piles that are driven together side by side.

### *Slabs*

Slabs cost less to build, but the structure cannot have any below ground space. Slab foundations are simply concrete poured over gravel or soil. To properly create a slab, the concrete needs to be reinforced and vapor proofed with a footing that is sturdy. It will be poured over crushed stone that has been compacted. The slab should be anchored to the ground to resist changes from the environment. A slow pouring of concrete is used to reduce lateral pressure.

Mat slabs are used in expansive soil. Rebars need to be placed 3 inches over the mud slab. When the concrete is poured, it needs to be at least 2 inches above top reinforcement bars.

Waffle slabs have indentations that are known as domes.

### *Combination*

In regions with warm climates, a combined slab and foundation may be used as long as the soil is compatible. This type of foundation uses a footing with a shallow perimeter that is poured over a vapor barrier with the slab.

In regions where the ground is likely to freeze, the structure walls must have the support of the foundation that extends below the frost line. Additionally, air entrapment should be added to the concrete mixture. The foundation walls and slab are typically separated in this instance.

When constructing bridges or multistory buildings, a voided (hollow core slab) is used. This is a slab of prestressed concrete that has been precast.

- **Flexural Strength –** a beam or slab's ability to resist bending or failure. Written as MR (Modulus Rupture) in psi. The strength is found by loading 6x6 inch concrete beams that are not reinforced using a span that is three times the depth.
- **Square foundation –** this will stress the soil roughly two times the foundation width in depth.
- **Strip foundation –** is longer than its width and can stress the soil depth that is multiple times the foundation.
- **Grade slab –** provides a base that is stable and requires the surrounding soil to be excavated.
- **Grade beam –** distributes the structure's weight over soil when it is not stable and reduce defection. They are typically concrete reinforced with steel mesh or rebar, and can be supported by pipe fitting, placed directly on the ground, or placed in the ground.
- **Batter board –** used to outline the foundation's location. They are horizontal bars that fix to posts and establish positions of corner stakes. Batter boards are installed after determining the grading corners, and the top represents the foundation wall's height. They are placed, at a minimum of 4 feet from each other at the excavation point.

Foundation pressure comes from hydrostatic water pressure along with the earth. Although concrete will both expand and contract, it is most likely to shrink, which causes cracking. Control joints can reduce cracking caused by the rapid drying or extra water in the mix. Joints need to be two or three times the concrete's thickness and at the same depth as the slab.

Control joints may be placed on the surface of the concrete to control random cracking. Without vertical steel reinforcement, shear failures and other horizontal displacements may occur.

- A control joint is a contraction joint that is used to create weakness in planes, which causes the cracks to develop at planned locations. It is also used to develop sections of walls made from masonry.
- An isolation joint acts for expansion. It isolates the slab and provides room for the movement necessary to reduce cracking.
- Joints should not be spaced more than 2 ½ times the thickness of the joints.
- Square panels used should have a length no more than 1 ½ of the width.
- All joint locations should be determined before construction begins.

### *Settlements and footing*

Footings need to support walls and columns, and the most common footing support is the isolated footing. The columns on the exterior of the building are combined footings when the building's projection is restricted. The concrete used to create footings needs a compressive strength that is at least 2,500 psi. A footing that has a slope of 10% must be stepped.

- Footing on rock or soil that supports light loads must be at least 8 inches.
- 3-story construction that has a light frame requires footings that are 8 inches thick and 18 inches wide.

### *Forms*

Formwork is the mold that holds the concrete temporarily until it sets and is cured, and the ACI governs the formwork setup. The weight of the formwork and the concrete combine to create the dead load. Concrete form liners may be constructed out of fiberglass, steel, or plywood. They are typically made from steel or timber, and the most cost effective timber is kiln-dried pine.

Steel allows heat to dissipate, which is why it is preferable to heat retaining timber. Vibrating the concrete will help prevent rapid stiffening, and needs to penetrate into previous layers by a few inches. The highest deflection limit in formwork is: span/360(with a sheathing maximum of 1/16 inch and a joist and beams maximum of ¼ inch). The foundation wall forms are held together with snap ties or form ties. Form ties require a safety factor of 2:1.

Concrete that is used for a form should not be dropped more than 1 meter, which equals 3.281 feet. When concrete forms are cast in place, the sections are smaller and weigh less because. The benefit is that they are designed to resist rotation. Should concrete be cast against the soil, it requires a 3-inch cover at minimum. When nails are necessary for brace forms, they should be duplex or double headed.

The slope away from a foundation wall should be at least 6 inches from the first 10 feet. Every foundation wall requires a footing that falls below the frost grade. It is possible to use building forms to create foundation walls above the footings. Precast foundation forms are built offsite and installed with a crane. Insulation foundation walls are made part of the foundation once they are installed. Permanent Insulated Framework are put together from insulating concrete forms and constructed on site. The stay-in-place structural formworks are put together on site as well. They are comprised of fiber reinforced or prefabricated plastics.

### *Formwork and Load Terms:*

- **Vertical formwork** – supports pressure that is lateral and includes wind load.
- **Horizontal formwork** – such as slabs, rests on joists and are usually made of plywood.
- **Braces** – are wall form parts used to keep the form erect in lateral pressure.
- **Sheathing** – holds the wall in its shape until the concrete sets completely.
- **Bucks** – used to make openings in the concrete.
- **Cleanout** – openings in column forms that provide room to remove the debris.
- **Slip-form** – a form created in place with the extrusion method.

Structural slabs are similar to foundational slabs, except that they are concrete floors. When they are poured onto subgrades directly, the term is slab on grade. Cement floors may be finished with slumps that contain hard, dense aggregates. This low slump should not be lower than an inch. Concrete slabs must have a psi of 3,500 when used for a garage.

### *Precasting*

Truck and crawler mounted cranes are typically used with precast material, but the mobile luffing-jib crane is the most versatile. When the construction is overhead, the telescoping boom crane is used. The stationary tower crane will not interfere with the cladding or external walls. Crane accessibility and size need to be considered when moving forms that are precast. The hoisting equipment, jib, and cables will establish the crane's capabilities.

- A single vertical hitch wire rope sling has a safe working load of 2,550 pounds and has a rope with a diameter of 3/8 of an inch.
- A sling angle must not be over 45° from the horizontal.
- The hardware used to lift precast concrete safety factor that is at least 5 to 1.
- A 4 point pick is necessary when lifting a double T panel that is precast.
- Beam reactions can result in column top deformations due to eccentric loads.
- Precast items that are not prestressed require external bracing or strongback.
- All precast concrete connections need bolts with a diameter of ½ of an inch.

- Bearing pads need to be made out of plastic or elastomerics.
- Braces must remain on walls that are precast until it is stable.
- •he span of a single support crane is generally 60 feet.

### *Shotcrete*

Shotcrete is an alternative to formwork. The concrete mixture is sprayed onto surfaces. Shotcrete uses aggregate that is smaller than ¾ of an inch, and reinforcement bars used are typically No. 5. The smallest clearance used between the bars is 2 ½ inches.

Shotcrete needs to be held at 40° or higher, and it needs to remain moist while it is curing for at least 24 hours. A strength test must be conducted every 50 yards when using shotcrete.

### *Pavement*

There are two basic pavement types, flexible and rigid. Flexible pavement allows for ground movement and does not have any reinforcement such as blacktop. Flexible bituminous pavement is used for its ease of maintenance and basic repair of sections. Rigid pavement is cement concrete that can be found in slabs.

- Concrete curb bases that have granular materials need to be set at a 6 inch depth.
- When paved sidewalks are born against structures, joints should be placed at intervals every 30 feet.

### *Using Concrete in Construction:*

- When concrete needs to be placed underwater, the tremie method is used to pour it.
- Concrete walls need to be damp proofed before any backfill.
- A standard concrete block has a nominal size of 8" x 8" x 16".
- The standard mortar joint is necessary for concrete blocks 3/8 of an inch wide.
- Joint reinforcement is needed with every second course in a stack block pattern.
- Lintels are used to cover the openings for windows and doors in concrete walls. When used for support, they need to be at least 4 inches long.

## MASONRY

Masonry is a combination of different materials that are combined with grout, mortar, or other joining methods. It is heat resistant and prevents the spread of fire. Slurry or grout is made up of bentonite, additives, and the stable colloidal suspension of powder cement. Grout is the material used to fill cavities and other spaces. The difference between grout and mortar is aggregate. Mortar has fine aggregate, but grout does not always have aggregate. Weight bearing masonry walls should be 8 inches thick to bear loads, according to the IBC.

### *Masonry Units and Walls*

- **Concrete masonry Unit (CMU)** – are priced low and provide fire resistance, making it the most commonly used construction material. The psi is at least 1,000.
- o Mortar joints in CMU are typically 3/8 of an inch thick.
- o 8 x 8 x 16 CMU has the strongest aggregate made of sand and gravel, and will weigh 40 pounds.
- o Pumice has the least weight of any CMU per cubic foot.
- o Two core CMU is usually selected in cases of reinforcement.
- **Ashlar masonry** – made of rectangular units of different sizes from sawed dressed, or square beds surfaces that are bonded and put together with mortar.

- o Coursed ashlar masonry – a type of ashlar masonry that that creates a course of stones with equal height.
- o Random ashlar – a type of ashlar masonry that is put together without any course or pattern.
- **Glass unit masonry** – are units of glass that are bonded with mortar.
- o Glass mortar joints are ¼ of an inch thick.
- **Plain masonry** – masonry that needs tensile strength to be considered but not the reinforcement stress.
- **Reinforced masonry** – reinforcement is used with the masonry to resist forces.
- **Unreinforced masonry** – the masonry is plain, without reinforcement.
- **Solid masonry** – has solid units that are placed adjacent to each other and have joints between, and the spaces are filled with mortar.
- **Clay masonry** – comprised of shale, fired clay, or burned clay and larger than brick.
- **Concrete masonry** – masonry that is more than 12 x 4 x 4 inches and comprised of cement and other aggregates.
- **Hollow masonry** – a cross-sectional area of planes that are parallel to the load bearing surface makes up 75% of the gross cross section or more as it is measured on the same plane.
- **Cavity** – a two-wythe wall of masonry or other units that is arranged to allow airspace so that they react to stress independently. Additionally, the inner and outer walls a connected with metal ties. Wall ties in brick cavities need to be placed 5/8 of an inch from the unit's edge. The average cavity is 2 inches.
- o Masonry pocket – opening to contain an end girder/beam. It requires ½ inch clearance.
- **Composite wall** – a wall combined of two masonry units or more where one is the backup and the other forms the facing elements.
- **Masonry bonded hollow wall** – the masonry is made of hollow units that have airspace in the wall and have facing and backing walls that are bonded.
- **Dry stacked wall** – also called a surface bonded wall, the concrete units are dry stacked before both sides are coated with a mortar that is surface bonding.
- **Parapet wall** – a section of wall that is above the roofline.
- **Masonry veneer wall** – a wall that is structurally independent and has masonry units on both sides but does not support loads. Brick veneer should be anchored with corrugated metal ties.
- **Masonry fire wall** – concrete or masonry wall that has no opening. The IBC recommends that the nearby combustible members have a 4 inch separation of the opposite wall sides.
- **Stucco masonry** – a finish on the exterior wall. Control joists need to be placed every 144 square feet to prevent stucco cracking. Stucco must be ½ an inch thick.
- **Efflorescence** – forms on masonry after water exposure.
- **Strap anchor** – connects masonry walls at their intersection.
- **Copings** – wall coverings that keep moisture from entering the top of the wall.
- **Tooled joints** – provide the greatest protection from moisture.
- **Control joints** – in masonry, require raking ¾ of an inch of mortar and then using a caulking compound to seal it.
- **Jack arch** – arches that are supported by steel and wider than 2 feet.

Masonry walls that are over 8 feet need to be braced.

### *Grout and Mortar*

Mortar is usually made of lime, sand, water, and Portland cement. The lime used in mortar is type S hydrated. It typically needs to be used within 2 ½ hours of mixing.

- **M mortar** – has the greatest strength (2,500 psi average compressive strength at 28 days)and is used for structures below grade.
- **S mortar** – has a great strength; used in areas where the wind speed is over 80 mph, (1,800 psi average compressive

strength at 28 days) and is used for a general purpose.

- **N mortar** – has a mid strength (750 psi average compression strength at 28 days) that is used in walls that are above grade and moderate areas of wind.
- **O mortar** – has a low strength (350 psi average compression strength at 28 days) that is used in interior walls that are load bearing.
- **K mortar** – typically used in restoration projects and areas that do not require strength.

The bond strength of mortar that is hardened is the most significant property. When mortar is used to fill in empty spaces, it is called tuck pointing.

Grouts may be coarse or fine depending on whether coarse aggregate is used in the mix. A coarse aggregate will not be able to fall through a ¼ inch sieve. Grouting is either low lifting or high lifting. High lifting is complicated, but it is used to grout an entire story of a structure. The grout lift should not exceed 5 feet. Low lifting is grouted the height of the scaffold before the next lift is done. Grout pours are consolidated by vibration and rodding when the pour is 12 inches and below.

Grout should not fall below 40 °; ideally, it should not fall below 50°.

### *Tools and equipment*

Masonry joints that are long and horizontal, are created using the sled runner jointers.

Brick hammers will cut bricks quickly, and may be used when jagged edges will be hidden by mortar.

Sandblasters used on brick should have ¼ inch nozzles and operate at a pressure between 60 and 120 pounds.

It is best to clean brick with hydrochloric acid or muriatic acid.

Trowels are useful for spreading and furrowing the mortar bed.

### *Blocks*

Masonry blocks should be laid so that the wide flange is up. Lead corners are typically laid 4 to 5 courses in height.

### *Bricks*

MW bricks are used in areas prone to freezing but are not wet. In areas that are wet and prone to freezing, SW bricks are necessary. All bricks that are considered solid will be at least 75% solid. The average size of a modular brick is 4 x 2 2/3 x 8 inches.

The leads of a structure are found in the corners when bricks are laid.

### *Bonds:*

Stacked bonds are the weakest bonds, and they are created by aligning the vertical joints.

Common bonds are patterns of 5 stretcher courses and a single header course.

### *Fireplaces*

Masonry fireplaces that are indoors need a back clearance of 4 inches and a front clearance of 2 inches. The hearth needs to be 8 inches on the sides of the fireplace and 16 inches in the front in most fireplaces. If the box is more than 6 feet squared, the hearth should be 12 inches on the sides and 20 inches in the front.

Chimneys walls must be at least 4 inches thick and must be at least 2 feet higher than other building elements that are within a 10-foot range.

## WOOD AND STRUCTURAL STEEL

The wood commonly used in construction is softwood. This includes the use of cedar, pine, redwood, spruce, and other coniferous trees. Hardwoods that are popular in construction are oak, cherry, maple, ash, and other deciduous trees. The choice of lumber will determine the finish of a project, which means the grade must be taken into accounts.

*Select Grades:*

B – has few if any defects

C – has a few defects

D – has large defects

*Common Grades:*

1. has few defects and tight knots
2. has defects and larger knots
3. has knotholes, loose knots, and other defects
4. is low quality wood
5. lowest quality and most defective appearance

Lumber that has a grain that separates lengthwise has what is known as a ring shake, which is the most commonly seen defect.

Wood that is natural and durable may be decay resistant or termite resistant. Redwood and eastern red cedar is termite resistant wood. Black walnut, black locust, redwood and cedar are decay resistant.

The standards for wood are established by the American Wood Council (AWC) along with state and local building organizations and codes. The standards outlined are found in the: Wood Frame Construction Manual for One and Two Family Dwellings, National Design Specifications for Wood Construction (NDS), Load and Resistance Factor Design for Engineered Wood Construction (LRFD).

When wood is inspected and approved, it will be stamped by an accredited organization that follows the guidelines of the American Standard Lumber Committee in DOC PS 20.

The Northeastern Lumber Manufacturers Association (NELMA) does the grading of Eastern White Pine Lumber, Balsam Fir, Eastern Spruce, and SPF (Spruce-Pine-Fir), along with other softwood lumber from the east. There are five different grading elements:

1. 1The moisture content
2. The product grade
3. The species/grouping
4. ALSC supervisory agency
5. The Mill number ID or name

A great number of manufacturers are part of the Western Wood Products Association. The lumber grading is done by the Quality Services Division along with overseeing mill quality and grading machine stressed lumber and glued materials. These rules are used to create the standards used in the Softwood Lumber Standard PS 20.

Fireblocks are wooded blocks between wall space that prevent air from feeding a fire. According to the IBC, fireblocks need to be 2 inches thick when made of nominal lumber, or it may be two pieces of 1 inch lumber. The blocks need to be placed vertically, between the floor and ceiling, and they should be spaced horizontally at least every 10 feet.

### *Decay*

The rate of wood decay and hazard can be predicted using a climate index map. There is little resistance to decay in most wood, but there are chemical preservatives to address different sources of decay such as fungi or insects. Preservatives should maintain moisture levels at 19%. The level of protection will depend on the type of wood and preservative. Sapwood has the lowest decay resistance to decay than heartwood, but an effective preservative that is applied adequately can be effective on any wood and increase its life. It is particularly important to treat wood for decay and infestation if it touches soil. Wood that is below the water should be untreated.

Timber frames must have columns that are 8x8 inches at least when they support floors to have a ¾ hour fire rating.

Sunlight will draw moisture from wood siding, which causes blistering and peeling of paint.

### *Truss*

- Wood trusses must be at least 2 x 4 in diagonal bracing and lateral restraint.
- Ground braces with trusses require the clinching of 2 nails that are 16d.
- The greatest out-of-plumb tolerance of a 6 foot truss rise is 1 ½ inches.
- Trusses require a bearing support tolerance +/- ¼ inch.
- Temporary restraints must have a 15 foot spacing between bottom chord lateral restraint.
- Permanent restraints must have a 10 foot spacing between bottom chord lateral restraint.
- Diagonal web bracing requires two 16d nails be used at each point.
- Diagonal braces need to be installed at 45° and are necessary at every 10 spaces.
- Trusses that are not braced cannot carry loads.

Engineered wood products typically fall under code guidelines. Types of engineered wood includes:

- **Plywood** – when it is used for a concrete form, it must have a B-B quality.
- **Oriented strand board (OSB)** – panels created from strands of wooden rectangles that are layered lengthwise.
- **Laminated veneer lumber** – billets that are bonded with thin veneers of wood. Laminated decking is used when high traffic is expected.
- **Glulam** – glued laminated timber, dimensional timber layers are glued together. Curved beams should be on top or up and never drilled or notched unless it is part of their design.
- **Cross laminated timber** – lumber converted into a multilayer panel.
- **Parallel strand lumber** – strands of veneer bonded and placed in parallel form.
- **Finger jointed lumber** – lengths of wood that are created from short pieces.
- **I-joists** – floor and roof pieces that have an I shape.

## GYPSUM

Most gypsum wallboards are not used in damp areas unless they are green and moisture resistant. Type X gypsum boards are fire resistant according to ASTM requirements.

When installing drywall, the least expensive method that provides sound resistance is the resilient channel. Installing resilient channels requires fasteners that are 1 ¼ inch and type W or type S screws with bugle heads.

- The fasteners necessary to attach steel studs to runners are type S pan heads.
- Tapcon is necessary fastener for attaching steel framing to block surfaces or poured concrete.
- Screws that are 1 ¼ inch type W bugle heads are the minimum length for installing gypsum panels that are 5/8 of an inch.
- The 1 inch type S fastener is needed to attach a layer of drywall to metal studs.
- Annular drywall nails that are 1 ½ inches can be used to install drywall that is ¾ an inch.
- Wallboards that are ½ inch require center stud spacing of 24 inches and 7 inch spacing of fasteners.
- Stud spacing is 24 inches when gypsum is installed over them.
- Nonbearing interior walls require stud spacing at 28 inches.

Drywall joint compounds that can harden and finish the same day are powder setting joint compounds. When covering 1,000 square feet of drywall, 9.4 gallons of joint compound are needed. Joint compound is used to hide the heads of screws once the fasteners are replaced.

Drywall joints should be arranged on opposite sides of the partition in wood frames. This way, they appear on different wall studs before being sheet rocked. When multiple gypsum applications are necessary, the joists require 10 inch offset spacing.

When hanging sheetrock, it is important to make sure that the temperature is at least 50°. The drywall screws must remain at least 3/8 of an inch away from the edges during installation. The corners of sheetrock need to be reinforced at their outside corners by the corner bead.

- **Drywall** – interior wall made from wood pulp and plaster, and other elements. When it is used in moist areas, such as the bathroom, (MR) greenboard is necessary.
    - Blue board – absorbent veneer plaster with a gypsum base that is used on drywall.
    - Curved walls require ¼ inch of drywall.
- **Joint compounds** – plaster like compounds that cover joints, nails, etc. The dry time is affected by moisture and temperature. It should not be applied in temperatures below 55°. At 60° and 60% humidity, it will dry in 29 hours.

## STEEL CONSTRUCTION

The yield stress of structural steel needs to be defined to determine at which point it will not be acceptable. Steel standards are governed by both the ASTM and the AISC (American Institute of Steel Construction). When structural steel cannot be identified, tests need to be done. It is important to protect steel with paint or other applications. Painted steel, which is cold-formed steel, and other steel that is used in construction must adhere to the guidelines of AISC 360. When creating joints, welding is more expensive than bolting. However, it is cheaper when done with in shop conditions. Welding requires both extra labor and ultrasonic and/or radiographic inspection.

The manufacture, design, and application of joist girders and open web joists fall under the Steel Joist Institute (SJI) specifications. The support of one way roof or floor systems should be parallel chord and open web composite steel joists. The load carrying members may be cold-formed or hot-rolled. The SJI outlines the following joists:

- **K-series (open web steel)** – offer support for building roofs and floors, and have a 30-inch depth and 2 ½ inch bearing depth at most. The most commonly used is a Warren joist or Modified Warren joist. The end of the joist is attached with 2 1/8 inch fillet welds that are an inch long or 2 bolts that are ½ inch each. A flex or bow in an open web joist is a camber. These joists are also called bar joists, shortspans, and composite joists. When bar joists are not even, they are sweeps.

When open web joists are bottom bearing, they need to be erected with the right side up. Bottom bearing joists need to be restrained with bolted diagonal bridging at the end.

In a 60 foot joist, the camber is 1 ½ inches long.

Open web joists require at least 4 inches of bearing depth in masonry walls.

- **DLH/LH** – series Deep Longspan and longspan – joists that are used to extend the loads and spans the K-series cannot. Longspan joists have a 5 inch bearing depth, and their greatest depth is 48 inches. Deep longspan joists haves depth from 52 to 72 inches and lengths that are 61 to 144 feet. They should be attached with 2 ¼ inch fillet welds that are 2 inches long or 2 bolts that are ¾ inch each. The final 2 numbers in the designation are the chord number designation.

The DHL/LH joists require steel plates anchored at 6 inches when there is bearing on masonry or concrete support. Steel plates should not be more than ½ inch away from concrete or masonry walls.

Steel joists that are under 60 feet may be designed in a way that allows a single employee to release the hoisting cable without erection bridging. Steel joist bridging can hoist 1,000 pounds at most. When joist spans are over 100 feet, the hoisting cable is released after the diagonal bridge is installed. Bridging is installed for 100 foot joists by the placing the joists in the appropriate position and held until the joists are attached. Unbridged joists are not safe for bearing loads.

K-series joists that require the support of girders need to rest on the chord panel tops.

Columns normally support joist girders, and they typically have a bearing depth of 7 ½ inches when they are underslung. A nominal girder will have a 36-inch depth at the mid-span. The first two numbers of the designation number is the depth and the next number is the joist spacing.

When vertical stabilizer plates are used to stabilize the chords at the bottom, they prevent unbridged girders from toppling over. The plates need to be 6 x 6 inches at least to be effective.

The bearing details of joists on perimeter or interior joist girders need the reaction to pass the centroid of the girder. The end of a floor joist requires a wood or joist hanger of 1 to 1 ½ inches for support. Floor joists require 2 x 6 lumber and should not have holes closer than 2 inches from the edge. When a type of lateral is placed between floor joists to prevent lateral distortion and warping, it is called bridging. Tee shaped joists can provide support up to 60 feet. It is important that the center 1/3 of the joist not be notched. When notches are done at the top or bottom, they should be 1/6 of the joist's depth.

Base plates are used to help columns distribute vertical loads, and they are installed with shim packs that fit into crevices. Steel columns must be anchored by at least 4 anchor rods and anchor bolts. Perimeter columns need to extend 48 inches over a finished floor.

When the connections are between members made of steel and other materials, they will vary greatly because the strengths will vary. The same is true of connections made of different types of steel.

When stress is transferred to a bar interface, it will alter the tensile stress of the bar used as reinforcement. To protect against bond failure, the bar must extend past the point of yield stress and would be the same as the development length. The criteria for placing the bars are proper spacing and enough room to provide the necessary cover of the bars. The tension cross brace in steel frames provide vertical and horizontal stability while allowing for load reversals.

### *Reinforced Beams and Ties*

- The beams used at the perimeter of the structure are spandrel beams.
- Cantilevered beams need tension bars placed at the top.
- Beam bolsters are 5 feet long.
- Stirrups may be placed in beams to resist diagonal tension. They are U or W shaped.
- There are 11 reinforcement bar sizes.
- When bars are at right angles, temperature steel carries the stress.
- A No. 5 rebar has a .625 inch diameter.
- Spiral bars must be a no smaller than 3/8 inch in diameter and require spacing between 1 and 3 inches.

- Longitudinal reinforcing bars have the greatest tolerance placement.
- There is no exact spacing of bars used in long run walls or slabs.
- When tying reinforcing bars to maintain position, 16 gage wire is used.
- Wrap and snap ties are necessary for concrete pours.
- Wall reinforcement ties should be spaced 4 to 6 feet away from each other.
- The last bars placed are temperature reinforcement.
- Rafter ties must be spaced 4 feet apart from each other.
- Joist headers over 6 feet require hangers.

When bolts are used in connections, the bearing type can cause the load direction to change. This occurs if the whole is larger than the bolt and allows movement. The hole should only be 1/16 of an inch oversized. The most commonly used bolt is the A325.

### *Welding:*

- Longspan joists that are welded to steel supports require ¼ inch fillet welds that are 2 inches long.
- Two bolts ¾ inches in diameter are necessary when welding two joist girders made of steel.
- When steel joist are welded in place, they should be welded at each end on one side.
- Welded horizontal bridges require at least 2-inch laps.
- Longspan joists should be attached at the ends with 2 bolts ¾ inch each or 2 ¼ inch welds that are 2 inches long.
- Spot welding/ tack welding will lower the bar's strength by 35% to 40%.

### *Pipe Columns:*

Pipe columns are steel pipes filled with concrete. They must not be closer to than 1 inch to the exterior steel shell. When the pipe columns are secondary, such as in a basement, they need a 3-inch diameter. In 3 story or 40 foot structures, their diameter needs to be 4 inches.

## TRANSPORTATION/STORAGE

When joists are shipped, they need to be upside down. Joists should be unloaded from flatbeds in bundles that do not exceed 1,000 pounds. Cranes are necessary to remove the bundles. Removal requires the use of cables through the web system that are spaced evenly at the bottom chord. After joists are removed, they should be kept in the same positions they traveled in.

Post tension cables require cradle coils and nylon straps to be unloaded, and they need to be stored on dunnage so that the tendons are not touching the ground

Drywall needs to be stored in a flat position and in the middle of a dry room.

Trusses need to be unloaded with cranes that do not have web members attached. Connecting the top chord with a closed loop attachment should lift trusses. Trusses need to be stored indoors, with adequate ventilation, when they are kept for more than a week. If they are in a horizontal position for this time, they need to be spaced 8 to 10 feet on blocking centers.

Steel decking bundles weigh 4,000 pounds when they are shipped. Steel decks need to be lifted with both chokers. When storing decks, they should be elevated at one end and not touch the ground.

# INTERIOR ASSEMBLY/INSTALLATION TYPES

### Doors:

There are exterior and interior doors. The typical height of a door is 80 inches. When installing exterior doors, the 15 pounds of felt flashing are placed in the rough opening before the frame. Bifold doors require the top track to be installed before the lower/bottom track. An interior door that is 1 3/8 requires hinges that are 3.5 x 3.5 inches. When door stops are installed they need to be nailed to the side with the lock first.

Doors frames that run from the floor to the ceiling may act the same way as control joists.

### Stairs:

- **Winders** – stairs that radiate.
- **Total run** – the complete horizontal length of the stairway.
- **Riser** – the vertical portion of the stair is typically between 4 and 7 inches per step; 7 is ADA compliant.
- **Tread** – the horizontal portion of the stair. They should be 11 inches, according to the IBC.
- **Stair stringer** – supports the tread and riser, and requires 3 ½ inches past the notch. Stairs width more than 2 feet and 6 inches require a third stringer in the center of the stairs.

### Cabinets:

A standard wall cabinet is 12 inches deep. Base cabinets are typically 32 ½ inches high and 24 inches deep. When cabinets only span a single stud, 2 #10 screws need to be used along with 2 toggle bolts that are 3/16 x 3 ½ inches.

### Flooring

The final large project is installing a finished floor, which occurs after the electrical, plumbing, and plastering is finished. Wood flooring should be kept in the building for a minimum of 4 days before installation. Before installing a subfloor the area needs to be swept and 15 pounds of asphalt paper paid. This should be done before maple flooring is installed. The most common wood floors are Maple, Birch, and Beech. The groove of tongue and groove flooring needs to face the wall, and the first board should be ½ inch to 5/8 inches away from the frame wall.

When installing tile, the base should be the backerboard.

In floor slabs, the stirrup location has a maximum variation of +/- 1 inch.

### Ceilings

In furred ceilings, the furring channels should be attached at right angles to the bar joists and have a 24 inch maximum center.

# ROOFING

### Roof Types

The pitch (also slope) and materials for the range are used to define the roof. The rise to the rafters ratio is the pitch. Express pitch is the vertical rise of the roof over the 12-inch distance horizontally. A uniform pitch will have a valley rafter create a 45° angle with the main ridge board, which should be an inch thick. The formula used to determine the slope or pitch is

:

### Rise/Run

**Fascia** is the board gutters are connected to on the exterior. Fascia itself is nailed to the rafter tails. Should it be spliced to the joint, it needs to be metered and fall on the rafter tail's end. The soffit or eave is below the fascia. When plywood is used as a soffit, the nails should be 6 inches a part. The same spacing is used in roof sheathing.

**Flat roofing** – a roof with a slope under 1:12.

**Low sloped –** a roof with a slope that is only slightly pitched (under 4:12 to 2:12).

**Built-up roof (BUR) –** a roof has layers that have bituminous material that are lapped and cemented together and a slope of ¼ :12 or 2%. The vapor retarder used in BUR is usually 40 to 80 pounds per square. When done correctly, the roof should last 20 years.

**Single-ply membrane –** a roof with a sheet of synthetic rubber, plastic, and modified bitumen with a UV protected topcoat.

**Roll roofing –** a roof that is saturated with asphalt over the deck that may be single or two-ply. The normal exposure is 17 inches, and the strip should over hang by ¼ inch. The slope should be at least 1:12 or 8%. This type of roofing should be installed when the temperature is more than 45°. The strips need to be shortened an allowed to warm in the sun if the temperature is lower.

**Steep sloped –** a roof that has a slope over 1:12. The materials used are typically cedar shakes, cedar shingles, asphalt **shingles, and concrete tiles.**

**High sloped –** a roof with pitch from 4:12 to 21:12.

**Mansard –** a roof with a pitch at 21:12 or over.

Asphalt roofs have a flashpoint between 437° and 500°. The asphalt most commonly used on roofs is type III, and it cannot be heated past 475°. The seams in the roof are sealed with the hot mop. When using asphalt shingles, two fasteners are necessary for a single shingle and four fasteners need to be used for each strip. The lowest slope for asphalt shingles is 2:12. The manufacturer instructions must be followed during installation.

Cedar shingles come in bundles of four. Wooden shingles need a side lap or offset of 1 ½ inches and require 2 nails each. When they are installed on 1 x 4 sheathing that is non-continuous, they need to be centered and spaced at equal distances. The slope of the roof needs to be at least 3:12.

When the slope is more than 33% (4:12), it is safe to use wooden shakes. Spaced and open sheathing will promote even drying with wooden shakes and improve ventilation. Corrosion resistant fasteners must be used, and the penetration should be ¾ in into the sheath. Ventilation requires the area that is net free not be under the ventilation's square footage per 150 square feet of the entire area or 1/150 of the space. (Floor ventilation uses the same ratio.)

Tile roofs may be clay or concrete, and they require fasteners that are at least ¾ of an inch. Tiles typically weigh 900 pounds per square. Field tiles require 3-inch metal cap overlaps. Clay tiles must comply with ASTM C1167 and require slopes that are at least 2.5:12. Concrete tiles used around roof valleys must have end laps that are at least 4 inches and should extend from the centerline at least 11 inches.

When slate is used on open valleys, the flashing should be .0179 zinc coated or 16-ounce copper. Slate requires the roof have a slope of at least 4:12 or 33% and metal flashing that is .0179 inch zinc-coated G-90.

*There are different components in roofing:*

- **Roof section –** a portion of a roof that uses flashing, existing joints, parapet walls, elevation differences, legal description, or roof type difference. It excludes any portion that has an existing system tie off.
- **Roof assembly –** anything that offers protection and resistance from loads and weather. This includes insulation, roof deck, roof covering, thermal barrier, and others.
- **Roof deck –** is a sloped or flat surface that does not include supporting members. It is a substrate to apply weatherproofing and roofing, and the deck needs to support live loads. Plywood or wood plank is used to make combustible decks, and concrete, gypsum, and corrugated metal are used to create non-combustible decks.
- **Roof covering –** are fire classification, weathering, etc. that are applied to the roof deck. They need to be approved and applied correctly, and are required by the IBC when the roof or insulation is combustible.
- o A covering with a layer or more of polymer modified asphalt sheets is a modified bitumem roof covering. They may require a ballast layer or held with a substrate.
- **Built-up roof covering –** felt, in multi layers, are bonded together and surfaced with a smooth coating, cap sheet, mineral aggregate, etc.

- **Interlayment –** felt layer or layer of nonbituminous saturated felt that is shingled and has a width of 18 in or more.
- **Metal roof panel –** is a metal sheet that is interlocking and has a 3 square foot sheet installed weather exposure.
- **Metal roof shingle –** has a weather exposure installed that is smaller than 3 square feet.
- **Mechanical equipment screen –** a rooftop structure that is partially enclosed and used to hide HVAC equipment.
- **Penthouse –** a structure above the roof that is fully enclosed and takes up under 1/3 of the roof's space. Bulkheads, towers, tanks, spires, domes, etc. are not included in the penthouse.
- **Saddle –** also called a cricket, is the raised area that is around the chimney's upper side and should be at least 30 inches.

### *Requirements*

To keep moisture out of walls and roofs, flashing is used. Flashing is the installed where the slope or direction of the roof changes as well as at gutters and intersections of the roof. It is not necessary for hip ridge junctions. Flashing is placed beneath the sheathing and framing, at the brick course.

When parapet walls are sealed, weatherproof and noncombustible materials are used, they need to be at least the same thickness of the wall. The parapet wall must not be fewer than 30 inches higher than the intersection between the roof surface and wall intersect. This is not true when the roof is sloped and drains, which requires a system for drainage.

Downspouts transfer water from gutters, scuppers, and conductor heads to lower roofs, water runoff, or the ground. Overflow scuppers need to be above the roof covering of parapets and walls when the drainage system in not set up. Roof downspouts and condensate lines need to be one foot away from the sidewall at a minimum. When the drain spouts are used, the splash blocks need to be 3 inches long.

When using fire retardant shingles, they must be treated with the vacuum pressured method. They also need to be identified by a label or marking approved by the UL.

Membranes that are only attached at the substrate to the roof's perimeter and penetrations are loose-laid membranes. A ballast is needed to keep the membrane in position. Membranes on smooth surface roofs will not have any aggregate or mineral granule surfacing. Ice dams' membranes need to reach 24 inches into the structure's exterior wall line.

### *Roof Loads*

Wind deflection at the roof edge, obstruction, or peak that creates a drop in the air pressure is wind uplift. This affects the roof by causing the membrane to pull away from the roof as it expands. The requirements for the wind and snow loads vary with each region. County and city requirements also need to be consulted.

### *Classes:*

A – the assembled roof is identified by the correct testing agency as effective in severe fires and is permissible in all construction, such as metal shingles.

B – the assembled roof is identified by the correct testing agency as effective in moderate fires.

C – the assembled roof is identified by the correct testing agency as effective in light fires.

Non-classified – uses materials that are approved but not included in the other classes.

### *Materials*

All roof covering materials must be compatible with the other materials of the structure. If the materials do not have the necessary markings on the packaged materials, they need to be tested by an approved agency.

- **Asphalt shingles –** the simplest installation for steep roofing and least expensive roofing material. They must comply with ATSM D 225, 3462, 3161, and 7158 and are typically comprised of spun fiberglass or polyester along with saturation of modified bitumen/asphalt that is covered with ceramic granules. A three tabbed asphalt shingle requires 4 nails, and each sq/ft will require 2 ½ pounds of nails for installation. The nail must penetrate at least ¾ of an inch to comply with IBC regulations.

- **Cedar shakes/shingles –** are made of cedar and have different quality. The premium cedar is completely (100%) clear, edge grain, and heartwood. The next level of quality is Number 1, which has 20% flat grain maximum and is clear heartwood. The lowest quality is Number 2, which has the most defects and a higher percentage of flat grain in the shingle.
- **Concrete roof tile –** is comprised of cement, water, and sand.
    - Flat profile – the tile is without curves from the back.
    - Low profile – the tile has small curves (1:5 or under).
    - High profile – the tile has large curves (over 1:5).
- **Nails –** need to meet ASTM A 641 standard and be able to resist corrosion.
    - Class 1 – are resistant to corrosion because of electro galvanization, coating, mechanical galvanization, stainless steel, other metals, and hot dipped galvanization. A 16d nail is 3 ½ inches long. In moist frame, the nail pops will need to be reduced by 19%.
- **Wood screws –** need to meet ANSI/ASME B 18.6.1 standards and be able to resist corrosion due to galvanization, nonferrous material, stainless steel, coating, etc.
- **Clips –** need to meet the standards ASTM A 90/A 90M, TAS 114 Appendix E and be able to resist corrosion.
- **House wrap –** materials that take the place of asphalt-treated paper, or asphalt saturated felt. The high density polyethylene ventilates by permitting gas to pass through but not liquid.

A single square of shingles will typically cover 100 square feet. A bundle of shingles is a tab. Shingles should not be nailed within 6 inches of the valley. When roll paper endlaps are used, they should be offset by 6 inches.

### Underlay

Any sheet material or felt that is asphalt saturated and placed in the space between the roof deck and system is an underlay. Underlays serve two purposes: they act as a secondary barrier and separate the deck and cover. The requirements for the underlay will depend on the materials in the covering. In its role to protect from moisture, it needs a permeability rating of 1 or under. The underlay of a sloping roof does not act as a vapor barrier. The lap of underlay needs to be 4 inches at the end and 2 inches on the edge.

### Flashing

Sheet metal that is put over a joint and used to keep moisture out of a building is flashing. The terminations and intersections are found created by flashing and include valleys, rakes, chimneys, caves, skylights, etc. When done correctly, flashing will resist water penetration from wind pressure, gravity, and surface tension. Stainless steel is the most effective flashing material, but any material used for flashing need to be compatible, durable, and weather resistant. Metal flashing needs to be able to resist corrosion. The thickness should be at least .019 inches and No 26 gage galvanized to meet IBC regulations.

Flashing gables and eaves requires a placing at least 2 inches of drip edge metal on the surface as well as 1 ½ inch over decking edges that are exposed. The most on center spacing that a mechanically fastened drip edge may have is 12 inches. Drip edges are the a type of flashing with a lower edge that are attached to the roof deck below the felt and project outward to control dripping water or change the contact continuity of between wall components and the roof's perimeter. On the other hand, edge flashing is membrane that seals the edge of the roof's membrane.

Flashing needs to be replaced once it rusts or becomes damaged. Open valley flashing must be 26 inch gauge galvanized steel and at least 24 in. wide. Counterflashing may or may not be necessary, but both must be installed where the roof is at a vertical surface. Counterflashing is the vertical flashing that curves over the base flashing's top. Flash failure occurs with acid rain, salt, extreme heat, abrasive wind, and heavy snow.

Roof leaks may be discovered by noticing shingles that are warped, damaged, or warn. The inspection should be made around vent pipes where leaks are more common. Installing metal sheets below the shingles and caulking them with tar and granules may repair shingles made of asphalt.

### *Steel Roof Decking*

Steel decks are used to provide additional support beyond beams and joists, and there are different types of decks.

Composite floor decks are used so that the ends do not overlap. They have thickness ranges between .03 and .06 inches and a lowest weight of 4 psf. They need to be installed with the bare side on the top. Shear connector devices are used to mechanically connect the deck with the concrete. Decks can be connected with pneumatically driven pins, arc puddle welds, and self-drilling screws. Welds, button punches, and screws are used to connect laps with decking. Shear lugs are not recommended for welding composite decks.

When floor decks are covered in concrete, it needs to be spread in a uniform pattern towards the center.

Cellular decks are used to help chase electrical distribution. They are installed with the panels connecting end to end. There is no overlap.

Roof decks transfer the horizontal and vertical loads to the frame of the building. The typical roof deck has a 2-inch roof deck. They are posted as (IR) 1 ½ x 6 and have a weight of 2 to 4 psf. Roof decks should support 30 psf at a minimum. At most, a 6-inch opening is framed before penetration.

The weld perimeter of 75% is necessary when working with a weld that has a strong side lap. A fillet weld is used when the metal deck's flat side lap is not long enough.

Steel floor decks that are used as working platforms should be able to handle psf when used as work platforms. Employees must stay 6 feet away from the deck's end during installation. This is called the Leading Edge or Control Zone. The work area should be 12 feet wide at least.

## GLASS

Glass is used in many different structures, and the purpose of the glass determines which type is used.

- **Clear glass** – typically has a small amount of tint and is annealed.
- **Tinted glass** – decreases sunlight exposure with the use of metal oxides in the mixture.
- **Patterned/rolled/figured glass** – an ornamental glass that is used to prevent outside visibility and diffuse light.
- **Ceramic print glass** – used for privacy, this is a type of silk-screened glass.
- **Wired glass** – is fire resistant, and the wire keeps broken glass from falling.
- **Tempered glass/spandrel glass** – provides both strength and safety. The strength of the glass is 4 to 5 times other glass and comes from the high heat treatment and fast cooling, which creates a compressive stress. Manufacturers may include paper labels if they are removable.
  - Heat strengthened – tempered glass that uses thermal strengthening and has a great mechanical strength.
- **Reflective glass** – creates a mirrored refection with a metallic coating on one side of the glass.
- **Insulating glass** – a unit that is premade and has two glass panes or more with a cavity separating them. The joint and cavity are protected by hermetically sealed edges. Filled desiccants are used to control noise and moisture
- **Laminated glass** – layers and plastic Polyvinal butyral that have been treated are combined with glass layers. It is a strong noise barrier, thermal resistant, and shatter resistant, resisting penetration and absorbing forceful impact.

### *Glazing*

A transparent coating is a glaze. On windows, glazing is the glass that is held in place by glazing putty. Other materials that are mixed, made, or treated are safety glazes. Examples include laminated, wired, and tempered glass. Safety glazing is not necessary if there is 1 ½ bar that can resist loads of 50 pounds per linear foot.

### *Other Glazes:*

- Insulted glaze: a method of double glazing in which krypton or argon gas fills the space between panes to increase the thermal performance.

- **Low Emissivity glaze –** limits the rate at which infrared radiation is transferred from the warm plane to the cold, using a coating of metallic oxide.
- **Reflective window glaze –** blocks out light to limit solar radiation.
- **Spectrally selective glaze –** insulated glass that allows light through but prevents 40% to 70% of heat to be transmitted.

The IBC rates wired glass window panels that are 100 square inches as having 1 to 1 ½ hours of fire protection.

## SAFETY

Safety engineers have the responsibility to protect the work environment, employees, and property. This is done by predicting the conditions and policies that present hazards; developing programs that address hazards; monitoring control programs; and writing safety plans and statements for the future.

Safety plans have their own safety life cycles that move through the phases:

- Initiation
- Safety requirement specifications
- Covering design
- Safety feature development
- Decommissioning

Employers are responsible for providing a safe workspace, and a safe space is sure to increase morale and profits. Any employer with more than 10 employees must provide a written emergency plan outlined in OSHA.

The enforcement of OSHA regulations is done by the industrial hygienists (IH), and they make up more than 40% of the OSHA compliance officers. They play a role in developing standards and provide support to regional and national offices. The IH role also includes:

- Aid in field procedures
- Interpret OSHA standards
- Identify and analyze hazards and stressors
- Find measures to control hazardous conditions

OSHA Forms 300, 300A, and 301 are injury and illness logs, and they must be kept a minimum of 5 years from the incident. Form 301 addresses individual injuries while form 300 outlines and describes the case. Material Safety Data Sheets (MSDS) should be kept on file for every chemical used and consulted if an employee is exposed to a harmful substance. An MSDS must include: 1) the name 2) the ingredients and health information 3) Safe handling and use 4) contact information for the manufacturer or importer. When an MSDS is amended, the label must be amended on the worksite. All employees should be trained in the use of MSDS.

Health and safety programs have the following elements:

- The commitment and involvement of both management and employees
- Continual analysis of the worksite
- Control and prevent hazards and exposure

- Hazard trainings for supervisors, managers, and employees.

In the event that 3 or more employees are hospitalized, OSHA needs to be notified within 8 hours.

### *Violations:*

- Willful violations have $5,000 fines at minimum, but they do not exceed $70,000.
- Citations for a serious violation have $7,000 fines at minimum, but they do not exceed $70,000.
- Failure to fix violations carries a $7,000 fine per day.
- Violation of Section 6 state plans that result in death is a $10,000 fine and/or 6 months in prison. A repeat of this will result in a $20,000 fine and/or a year in prison.
- Making a false statement results in a $10,000 fine and/or 6 months in prison.

OSHA inspections may be programmed or unprogrammed. Programmed inspections occur in areas with high rate of injury. The main risks associated with construction are vehicle sediment, open burning of debris becoming uncontrolled, dust, CFCs, and combustion gases.

### *IBC (ICC) Construction Safety*

- If asbestos is found on site, a certified inspector's inspection and notice of intent must be filed within 10 days.
- All stumps and roots must be removed from the soil up to 12 inches deep.
- The fill slope must not exceed 1:2 ratio or 50%.
- 60 foot high projects must be at least 5 feet from the street and have covered walkways.
- Walkways must be 4 feet wide and always lit.
- Fencing must be at least 8 feet high.
- Neighboring properties must be given 10 days' notice before the project begins.

### *Lead Paint Law:*

If a building has lead paint, the "Protect your family from lead paint in your home" pamphlet must be provided. Proof of distribution must be kept for 3 years. Any violation of the lead paint law is a $37,500 fine per day. The EPA has a Lead Renovation, Repair and Painting Rule, which requires contracts working on child related projects that contain lead have EPA certification or certification from and EPA approved state.

### *Safety Hazards*

There are three federal laws that protect the health and safety of employees:

- Metallic and Nonmetallic Mines Safety Act (1966)
- Federal Coal Mine Health and Safety Act of 1969
- Occupational Safety and Health Act of 1970

Almost all employers are required to follow OSHA regulations.

## *Controls*

Preventing the exposure to hazards is primarily done through engineering controls, work practice controls, and administrative controls. Engineering controls remove the hazards or reduce them by limiting exposure and isolating hazards. Examples include ventilation systems and replacing toxic chemicals.

Work practice controls change the way that a job is completed. Typical controls include:

- Procedures that limit exposure
- Inspect and maintain process controls
- Procedures that implement good housekeeping
- Appropriate supervision
- Forbidding food, drink, gum chewing, and cosmetic application in work areas.

Administrative controls limit hazard exposure through scheduling. If the engineering or workplace controls do not provide adequate protection or exposure limits, the appropriate protective equipment must be used.

## *Personal Protective Equipment PPE*

Personal Protective Equipment (PPE) and administrative controls are at the method of control. PPEs are typically used with other methods of control. PPE requires the following manufacture instructions in use as well as storage and cleaning. Signs must be displayed in areas where PPEs are required.

Typical hazards include: air contamination, chemicals/toxins, biological (bacteria, etc., physical (temperature, vibration, etc.), and ergonomic.

## *Exposure*

Contact between one or more pollutants and the body is exposure. Exposure may be evaluated by 1) measuring the intensity 2) determining the duration, exposure, and frequency 3) compare the internal, regulatory, and professional standards 4) weigh all factors before making a judgment.

The exposure assessments include:

- Route – skin, inhalation, injection, and ingestion
- Magnitude – level of media concentration (f/cm3, mg/m3, ppm)
- Duration – over life, days, hours, and minutes
- Frequency – season, weeks, days

Safe exposure is defined by the threshold limit value (TLV) of a substance. TLV is the concentration that it is safe to expose employees to on a regular basis. When employees are only exposed to a substance for 15 minutes safely, the term used is short-term exposure (STEL). If the concentration can't be measured because you are lacking technology, it is ceiling concentration after 15 minutes. Ceiling also refers to instant concentration.

Skin notation is used for any substance that is exposed through the skin adsorption. Dermal contact, along with inhalation exposure, that is known to potentially cause sensitization in workers are listed substances and sensitizer (SEN).

Concentrations that are over the TLV must be balanced with lower concentrations so that the TWA of 8 hours is under TLV. Typically, up to 30 minutes at 3 times the TLV is safe, but 5 times the TLV is not.

OSHA's permissible exposure limit (PEL) is the 8 hour weighted average at which the concentration is expressed. Half of the PEL is an action limit. Short-term exposure (STEL) limit is the 15 minute weighted average in which concentration is expressed. A concentration should not ever go over the ceiling, which is a 10 or 15 min. TWA.

When more than 30 minutes of exposure to a substance would be fatal, it is designated immediately dangerous to life and health (IDLH). It is commonly used with respirators.

### *Carcinogens*

The National Toxicology Program (NTP) and the International Agency for Research on Cancer (IARC) classify carcinogens, not OSHA.

Carcinogens are classified in the following manner:

A1 – a known carcinogen to humans

A2 – a possible human carcinogen

A3 – a known carcinogen to animals but unknown to humans

A4 – not a known carcinogen to humans

A5 – not believed to be a human carcinogen

### *Aerosol*

Solid or liquid particles are suspended in the air are air contaminants or aerosols. Solis aerosols are typically particles given of from the workspace such as dust, grinding, or cutting material. Liquid aerosols, on the other hand, typically come from condensation or the breaking of liquids. The sizes of both solid and liquid particles depend on energy input. Solids that come as a result of carbonaceous material not combusting completely, the sizes will be a large variety. Fibers are a specific type of solid particles that are fibrous and typically come from ceramic fibers, asbestos, and fiberglass. When the particles released are biologic, there is a risk of allergies, irritation, and infection.

The particle concentration of aerosols uses the formula:

Contaminated air mass/ air volumes

The unit's density sphere diameter that a settling velocity that is the same as the particle is the definition of the Aerodynamic Equivalent Diameter (AED)

To determine the risk of disease, the following functions apply:

- Clearance of the path or destination of particles
- Particle chemical properties
- The deposition site of the respiratory system

Sedimentation is the gravitational settling of the lung that is the particle velocity function and mass. Diffusion in the lung is the particle diameter, velocity, concentration, and distance function.

### *Gas*

A state of matter that has no form at room temperature is a gas. Gas also has a low viscosity or density that will distribute itself uniformly. Pressure that occurs when a liquid or solid has an equilibrium with the vapor is vapor pressure, which is measured mmHg. A volatile chemical would have a higher pressure, and higher temperatures will increase the pressure along with the concentration's equilibrium.

Diffusion covers gas and vapors because they are molecules. The solubility of the gas will determine its absorption in the mucous membranes. Gases and vapors may also be irritants or toxic to the system.

The density of a gas is affected by temperature, pressure, and volume, as the following laws explain:

- Boyle's Law – the volume that a gas occupies at a constant temperature is proportionally inverse to the pressure. The higher the pressure, the more the volume drops.
- Charles' Law – when gas is exposed to constant pressure, it will keep a volume that remains in proportion with the temperature.

The critical variables of gases that affect Fire and Explosive Hazards are:

UEL – above this, there is not enough oxygen for an explosion

LEL – below this, there is not enough fuel for an explosion

Flashpoint – the lowest a temperature can be when a liquid sends off enough vapor to create a mixture that ignites

### Safety Factor

A figure that is typically used to offer a design margin on top of the theoretical design capacity is a factor of safety, also called a safety factor. The safety factor determines calculations, estimates material strength and quality and other factors in the design process that are not certain. The calculation is:

- Component strength/component load

In partial safety factors, there are indicators that will provide the structural dimensions as they relate to loading.

The materials used and the purpose of the item determines the number of the safety factor. These can be calculated with the help of the design and engineering standards. It is not usually necessary to use arbitrary standards.

Safety factors are decided for each section of the unit, but similar factors for each part does not guarantee a uniform safety factor for the unit. The safety factor of one part of the unit will affect the safety factor of the entire unit and the stress that it can handle. The likelihood of failure increases with a factor below one.

### Vibrations

Mechanical vibrations can travel to the hands and arms of workers and can occur when hand tools are used. This is called hand-arm vibration. When employees are sitting or standing and the mechanical vibrations come from a supporting surface, whole-body vibration occurs.

The vibrations from hand tools can cause hand-arm vibration syndrome (HAVS) as damage to blood vessels result in damage to the skin, muscles, and nerves. The chance of damage increases when the vibration exposure occurs with other risk factors that affect blood supply. HAVS will cause Reynaud's Syndrome, which is also called white finger or dead finger.

The best method for preventing HAVS is to avoid using a use non-vibrating tools or vibrating tools that have anti-vibration attributes when necessary. Place limitations on the time using vibration tools and keep the tools in good working order to help prevent injuries.

### Ergonomics

Practicing safe ergonomics is necessary to prevent injury in the workplace, particularly for manual tasks. Manual activities include manipulating, throwing, carrying, striking, grasping, lifting, pushing, pulling, restraining, or lowering objects. These activities increase the risk of developing a number of musculoskeletal injuries, including carpel tunnel and tendonitis. These injuries usually occur as a result of prolonged exposure to the activities. Five activities are risk factors for musculoskeletal injury:

- **Vibration –** hand-arm vibration will damage the vascular system and the peripheral nerves.
- **Repetition –** performing the same type of movement repeatedly causes repetition. Short cycles of activities (30

seconds) become a risk when they are done for an hour or more.

- **Static/awkward posture –** Any body position that is not neutral is awkward. This type of positioning will affect nervous tissue and cause the muscles to operate below capacity and increases the risk of injury.
- **Duration –** how long an activity takes is the duration. Longer duration increases the risk of injury.
- **Exertions that are forceful –** When exertions are forceful, the loads on the tendons, muscles, etc. are strong, causing fatigue that the body cannot recover from easily. When recovery does not occur, musculoskeletal injuries develop.

It is important to manage risks of manual tasks and other activities by 1) identifying and prioritizing tasks that are hazardous 2) making a risk assessment 3) control the risk 4) monitor and review activities.

There is a hierarchy of controls ranks the control options. Manual task control options are they are both administrative controls and design controls.

**Administrative control –** (less effective than design) uses ongoing supervision to address the amount of time that people are exposed to the risks and trains employees to use safe methods of work. This type of control is most effective as part of a comprehensive strategy or in the interim.

**Design control –** addresses the designs of tools, tasks, the workplace, etc. and redesigns as necessary to decrease risk and prevent injury.

### *Trips and Falls*

Most industrial accidents fall under the categories trips, slips, and falls, and they follow the cars and vehicles in fatalities. When these accidents are not fatal, they can result in lacerations, sprains, cuts, broken bones, and injuries to the head and back. OSHA's General Clause, Section 5 (a)(1), governs the employer responsibilities regarding hazard safety and health standards. Hazards addressed are:

- **1910.22 –** work and walking surfaces
- **1910.27 –** fixed ladders

The above standards do not apply to agriculture work, domestic work, or mining, but they do apply to the all other places of permanent employment.

Keeping a clean environment and removing contaminants can prevent many accidents. A contaminant is anything that falls to the floor such as oil, dust, shavings, etc. Cleaning floors will make sure that they are:

- Free of contaminants
- Preventing the buildup of residue
- Not becoming slippery
- Able to stay slip resistant

Floors need to be slip resistant, which requires grip. This is particularly true in wet or contaminated areas and places where thick or viscous contaminants are used. Floors that are cluttered or uneven will increase the risk of tripping.

It is possible to reduce the risk of tripping by practicing good housekeeping; fixing curled linoleum, holes, or uneven surfaces; using storage; tacking carpet and linoleum edges; and highlighting uneven areas.

*Terms to remember:*

- **Floor hole –** a hole that is larger than 1 inch but smaller than 12 inches that is made of any material on any walking surface.
- **Floor opening –** a hole that is over 12 inches in a walking surface and could result in a fall. These include ladder openings, manholes, hatchways, or pits but Not conveyers, elevators, dumbwaiters, or machinery.
- **Wall hole –** a hole in the wall that is over an inch in height but under 30 inches. Ventilation and drain scuppers fall into this category.
- **Wall opening –** a hole that is 30 inches high and 18 inches wide at minimum, which allows people to fall through. This includes chutes and yardarm doorways.
- **Platform –** is an elevated space for work, Examples include balconies and machine platforms.
- **Standard railing –** a barrier constructed to prevent falling, typically around a ramp, runway, platform, hole, or wall opening.
- **Stair railing –** a barrier that is constructed around stairs to prevent falling. Handrails are necessary when there are 4 risers or more over 30 inches.
- **Stairway** – the succession of stairs that leads between floors, platforms, and rooms, equipment, etc. Stairs should be installed at a 30° to 50° angle.
- **Ladder –** used to ascend and descend, they have two side rails that are connected by crosspieces (steps) and even intervals.
- **Extension ladder –** a ladder that is portable, not self-supporting, and adjustable.
- **Sectional ladder –** a ladder that not self-supporting, portable, and not adjustable in length and has the two sections or more.
- **Trestle ladder –** a ladder that is self-supporting, not adjustable, and portable. The two sections have equal angles at the base and hinges.
- **Special purpose ladder –** a ladder that is portable and modified specific uses.
- **Climbing ladder –** a ladder that is typically connected to a scaffold.
- **Ladder safety device –** outside of cages or wells, the devices that reduce risk such as sliding attachments, belts, and breaks.
- **Fixed ladder –** needs to extend 42 inches over the top of the platform and has a 7 inch clearance between rungs.
- **Portable ladder –** moveable and need to extend 3 feet over the surface.
- **Well –** a ladder enclosure that is around a fixed ladder.
- **Grab bar –** ladder handholds that are beside or above ladders to offer more access.
- **Manually propelled mobile scaffold –** a scaffold that rolls on casters, which also support it.
- **Light duty scaffold –** a scaffold created for light loads, below 25 pounds sq/ft.
- **Needle beam scaffold –** a light scaffold that supports the platform using needle beams.
- **Medium duty scaffold –** a scaffold that handles medium loads, below 50b pounds sq/ft.
- **Outrigger scaffold –** a scaffold that uses outriggers and thrust-outs for support. They project past the building's face or wall and have secure inboards inside the structure.
- **Tube and coupler scaffold –** a scaffold that uses tubing in the assembly in place of runners, ties, posts, bearers, and braces. Couplers are used to connect different members and bring the uprights together.
- **Tubular welded frame scaffold –** a scaffold that is frame metal, panel, or sectional and created from sections (posts and horizontal bearer with intermediate members) that are premade and welded.
- **Two-point suspension scaffold –** a scaffold that swings with hangers that support the platform at two points. The hangers are called stirrups and they allow the platform to be lifted and lowered as they suspend from overhead supports.
- **Window jack scaffold –** a scaffold with a jack or bracket that supports the platform. The jack is projected through a window.
- **Catenary scaffold –** a suspension scaffold that has the support of continuous horizontal and parallel ropes to create a vertical pickup. It should not have more than 2 platforms.
- **Bearer –** a part of a scaffold that is horizontal, has ledgers that support it, and hold the platform.

- **Brace –** a connector that holds two scaffold members in a fixed position.

Scaffold need to be tied to the structure horizontally at 30 feet and vertically at 20 feet. Anchor bolts, reveal bolts, etc. must be used to adhere scaffolds to permanent structures according to Regulation (Standards – 29 CFR) and safety requirement 1910.28. The complete OSHA standard for scaffolding can be found at:

https://www.osha.gov/pls/oshaweb/owadisp.show_document?p_id=9720&p_table=STANDARDS

- A scaffold needs to support 4 times the maximum load along with its own weight.
- Only 1 inch of space is allowed between scaffold boards.
- Walkways and platforms on scaffolds need to be 18 inches wide.
- A width of 12 inches is necessary for roof brackets, pump jacks and ladder jack and top plate scaffolds.
- If there is not room for 18-inch platforms, walkways, etc., the guardrails and other fall protection systems must be provided.
- Without guardrails, the greatest horizontal distance allowed between the work face and scaffold platform is 14 inches.
- Outrigger scaffolds have a 3 inch space from the face.
- The working distance between the face and plaster or lathing is no more than 18 inches.
- Scaffold platforms must extend 6 inches over the centerline unless there are hooks or another method of restraint.
- A platform that is 10 feet or fewer must not extend more than 12 inches past the support. Platforms over 10 feet must not extend 18 inches past.
- Scaffolds that overlap should do so by 12 inches.
- Wood platforms may have preservatives and finishes, but they may not be painted.
- Scaffolds parts from different manufacturers must not be combined unless they can be joined without force and compromising the integrity.
- Base plates and mudsills are necessary for supported scaffold poles.
- Four wraps of suspension rope must be used with winding drum hoists on suspension scaffolds. The rope is placed at the lowest point of travel.
- Ropes must be replaced once they are defective.
- Scaffold platforms that are 2 feet above or below ladder or stair access must not be cross braced.
- Steps to platforms must be 16 inches wide.
- Attachable ladders that are must have rest platforms every 35 feet when the scaffold is over 35 feet high.
- Scaffold require a 3 foot clearance with power lines that have fewer than 300 volts.
- The utility/power company must be notified when the scaffold needs to be closer than the minimum distance.
- Platforms cannot deflect over 1/60 once they are loaded.
- Protection from falls is necessary at 10 feet.
- Guardrails and personal fall systems are necessary for employees on single point or two point adjustable suspension scaffolds.
- Horizontal lifelines should be secured to two structural members or more.
- The open ends and sides of platforms are where guardrails should be installed.
- Scaffolding guardrails have a minimum height of 38 inches.
- Crossbracing may be used instead of a midrail if the crosspoint of two braces is between 20 and 30 inches above the platform.
- If the crosspoint between braces is 38 to 48 inches over the platform, scaffolding crossbracing may be at the toprail.
- Toeboards need to be 3 ½ inches more than the walking surface, and the clearance should not be over ¼ of an inch.
- The outside face of double and single pole scaffolds require diagonal bracing in both directions.

- The current platform of pole scaffolds and platforms should not be moved until new bearers are set.
- Bearers are to extend more than 3 inches over a runner's outside edge.
- Ladder jack scaffolds should not be more than 20 feet.
- Casters and wheels must remain locked with swivel or positive wheel locks.
- Intermediate ties on a base that is 36 inches need to be no more than 20 feet.
- Float and ship scaffolds can support 750 pounds.
- No more than 6 feet is permitted between the work and walking levels without side protective sides or edges that demand a fall protection system.
- Employees on leading edges require protection when the lower level is 6 feet away or more.
- Employees must be protected from any fall of 6 feet or more with a safety net, fall arrest system, or protection device.

The top of a guardrail needs to be 42 inches (3 inches +/- ) from the ground and need to be ¼ of an inch. Mesh must extend from the top of the guardrail to the walking surface. Mesh, screens, midrails, etc. need to be installed with guardrails that lack a wall or parapet and are 21 inches high. Balusters in guardrail systems need to be 19 inches apart. Guardrail systems need to be able to resist 200 pounds. When wire rope substitutes the top of a guardrail, it is flagged every 6 feet.

Safety nets must be as close to the employees as possible. They may not be more than 30 feet away. The safety net needs to be tested with a 400 pound bag of sand before use. They must not be spaced more than 6 inches apart.

Horizontal lifelines require a safety factor of 2, and the attachment points of the harness need to be in the back, in the center between the shoulders.

Before any fall arrest system is used, it must be inspected discarded if it is not in safe working order.

## FIRE SAFETY

Every employer must make fire safety a high priority. Failure to engage in fire safety can lead to injury and death as well as expensive property damage. A safety program will increase the chance of survival and reduce fire damage. There are 4 different fire codes that other codes are modeled on: The National Fire Prevention Code, the Standard Fire Prevention Code, the Uniform Fire Code, the NFPA 1- Fire Prevention Code. The Fire Code works with the Building Code and varies with each jurisdiction that creates the minimum requirements for addressing hazards. Most fire safety codes have a section on administration that defines rules and guidelines and how they need to be enforced. The Fire Code works with the Building Code and varies with each jurisdiction that creates the minimum requirements for addressing hazards. Most fire safety codes have a section on administration that defines rules and guidelines and how they need to be enforced. Administration addresses hazardous containers, storage, and transportation as well as the industrial process, occupancy, and exhibition. Fire testing for buildings must follow the standard E 119 Chapter 35, ASTM.

- Passive fire protection (PFP) – protects from hazards with fire resistance materials in the walls and floor and create compartments and separations to prevent fires from spreading and improve evacuation and firefighting.
- Active fire protection(AFP) – finds and suppresses fires, and it may be done manually or automatically. Sprinkler systems and fire extinguishers are examples of active protection.

When used together, AFP and PFP provide the safest environment.

In sprinkler systems, the standpipe is the pipe that connects to the system and filled with water to keep the pressure steady. There are three classes of standpipe:

**I** – Used in advanced fires by firefighters and has strong pressure. Necessary when there is more than 30 feet between the top and bottom floor. The hose must be 100 feet long.

**II –** Used by occupants and has a limited reach. The hose should be 75 feet long.

**III –** Used by firefighters and has a strong stream. Necessary when there is more than 30 feet between the top and bottom floor. The hose must be 100 feet long.

The owner/operator must have a copy of the current fire code to ensure that the design adheres to the standards and a fire safety plan is in place. It is important to train employees how to recognize fire hazards and act in emergencies. The safety plan must consider the number of employees, the structure, industry, and the fire protection that is available. It is also important to make sure that the fire doors and exits are clear and marked, but the doors may have a delay if they have an alarm as part of the design. Additionally, employees should be taught how to use fire extinguishers.

Under OSHA, employer emergency action plans are necessary for:

- Systems for fire detection – 1910.164
- Process of safety management of chemicals that are highly hazardous – 1910.119
- Handling grain – 1910.272
- General fixed extinguishing system – 1910.160
- Methylenedianiline – 1910.1050
- Ethylene oxide – 1910.1047
- •Butadiene 1, 3 – 1910.1051

Fire prevention plans are necessary for Methylenedianiline – 1910.1050, Ethylene oxide – 1910.1047, and Butadiene 1, 3 – 1910.1051, according to OSHA standards.

Containers of flammable waste must be covered while stored, and no more than 25 gallons may be kept beyond the authorized cabinet. Only 60 gallons of flammable liquids from categories 1,2,3 may be stored. The limit on category 4 liquids is 60 gallons.

Fire resistant containers with covers are needed to store solvent waste or empty volatile containers.

Employers who fall under these standards must provide fire extinguishers and also:

- Develop a temporary fire watch – employees who will take action if the suppression system fails.
- Include the watch in the fire action plan.
- Post health hazard signs.

A 2A fire extinguisher may be substituted with two fire pails and a 55 gallon water drum.

Class A fire extinguishers – are used on wood, paper, and other combustibles.

Class B fire extinguishers – are used on gas, liquid, and grease.

Class C fire extinguishers – are used for electrical fires.

Class D fire extinguishers – are used for metals, including magnesium, titanium, zirconium, sodium, and potassium.

## GENERAL SAFETY

### *Noise*

It is possible to prevent noise with certain elements, and rating them using the sound transmission (STC) rating. The STC class number identifies the resistance to airborne sound. The STC rages between 25 and 60, and an STC over 60 is considered to be excellent sound proofing. For example, the resilient clips for 3/8 gypsum backer board ½ inch is a 52 STC.

Employers must follow the noise exposure levels outlined by the Hearing Conservation Amendment and OSHA's Occupational Noise Standard, 29 CFR 1910.95. When noise is excessive, it will damage hearing, and most hearing loss occurs at work. There are different pressure wave characteristics in noise.

*Terms to remember:*

**Amplitude** – sound pressure that is calculated with dB (decibels).

**Frequency – is the vibration rate in a unit of time. It is calculated using Hz (cycles per second).**

**Octave band** – characterizes noise's frequency dependence by implementing standardized notation. They operate by quantifying different effective frequencies.

**Decibel** – a scale that quantifies sound and is log-based.

**dbA** – a sound weighting measurement that determines risks.

**dBC** – helps find the correct method of hearing protection.

**SPL** – sound pressure level that is the sound pressure and reference level ratio.

A young adult should be able to hear at a range of 20 to 20,000 Hz. Hearing loss risk occurs when there is exposure over the SPL for 8 hours, which is usually over 90 dBA. There are variables to this. An increase of 5 dBA will decrease the necessary time for damage by 4 hours.

The two factors that affect noise are loudness and duration. The duration of exposure to sound over 85 dB is excessive when it is continuous (over 8 hrs). Prolonged exposure can cause more than hearing loss. It alters the nervous system, causing an increase in blood pressure and heart rate, and it increases the production of stress hormones.

Employees must not be exposed to peak sound over 140 dB for impulsive or impact noise.

OSHA's Safe Exposure Levels

| Duration | dBA |
|---|---|
| 8 hrs | 90 |
| 6 hrs | 92 |
| 4 hrs | 95 |
| 3 hrs | 97 |
| 2 hrs | 100 |
| 1 ½ | 102 |
| 1 | 105 |
| ½ | 110 |
| ¼ | 115 |

When it is not possible to reduce the noise level, it is necessary to provide personal hearing protectors. In most cases, however, noise control is possible and needs to be addressed. Sound level meters (SLM) and a noise dose meter (NDM) are used to assess and control noise levels. Noise control efforts may be administrative or engineering.

- **Engineering noise control** – steps to reduce the noise of machinery in the environment. This includes the treatment of the noise source, transmission path, and the receiver.

- **Administrative noise control** – are used when the noise cannot be controlled. It addresses schedules, signage, and quiet areas.

### Asbestos

Discovering if a structure contains asbestos requires laboratory analysis of different sample materials. The removal of asbestos requires masks, gloves, and goggles that the employer must provide.

### Respiration

It is necessary to protect employees from respiratory hazards. Respirators need to be used in hazardous conditions when there is not enough oxygen in the atmosphere (below 19.5%). When a lack of oxygen creates a life-threatening environment, the term immediately dangerous to life or health (IDHL) applies.

Respirators can be both a benefit and a risk. As a risk, respirators can be expensive to use and keep up, and overexposure to oxygen is dangerous. The best option for protecting employees from hazards is providing a safe environment that does not require the need for respirators. This is achieved with engineering controls and using material that is not toxic.

Air-purifying respirators (APRs) use filters, canisters, and cartridges to take particulates, vapor, gas, and any combination thereof out of the air. They are not designed for IDHL environments. It is important to follow the National Institute for Occupational Safety and Health (NIOSH) guidelines for labeling and color-coding the elements of the respirator.

In atmospheres with high hazards, the atmosphere-supplying respirators (ASRs) are necessary. This type uses a compressor and pressurized cylinder with both a continuous flow feature and pressure demand feature maintains the pressure.

- **Positive pressure respirators** – push air past the respirator's inlet covering to maintain a higher pressure inside rather than outside the device.
- **Negative pressure respirators** – create differences in pressure and are tight-fitting.

### Ventilation

Ventilation is necessary to protect employees and create a safe work environment. It draws air that is contaminated with chemicals and vapors out of the workspace and pulls in clean, safe air. Ventilation, along with process change and alteration of chemicals to be less toxic or nontoxic, is an alternative method of control.

Industrial ventilation requires a ventilation engineer to design the system and troubleshoot any difficulties. Ventilation is necessary to address employee safety under three conditions:

- The oxygen falls below 19.5%.
- Contamination levels are over safe exposure limits
- Flammable vapors pass the lower explosive limit

It is necessary to implement ventilation and other engineering controls before using respirators. In any confined spaces with respiratory risk, ventilation is necessary. Typical risks include dust, toxins, lack of oxygen, and vapors that are flammable.

### Ventilation types and mechanics:

- **Indoor air** – ventilation that heats and/or cools the structure.
- **Dilution** – exhausts contaminated air while providing clean air to dilute the contamination. Exhaust fans are effective in dilution ventilation.
- **Local exhaust** – used when there is high exposure to toxic chemicals, dust, or fumes. It may also be used to help

control heating costs in cold weather. A fan draws air through the system moving it to an area of low pressure.

- **Ducts** – The portion of the ventilation system that carries air and contaminants. The air must move at a steady rate. If it moves too fast, it takes an abundance of energy. If it moves to slow, the contaminants can create a clog. Ducts may require air-cleaning devices, depending on the regulation and pollution levels.
- **Dust filters** – air cleaning devices that are commonly used to protect air ducts.
- **Axial (propeller) fan** – exhaust fan in which air is pulled through the fan. It is usually used for cooling or dilution ventilation.
- **Centrifugal fan** – pulls air into the fan's center and breathes it out at a 90° angle. It is usually used in a local exhaust ventilation system.
- **Rugged radial blade centrifugal fan** – a type of centrifugal fan that is strong and useful for areas with a great deal of dust.

### *Confined Spaces*

Confined spaces at work are clearly defined by OSHA as a space with "limited means of egress that is subject to accumulation of toxic or flammable contaminants or has an oxygen deficit atmosphere. They have enough room for an employee to fit and work, do not have easy means for entrance and exit, and should not be occupied for long periods of time. The greatest threat that these small spaces pose is death by asphyxiation. Most accidents occur when employees fail to take appropriate hazard precautions.

### *Hazards in small spaces:*

- **Oxygen deficiency** – Oxygen levels below 19.5% require respirators. The oxygen levels should always be measured with an oxygen meter.
- **Flammable and combustible gas** – The space should remain vacant if it has 10% LEL or more, according to OSHA. The lower explosive limit (LEL) is measured using a combustible gas indicator or explosion meter.
- **Toxic gases** - safe levels of toxic gases depend on the type of gas in the space. The space is safe if the gas levels are under PEL, according to OSHA. Respirators and/or ventilation is necessary for higher levels.

Safe levels for entry to a confined space:

- **O2** – (oxygen) total volume of 19.5 to 23%
- **CO** – (carbon monoxide) ppm of 0 to 25
- **H2S** – (hydrogen sulfide) ppm of 0 to 10
- **LEL** – (lower explosive limit) less than 10% Of the LEL.

Physical hazards must also be monitored closely. Mechanical equipment should not be allowed in the space, and hazards need to be zero energy systems before they are allowed into the space. Ladders must be provided at the entrance/exit if there is risk of a fall. Other steps should also be taken to prevent falls.

When there are chemical or gas lines present, isolation procedures are necessary. Isolation can be accomplished by the following procedures:

- Double block and bleed
- Blanking and blinding
- Misalignment

Certain confined spaces will require permits for entry. The permit must be issued by a supervisor and include the date and location as well as the type of work to be done and how long the work should take. It must also provide evidence of atmosphere testing along with an evaluation of risks and the precautions taken to ensure safety. Entering this space requires an attendant to do the following:

- Stay outside during operations for entry
- Be aware of both potential and current hazards
- Communicate with entrants to monitor their condition
- Initiate rescues that are non entry
- Order emergency evacuations when necessary
- Keep the space clear of unauthorized individuals

Attendants are not allowed to enter the confined space under any circumstances, but they do need to alert emergency personnel of emergencies and maintain provisions that are necessary to remove unconscious individuals, including tripods and lifelines. There should be check in/check out procedure anytime employees go underground or into confined spaces.

Each employee who works underground should be provided with 200 cubic feet of air each minute.

### *Electrical*

A safe work environment requires using electronic equipment safely and identifying risks and hazards early. There are three basic hazards that are common with electricity.

6. **Shocks** – electric shocks occur through direct contact with the current, a medium, or arc. Shocks can result in injury or death.
7. **Arcing** – arcing occurs when a current jumps between two electrodes. This can cause burn, fires, and explosions. The risk increases with high fault currents.
8. **Gases** – gases can cause illness or death when they are toxic. Arcing and burns from electrical currents can cause reactions that release contaminants.

### *Terms to remember:*

- **Appliance** – uses electricity voltage in an amount higher than extra low. It can convert electricity to another energy form such as motion or heat. It may, or it will alter the character of the electricity.
- **Electrical equipment** – is any piece of equipment with electronic use, including cables, appliances, fittings, wires, materials, insulation, apparatuses, conductors, etc.
- **Associated equipment for electronic lines** – is an object that is typically in lines to insulate, support, or operate electricity.
- **Electrical line** – transmits, supplies, or transforms electricity through a wire or conductor.
- **Electrical installation** – electrical equipment that is installed as a group.
- **Electrical work** – work that involves electrical equipment such as installation, tests, removal, replacement, construction, manufacture, alterations, maintenance, etc.
- **Disconnect** – parts in the installation that have to connection to the source of the electricity, and can be achieved by separation, isolation, breaking connections, and discharge.
- **De-energize** – typically employs the switching process to disconnect a line or apparatus from sources.
- **Discharged** – removes the residual electrical energy by connecting to the general mass of the earth.
- **Earthed** – a connection to the general mass of the earth electrically.
- **Isolation and access** – a process that is part of a safe system. It allows switching, isolating, de-energizing, discharging, applying earths and short circuits, etc. partially or completely.
- **Live** – it is connected to an electrical source.

- **Isolated –** not connected to a sources of power and will not become live without purposeful observation. (requires a safety sign)
- **Neutral –** a two-wire system that is earthed, or a three-wire or multi-wire conductor that has a constant potential in connection with outer or active conductors. It is necessary to treat neutral items as live.

The acts of reenergizing, switching, and de-energizing require safe systems to be in place. Isolation requires that all parts need to be de-energized. This needs to be proven. The isolation process also includes:

- The parts need to be de-engineered from any electrical sources.
- Take away hazards from other energy sources
- Prove that the different parts have been de-energized.

Locks, inoperable machines, or both are used to establish isolation. Make sure that the isolation points cannot be accessed easily and that the system cannot be accidentally compromised. The isolation needs to be carefully explained to employees, and signage needs to have clear warnings.

When equipment requires service or is not in working order, out of service tags are necessary. Out of order tags need to be white letters on a black background. Isolation is also a useful method to use with out service tags in order to ensure that the equipment is not used while a danger. If equipment could injure an employee, it must be guarded. Only employees trained to operate machinery should do so, and the Department of Industrial Relation safety code must be adhered to when machines are in operation.

Work with live electricity is not typically allowed. On the rare occasion that it does happen, the worker must consider all materials as conductive unless there is proof that they are not. This consideration covers gases and liquids. When working close to live parts that are exposed, it is necessary to remove metallic objects beforehand. Additionally, it is important to make sure that precautions are taken when there are live parts close to earthed situations.

*Control measures:*

- Reduce fault level
- Isolate possible electrical sources
- Safety switch use
- Disable certain items that can create electricity (backup generators, auto-charge over systems, uninterruptible power supply, auto reclose, etc.)

It is necessary to provide proper working clearance so that the employees are positioned in ways to avoid contact with current. Barriers and signs are effective for the following:

- Warn individuals away from the current
- Protect employees
- Keep the workspace unobstructed
- Create safe pathways

Testing is necessary to ensure that the polarity is and connections are acceptable. Repeat these tests with any new work to ensure a safe environment and prevent accidents and injury. In cases where the safe system does not address the possibility of unintentional contact to live parts, the control measure that should be put in place is a safety observer.

Hand tools need to be double insulated if they are not grounded. All power tools require a positive on/off control that is can be turned on and off by the same finger(s). Electrical cords must be used correctly; they are not to be used to hoist equipment.

- Pneumatic nailers require a muzzle safety device if it has a psi over 100.
- Compressed air used to clean must not exceed 30 psi.
- Wheels that are abrasive require protection hoods or safety guards.
- Circular power saws must have guards above and below the base plate.

### *Rigging*

Equipment that lifts material to higher levels, such as cranes, falls under the category of rigging. OSHA Standard 1926 provides the guidelines for the use of riggings. This ruling demands that trained inspectors must inspect rigging each time before it is used. The inspector needs to address the ropes, hydraulic lines, airlines, electronic devices, fluid levels and other control mechanisms. Additionally, safety devices such as load indicators and boom kick outs need to be assessed. The inspection goes beyond the rigging to the ground where it assesses water accumulation, soil stability, etc. The rigging should not be used if any dangers are found.

Employee safety demands that operations requiring rigging be planned ahead of time. This is to protect the employees from cranes. This standard does not have to apply when cranes are operated by trained employees also who hook and unhook the steel before guiding it to the correct position. Self-closing latches need to be used when steel is rigged to keep everything in place.

Only operators and riggers who meet the requirements should complete rigging and latching. When establishing work standards, only one beam should be loaded at a time unless the crane is designed for more than a single load. In this case, no more than five items should be included in a single load. This type of operation requires additional training for the operating and rigging team. Always follow the manufacturer ratings when determining which type of load a rigging can handle.

Loads must be monitored carefully to prevent injury. Attempting to lift loads that are too heavy can overstress the rigging, put the machine off balance, and fall on site. These dangers can be avoided by following the ratings charts that OSHA requires for all cranes. The charts outline the loads that can cranes can handle. These loads should never be exceeded.

When securing equipment and beams to cranes, it is important to attach them at the points for their center of gravity. To prevent the anything from slipping outside the rigging, loads must be level and rigged from the top down. When there is more than one item in the load, the rigging should be done from the bottom to the top and spaced 2.1 meters (7 ft) from each other.

## SAFETY TRAINING

### *OSHA Standards/ 29 CFR Part 1926*

Employers are not responsible for CPR certification, but must provide other safety training. They are also responsible for medical care and first aid services. First aid kits need to be weatherproof and hold individually sealed package. Employers are responsible for the checking the contents weekly.

## SAFETY REQ.S

Construction areas must have the illumination of at least 3 ft candles when they are in use.

### *Sanitation:*

- Common cups may not be used for drinking, and single service cups must held in sanitary storage while receptacles are provided for used cups.
- Four toilets/urinals must be provided for every 200 employees.

### Safety:

Employee training records require written certification that is signed and dated by the employee. The employer is responsible for maintaining the records.

Bricklayers who reach 10 inches or more below the work surface need protection from falls. The same is true for employees who work on low slope or steep slope roofs.

The warning line must be at least 6 feet away from the roof edge when equipment is not in use, and it may be made up of chains, ropes, and scansions. Two warning lines will provide an access path to connect work areas and offer points of access in storage and hoisting areas. They should be flagged at 6 feet and capable of withstanding 16 pounds of force.

When holes are covered, the covers should be able to support two times the combined weight of the equipment, employees, and materials. The covers need to provide hazard warnings by implementing a color coding system and using the word "cover" or "hole."

Hoist towers need to be enclosed to the complete height on the side (or multiple sides) used as an entrance/exit when they are outside the structure. They must be enclosed on all sides when it is inside the structure. Hoisting cables must not be released until the steel joist is stabilized and bolted.

When operating around power lines, they must be considered live unless they are de-energized or clearly grounded. There needs to be a 10-foot clearance if the power lines are rated 50 KV.

Fire blocks are necessary when walls are over 10 feet high.

### Safety Gear:

- Employers must provide safety glasses or other methods of eye protection at their own cost.
- When rubber gloves are necessary, they should be tested with air.
- Employers have the right to demand the use of helmets, but they do not have to provide them, although they must supply adequate head protection according to OSHA.
- Safety belt lanyards must be nylon that is a minimum of ½ inch and no longer than 6 feet. The breaking strength must be 5,400 pounds. A lanyard should be anchored to the structure and the snap hook must not be clipped to itself. Lanyards that are discovered to be defective must be immediately removed.

Temporary heaters must be kept at least 10 feet from a combustible tarpaulin. Temporary heaters such as circulating heaters require a side and rear clearance of 12 inches and a chimney clearance of 18 inches.

## STORAGE

In a building that is under construction, material is not stored with 10 feet of the exterior walls. Bricks may not be stacked more than 7 feet high, and tapering is necessary at 4 feet. Masonry needs to be tapered when stacked over 6 feet high.

Lumber shall not be stored in piles over 20 when done with equipment or 16 feet when done manually. Before stacking lumber, it is necessary to remove the nails.

### Disposal

A 42-inch high barricade that is 6 feet away from the edge of the opening is necessary when debris is dropped through a hole without a chute. A chute is necessary when the material is dropped 20 feet or more beyond exterior walls. Chutes need to be surrounded by barricades that are 42 inches high.

Gas cylinders must remain upright. Cylinders require tilting and rolling of the bottom edge. Regulators need to be removed from gas cylinders before installing protection caps unless the cylinders are secured in specific carriers. Cylinders that contain oxygen must remain separated from fuel gas and other combustibles by 20 feet.

Warm water is needed to loosen frozen caps on gas cylinders. When opening fuel gas cylinders, leave the wrench on the stem incase there is an emergency. Before each shift, check oxygen and acetylene hoses.

## *Percent*

### *"Percent" is a portion of 100.*

How do I change a decimal to a percentage?

Move the decimal two places to the right of the number.

Example:

.34 = 34%

.07 = 7%

.1 = 10%

How do I change a fraction to a percentage?

The first step is to convert the fraction to a decimal. Do so by dividing the denominator into the numerator. Now, move the decimal two places to the right of the number and add the percentage sign.

Example:

¾ = .75 = 75%

¼ = .25 = 25%

How do I change a percentage to a decimal?

Move the decimal two places to the left of the number and remove the percentage symbol.

Example:

64% = .64

5% = .05

How do I change a percentage to a fraction?

Divide the number by 100. Reduce to lowest terms.

Example:

50% = 50/100 = ½

64% = 64/100 = 16/25

How do I change a percentage that is greater than 100 to a decimal or mixed fraction?

To change to a decimal:

Add a decimal point two places to the left of the number –

395% = 3.95

200% = 2.0

850% = 8.5

To change to a mixed fraction –

375% = 3.75 = 3+ 75/100 = 3 + ¾ = 3 ¾

375% = 3 ¾

525% = 5.25 = 5 + 25/100 = 5 + ¼ = 5 ¼

525% = 5 ¼

Conversions Commonly Seen in Real Estate:

| Fraction | Decimal | Percentage |
|---|---|---|
| ½ | .5 | 50% |
| ¼ | .25 | 25% |
| 1/3 | .333… | 33.3…% |
| 2/3 | .666… | 66.6…% |
| 1/10 | .1 | 10% |
| 1/8 | .125 | 12.5% |
| 1/6 | .1666… | 16.6…% |
| 1/5 | .2 | 20% |

## *Ratios*

Ratios are basic methods of comparison. They are used in construction for business and building purposes. Ratios show how many times one number is found in another, like fractions. For example, liquidity is seen in the current ratio:

Assets/Liability

20,000/10,000 = 2:0

## *Algebra*

Equations

To solve an equation, you must determine that is equal to the unidentified variable.

Things to remember about equations:

- There are two sides to an equation that are separated by an equal sign.
- An operation performed in an equation must be done at each side.
- The first step is to get the variables on one side and numbers on the other.
- You will usually have to divide both sides of the equation using the coefficient. This will enable the variable to equal an exact number.

Example:

x + 8 = 12

x +8 - 8 = 12-8

x = 4

How do I check an equation to make sure it is correct? Once you've solved the equation, take the number equal to the variable and input into the original equation.

Example:

x = 4

Original equation: x + 8 = 12

4 + 8 = 12

x = 4

### *Algebraic Fractions*

Example:

How do I solve subtraction on two fractions with different denominators?

x/4 - x/8

x/4 - x/8 = x(2)/4 (2) - x/8

2x/8 - x/8 = x/8

### *Converting Measurements*

It is important to be able to convert measurements accurately in order to ensure accurate construction.

### *Measurement Tables:*

Length

1 foot = 12 in

1 yard = 3 ft

1 mile = 1,760 yd

### *Metric*

| | |
|---|---|
| 1 inch = 25.4 mm | .0394 inches = 1 m |
| 1 inch = 2.54 cm | .3937 inches = 1 cm |
| 1 foot = .3048 m | 3.28208 feet = 1 m |
| 1 yard = .9114 m | 1.0936 yard = 1 m |
| 1 mile = 1.6093 km | .6214 mile = 1 km |

### *Area*

1 mile = 640 acres

1 acre = 4840 yd2

1 square yard = 9 ft2

## Metric

1 inch squared = 645.2 mm2 .0016 inches2 = 1mm2

1 inch squared = 6.4516 cm2 1.1550 inches2 = 1 cm2

1 square foot = .0929 m2 10.764 feet2 = 1m2

1 square yard = .8361 m2 1.1960 yard2 = 1 m2

1 square mile = 2.590 km2 .3861 mile2 = 1 km2

## Volume

1 pint = 20 oz.

1 gallon = 8 pints

## Metric

1 inch3 = 16.387 cm3 .0610 inches3 = 1 cm3

1 foot 3 = 28.329 dm3 .0353 feet3 = 1 dm3

1 foot 3 = .0283 m3 35.3147 feet3 = 1m3

1 yard 3 = .7646 m3 1.3080 yard3 = 1m3

1 pint = .5683 l 1.76 pint = 1l

1 pint = .4733 (US liters) 2.113 (US pint) = 1l

## Mass

16 ounces = 1 lb

1 ton = 1,000 lb

1 ton = 20 cwt

1 cwt = 112 lbs

1 stone = 14 lbs

1 ounce = 437.5 grains

## Metric

1 milligram = .0154 grain 64.935 milligram = 1 grain

1 gram = .0353 oz 28.35 grams = 1 oz

1 kilogram = 2.2046 lb .4536 kilograms = 1lb

1 tonne = .9842 ton 1.016 tonnes = 1 ton

## Geometric Formulas

Area Formulas

Circle: A = πr2

Sphere: A = 4πr2

Rectangle: A = lw

Square: A = s2

Triangle: A = bh/2

Parallelogram: A = bh

Ellipse: π*a*b

Polygon: (nsr)/2

Trapezoid: 5h(a+b)

### Symbols

$\pi$: = 3.141592654 or 3.14

r: Radius

l: Length

w: Width

s: Side length

b: Base

h: Height

n: number of sides

Examples of area:

Area of circle

Area of rectangle

l

_______r

w w

5mm

3mm

Example

$A = \pi r2$

A= lw

$A = \pi \times (5x5)$

A = 5mm x 3 mm = 15 mm$^2$

$A = \pi \times 25$

A = 3.14 x 25

A = 78.54

### Perimeter

Perimeter refers to the total distance around a two-dimensional figure.

It is simply calculated by adding together all of the sides of the figure.

Example:

5

8 8

3



FLORIDA CONSTRUCTIONSCHOOL

2

2

Perimeter = 8 + 8 + 5 + 2 = 23

Formula for circumference: C = 2πr

### *Volume*

Volume is necessary for filling three-dimensional shapes.

Cube: side3

Sphere: (4/3) × π × radius3

Rectangle: side1 × side2 × side3

Cylinder: π × radius2 × height

Ellipses: (4/3) × pi × radius1 × radius2 × radius3

Pyramid: (1/3) × area of base × height

### *Slope*

The formula for discovering slope factor is:

√(42 + 12 2)) /12

### *Angles*

The Pythagorean Theorem is essential to construction success. It is used with right triangles, and the formula is:

a2 + b2 = c2

Example:

50

80

802 = 502 + b2

6400 = 2500 + b2

3,900 = b2

62.45

### *Terms:*

**Right angle:** a 90° angle.

**Hypotenuse:** the side of across from the right angle.

**Diagonal:** the line that connects the polygon vertices that are not adjacent.

**Altitude:** the distance from the base to the vertex.

**Base:** the bottom of the figure, plane or 3-D.

**Isosceles right triangle:** right triangle with two equal sides.

Equilateral triangle: a triangle with all sides equal.

### *Board Lumber*

Hardwoods are board lumber, and they are sold by the board foot. A board foot is 1/12 of a cubic foot or 12 x 12 x 1.

The lumber's thickness is provided in fourths. For example, 4/4 equals 1 inch. The formula for finding board feet is:

length x width x thickness/144

Discovering the board feet allows you to determine the cost.

Example:

An oak is $15 a BF; how much are 10 BF?

10 x 15 = $150

## ACCOUNTING

A construction project requires a basic understanding of accounting principles.

### *Terms to Remember:*

- **Source documents –** are documents that are related to a project such as receipts, invoices, time cards, etc.
- **Financial statements –** includes cash flow statement, balance sheet, and income statement.
- **Asset –** any money or items owned by the business
- **Balance sheet –** includes the equity, assets, and liabilities.
- **Fixed asset –** tangible assets such as land and buildings.
- **Current asset –** cash or assets that can become cash within a year.
- **Liability –** all obligations and/or debts.
- **Current liability –** debts that need to be paid within a year.
- **Long term liability –** debt that needs to be paid after a year.
- **Income statement –** called the profit and loss statement (PNL) shows expenses and revenues.
- **Cash basis accounting** – that cash and payments are not accounted until they are received and paid.
- **Accrual accounting –** must be used in business over $5 million. The money is counted when orders are made, deliveries occur, or services occur.

### *Formulas:*

**Equity:** assets – liability

**Net working capital:** current assets – current liability

**Net income: revenue –** expenses

**Debt Ratio:** liabilities/assets

**Annual depreciation:** depreciation amount / years of depreciation

**Depreciation amount: cost –** value of salvage

**Gross profit: income -** cost of goods

**Liquidity ratio:** current assets/current liability

**Cost-volume profit:** sales revenue – variable costs – fixed costs = profit

# GLOSSARY OF CONSTRUCTION TERMINOLOGY

**Abrasion –** Wearing away by friction.

**Absorption bed –** A wide trench exceeding 36 in. (910mm) in width containing a minimum of 12 in. (305mm) of clean, coarse aggregate and a system of two or more distribution pipes through which treated sewage may seep into the surrounding soil. (Also called seepage bed.)

**Absorption field –** An arrangement of absorption trenches through which treated sewage is absorbed into the soil. (Also called disposal field.)

**Absorption of sound –** The ability of a material to absorb rather than reflect sound waves striking it by converting sound energy to heat energy within the material.

**Absorption of water by clay masonry –** The weight of water a brick or other clay masonry unit absorbs when immersed in either cold or boiling water for a stated length of time, expressed as a percentage of the weight of the dry unit.

**Absorption of water by concrete masonry units (CMU) –** The weight of water a concrete masonry unit absorbs when immersed in water, expressed in pounds of water per cubic foot of concrete.

**Absorption rate –** The weight of water absorbed when a clay brick is partially immersed for 1 minute, usually expressed in either grams or ounces per minute. (Also called suction or initial rate of absorption.)

**Absorption trench –** A trench not more than 36 in. (910mm) in width, containing a minimum of 12 in. (305mm) of clean, coarse aggregate and a distribution pipe, through which treated sewage is allowed to seep into the soil.

**Absorption unit –** See sabin.

**Accelerator –** An admixture used n concrete to hasten its set and increase the rate of strength gain (the opposite of a retarder).

**Accessible –** Describes a site, building, facility, or portion there of that complies with current standards and can be approached, entered, and used by a physically handicapped person.

**Accessible route –** A continuous, unobstructed path connecting all accessible elements and spaces in a building or facility that can be negotiated by a person with a severe disability using a wheelchair and that is also safe for and usable by people with other disabilities.

**Acid –** Corrosive, chemical substance that attacks many common building materials, decorative finished, coatings, paints, and transparent finishes.

**Acid resistant brick –** See under brick masonry unit.

**Acoustical correction –** The planning, shaping, and equipping of a space to establish the best possible hearing conditions for faithful reproduction of wanted sound within the space. (See also acoustics.)

**Acoustics –** The science of sound; the production, transmission, and effect of sound. (See also acoustical correction, architectural acoustics, and room acoustics.)

**Acrylic –** In carpet, a generic term including acrylic and modified acrylic (modacrylic) fibers. Acrylic is a polymer composed of at least 85% by weight of acrylonitrile. In glazing applications, a transparent plastic material.

**Actual dimension –** The actual measured dimension of a masonry unit, piece of lumber or other construction material or assembly. See also nominal dimension.

**Actual size –** See size.

**Adaptability –** The capability of certain building spaces and elements, such as kitchen counters, sinks, and grab bars, to be altered or added so as to accommodate the needs of persons with and without disabilities, or to accommodate the needs of persons with different types or degrees of disability.

**Adhesion –** The property of a paint film that enables it to stick to a surface.

**Adhesive, drywall –** Adhesives specifically intended for the application of gypsum board. A contact adhesive is an adhesive used to bond layers of gypsum board or for bonding gypsum board to metal studs. A laminating adhesive is an adhesive used to bond layers of gypsum board. A stud adhesive is an adhesive used to attach gypsum board to wood supports.

**Adhesive, tile –** Prepared organic material, ready for use with no further addition of liquid or powder, which cures or sets by evaporation; distinguished from mortars by the absence of siliceous fillers (sand) that are included in mortars either at the plant or in the field.

**Ad mixture –** A material (other than Portland cement, water, or aggregate) used in concrete to alter its properties (such as accelerators, retarders, and air-retraining agents).

**Adobe brick –** See under brick masonry unit.

**Age hardening –** The continuing increase in strength for long periods of time of aluminum alloys after heat treatment.

**Agglomeration –** Process for increasing the particle size of iron ores to make them suitable for iron working and steelmaking.

**Aggregate –** A hard, inert material mixed with Portland cement and water to form concrete. Fine aggregate has pieces 1/4 in. (6.4mm) in diameter and smaller. Coarse aggregate has pieces larger than 1/4 in. (6.4mm) in diameter.

**Aging –** The period of time in which a heat-treatable aluminum alloy is allowed to remain at room temperature, after heat treatment (heating and quenching) to reach a stable state of increased strength. (See also artificial aging.)

**Airborne sound transmission –** See sound transmission.

**Air chamber –** A piece of pipe about 10 in. (250mm) long installed above the hot and cold valves of fixtures such as sinks, lavatories, and clothes washers to cushion the rush of water as the valve is closed and prevent water hammer.

**Air drying –** In coatings, paints, and transparent finishes, capable of forming a solid film when exposed to air at moderate atmospheric temperatures. Of wood, see seasoning.

**Air-entrained concrete –** Concrete containing minute bubbles of air up to about 7% by volume.

**Air-entraining agent –** An admixture used to produce air-entrained concrete.

**Air gap –** The unobstructed vertical distance between the mouth of a water outlet and the flood level rim of the water receptacle. The water outlet may be a faucet, spout, or other outlet; the receptacle may be a plumbing fixture, tank, or other receptacle.

**Alclad sheet –** A clad product with an aluminum or aluminum alloy coating having high resistance to corrosion. The coating is anodic to the core alloy it covers, thus protecting it physically and electrolytic ally against corrosion. (See also clad alloy.)

**Alkali –** A soluble mineral salt present in some soils. Alkalis are chemical substances characterized by their ability to combine with acids to form neutral salts. They are damaging too many coatings, paints, and transparent finishes.

**Allowable unit stress –** See under stress.

**Alloy designation -** A numerical system used in designating the various alloys of aluminum.

**Alloy element –** Element added in steelmaking to achieve desired properties.

**Alloy steel –** See under steel.

**Alumina (AlO3) –** A hydrated form of aluminum oxide found in bauxite and in ordinary clays.

**Ambient sound –** A continuous background sound that is a composite of individual sounds coming from exterior sources, such as street traffic, and interior sources, such as ventilating equipment and appliances, none of which can be identified individually by a listener. (Also called background noise.)

**Ambulatory –** Able to walk without assistance or difficulty.

**Amperage –** Electrical rate of flow, measured in amperes (amps) and comparable to gallons per minute (gpm) in a fluid medium; the strength of a current of electricity.

**Ampere (amp) –** A unit of electrical current equivalent to that produced by 1 volt applied across a resistance of 1 ohm. One coulomb of electricity in every second.

**Anchor –** A piece of assemblage, usually metal, used to attach parts (e.g., plates, joists, trusses, studs, sills, masonry, windows, doors, and other building elements) to wood, concrete, or masonry.

**Angular course –** See under course.

**Angular measure –** The deviation between two lines that meet at a point, expressed in degrees, minutes, and seconds.

**Annealing –** See heat treatment.

**Annual growth ring –** The growth layer put on by a tree in a single growth year.

**Anodic coating –** A surface coating applied to an aluminum alloy by anodizing.

**Anodizing –** Applying an electrolytic oxide coating to an aluminum alloy by building up the natural surface film using an electrical current (usually de) through an oxygen-yielding electrolyte with the alloy serving as the anode.

**Antioxidant –** A compound added to other substances to retard oxidation, which deteriorates plastics.

**Antique finish –** A finish usually applied to furniture or woodwork to give the appearance of age.

**Arch –** A usually curved compressive structural member, spanning openings or recesses; also built flat.

- A back arch is a concealed arch carrying the backing of a wall where the exterior face is carried by a lintel.
- A jack arch is an arch having horizontal or nearly horizontal upper and lower surfaces. Also called a flat or straight arch.
- A major arch is an arch with a span greater than 6 ft (1800 mm) that carries a load that is equivalent to a uniform load greater than 1000 psf (4882 kg/m-). Typically known as a Tudor arch, semicircular arch, gothic arch, or parabolic arch. Has a rise-to- span ratio greater than O.IS.
- A minor arch is an arch with a maximum span of 6 ft (1800 mm) carrying a load that does not exceed 1000 psf (4882 kg/m"). Typically known as a jack arch, segmented arch, or multi-centered arch. Has a rise-to-span ratio less than or equal to O.IS.
- A relieving arch is an arch that is built over a lintel, flat arch, or smaller arch to divert loads, thus relieving the lower member from excessive loading. Also known as a discharging or safety arch.
- A trimmer arch is an arch, usually a low-rise type, of brick masonry unit used for supporting a fireplace hearth.

**Architectural acoustics –** The acoustics of buildings and other structures. (See also acoustics and room acoustics.)

**Architectural barrier –** A physical condition in a building or facility that creates unsafe or confusing conditions or prevents accessibility and free mobility.

**Architectural terra cotta –** Custom-made, hard-burned, glazed or unglazed clay building units, plain or ornamental that is machine extruded or hand molded. (See also ceramic veneer.)

**Area wall –** A retaining wall around below-grade basement windows.

**Aromatic solvents –** Group of organic compounds derived from coal or petroleum, such as benzene and toluene.

**Artificial aging –** The heating of an aluminum alloy for a controlled time at an elevated temperature to accelerate and increase its strength gain after heat treatment. (See also aging.)

**Ashlar masonry –** Masonry composed of rectangular units usually larger in size than brick with sawed, dressed, or square beds bonded with mortar. Ashlar masonry is also described according to its pattern bond, which may be coursed, random, or patterned.

**Atmospheric pressure steam curing –** See curing.

**Atmospheric vacuum breaker –** A simple mechanical device consisting essentially of a check valve in a supply line and a valve member (on the discharge side of the check valve) opening to the atmosphere when the pressure in a line drops to atmospheric. (Also called a siphon breaker.)

**Attenuation –** Reduction of the energy or intensity of sound.

**Audible cue –** See cue.

**Austenitic steel –** See grain structure.

**Autoclave –** See curing.

**Average transmission loss (tl) –** The numerical average of the transmission loss values of an assembly measured at nine frequencies. It is a single-number rating for comparing the airborne sound transmission through walls and floors.

**Axminster carpet –** See woven carpet.

**Back –** The side opposite the face. The poorer side of a plywood panel. The surface of gypsum board that will be placed toward the supports.

**Back arch –** See under arch.

**Back blocking –** A single-ply gypsum board installation procedure for reinforcing butt-end or edge joints to minimize surface imperfections such as cracking and ridging.

**Backflow –** The unintentional flow of water into the supply pipes of a plumbing system from a non-supply source.

**Background noise –** See ambient sound.

**Backing –** The carpet foundation of jute, kraft cord, cotton, rayon, or polypropylene yarn that secures the pile yarns and provides stiffness, strength, and dimensional stability.

**Backing board –** See under gypsum board.

**Backing, tile –** A suitable surface for the application of tile, such as a structural subfloor or wall surface.

**Backparging –** See parging.

**Backplate –** See under finished mill products.

**Back-siphonage –** A type of backflow, usually caused by a temporary occurrence of negative pressure (suction) in pipes.

**Backup –** The part of a masonry wall behind the exterior facing.

**Baking finish –** A coating that is baked at temperatures above 150°F (65.6°C) to dry and develop desired properties.

**Bark –** The outer corky layer of a tree composed of dry, dead tissue.

**Bars –** See under finished mill products.

**Base coat –** The first plaster layer in two-coat work; or either the scratch or brown coat in three-coat work.

**Base course –** The lowest course of masonry in a wall or pier.

**Base line –** A parallel of specified latitude, used in the rectangular survey system, serving as the main east-west reference line, with a principal meridian for a particular state or area.

**Basic stress –** See stress.

**Batter –** Recessing or sloping a wall back in successive courses; the opposite of corbel.

**Bauxite –** A raw ore of aluminum consisting of 45 to 60% aluminum oxide, 3 to 25% iron oxide, 2.5 to 18% silicon oxide, 2 to 5% titanium oxide, other impurities, and 12 to 30% water. This ore varies greatly in the proportions of its constituents, color, and consistency.

**Bayer process –** The process generally employed to refine alumina from bauxite.

**Beam –** A structural member transversely supporting a load.

**Bearding –** Long-fiber fuzz occurring on some loop pile fabrics, caused by fibers snagging and loosening due to inadequate anchorage.

**Bearing wall –** A wall that supports a vertical load in addition to its own weight. (See also non load-bearing wall.)

**Bed joint –** Horizontal layer of mortar in which a masonry unit is laid.

**Beneficiation –** Concentrating process used to increase the iron content of ores prior to use. (See also agglomeration.)

**Binder –** In paint and coatings, the vehicle ingredient with adhesive qualities (linseed oil, resins, etc.) that binds the pigment and other ingredients of a coating, paint, or transparent finish into a cohesive film and facilitates bonding with the underlying surfaces. In terrazzo, a cementitious or resinous material that gives the matrix adhesive and other important physical properties.

**Bleaching –** The process of lightening raw wood. The process of restoring discolored or stained wood to its normal color or making it lighter.

**Bleeding –** (1) In unit masonry, (a) the loss of water from a masonry unit having low suction when it comes in contact with mortar or (b) the loss of water from mortar due to low water retention when it contacts a masonry unit. Bleeding causes masonry units to float (see floating). (2) In concrete, the appearance of excess water rising to the surface shortly after placing of concrete. (3) In coatings, paints, and transparent finishes, discoloration of a finish coat by coloring matter from the underlying surface or coat of finishing material. (4) In plastics, the diffusion of a colorant out of a plastic part into adjacent materials blend to a common level. The meeting of two or more surfaces so that there is no abrupt rise or drop in the surface.

**Blistering –** The formation of bubbles or pimples on a coated, painted, or transparent finished surface caused by moisture in the underlying material (wood, masonry, concrete, etc.); caused by adding a coat of coating, paint, or transparent finish before the previous coat has dried thoroughly, or caused by excessive heat or grease under a coating, paint, or transparent finish.

**Blocking –** In masonry construction, a method of bonding two adjoining or intersecting walls, not built at the same time, by means of offsets whose vertical dimensions are not less than 8 in. (200 rnrn). In wood construction, short pieces of wood used as nailers, spacers, or fillers between wood members, between wood members and other construction, or between other materials.

**Blow molding –** Shaping thermoplastic materials into hollow form by air pressure and heat; usually performed on sheets or tubes.

Blushing – Describes opaque lacquer that loses its gloss and becomes flat or clear lacquer that turns white or milky.

**Board –** See under lumber.

**Board foot –** A measure of lumber. One board foot is the equivalent of a piece of lumber whose nominal dimensions are 1 in. (25 rnrn) thick, 12 in. (305 rnrn) wide, and 12 in. (305 mrn) long.

**Body –** Used to indicate thickness or thinness of a liquid coating, paint, or transparent finish material.

**Bond beam –** Course or courses of a masonry wall grouted and usually reinforced in the horizontal direction. Alternatively, may be made of reinforced concrete. Serves as a horizontal tie of wall bearing courses for structural members or itself as a flexural member.

**Bond course** – A masonry course in which the units overlap more than one wythe of masonry.

**Bonded rubber cushioning** – Rubber or latex cushioning adhered to a carpet at the mill.

**Bonder** – See header.

**Bonderizing** – Process to improve paint adhesion on steel by dipping lightly galvanized (see galvanizing) objects in a hot phosphate solution to form a surface film of zinc phosphate.

**Bond, pattern** – See pattern bond.

**Bond, structural** – Tying wythes of a masonry wall together by lapping units over one another or by connecting them with metal ties.

**Bond, tensile** – Adhesion between mortar and masonry units or reinforcement.

**Border** – The resilient flooring at the perimeter of a room adjacent to the walls, which is installed separately from the field.

**Bow** – See warp.

**Boxing** – Mixing a coating, paint, or transparent finish material by pouring it from one container to another several times. Boxing is not recommended for most such materials.

**Braille** – A special raised-touch alphabet for the blind using a cell of six dots.

**Brazing** – A welding process in which the filler metal is a nonferrous metal or alloy with a melting point higher than 800°F (426.67"C) but lower than that of the metals joined.

- A brazing alloy is an alloy used as filler metal for brazing. In aluminum the brazing alloy is usually in the 4000 Series of alloys.
- A brazing sheet is an unclad or specially clad sheet for brazing purposes, the surface of which has a lower melting point than the core. Brazing sheet of the clad type may be clad on either one or two surfaces.

**Breathe** – The ability of a coating, paint, or transparent finish film to permit the passage of moisture vapor without causing blistering, cracking, or peeling.

**Brick grade** – Designation for the durability of a unit, expressed as SW for severe weathering, MW for moderate weathering, and NW for negligible weathering.

**Brick masonry unit –** A unit that is formed into a rectangular prism while plastic.

- An acid-resistant brick is a clay brick suitable for use in contact with chemicals; designed primarily for use in the chemical industry. Usually used with acid-resistant mortars.
- An adobe brick is a large clay brick of varying size, roughly molded and sun dried.
- A building (common) brick is a clay brick for building purposes, not especially treated for texture or color. Formerly called common brick.
- A clay brick is a brick made of clay or shale, formed into a rectangular prism while plastic and burned (fired) in a kiln.
- A concrete brick is a brick made from Portland cement and an aggregate and cured either in normal atmosphere or using either low- or high-pressure steam. It is formed as a rectangular prism, usually not larger than 4 X 4 X 12 in. (l00 X 100 X 305 mm).
- An economy brick is a clay brick whose nominal dimensions are 4 X 4 X 8 in. (100 X 100 X 305 mm).
- An engineered brick is a clay brick whose nominal dimensions are 4 X 3.2 X 8 in. (l00 X 81.28 X 305 mm).
- A facing brick is a clay brick made especially for facing purposes, often with a finished surface texture. Such units are made of selected clays or treated to produce desired color.
- A fire brick is a brick made of refractory ceramic material that will resist high temperatures.
- A floor brick is a smooth, dense brick that is highly resistant to abrasion; used as a finished floor surface.
- A hollow brick is a clay or shale masonry unit whose net cross- sectional area in any plane parallel to the bearing surface is not less than 60% of its gross cross-sectional area measured in the same plane.
- Jumbo brick is a generic term indicating that a clay brick is larger than the standard. Some producers use this term to describe oversized brick of specific dimensions manufactured by them.
- A Norman brick is a clay brick whose nominal dimensions are 4 X 22/3 X 12 in. (l00 X 67.7 X 305 mm).
- A paving brick is a clay brick especially suitable for use in pavements where resistance to abrasion is important.
- A Roman brick is a clay brick whose nominal dimensions are 4 X 2 X 12 in. (l00 X 50 X 305 mm).
- An SCR brick is a clay brick whose nominal dimensions are 22/3 X 6 X 12 in. (67.7 X 150 X 305 mm). It Jays up three courses to 8 in. (203.2 mm) and produces a nominal 6-in. (150-mm)-thick wall. Developed by the Structural Clay Products Research Foundation.
- A sewer brick is a low-absorption, abrasive- resistant clay brick intended for use in drainage structures.

**Brick type –** Designation for facing brick that controls tolerance, chippage, and distortion. Expressed as FBS, FBX, and FBA for solid brick and HBS, HBX, HBA, and HBB for hollow brick.

**British thermal unit (Btu) –** A measure of heat quantity equal to the amount of heat required to raise 1 lb of water 1°F (0.5556°C) at sea level.

**Broadloom –** Carpet woven on a broad loom in widths of 6 ft (1800 mm) or more.

**Brown coat –** The second plaster layer in three-coat work, which provides additional strength and a suitably true and plane surface for the application of the finish coat.

**Brush –** A tool composed of bristles set into a handle; often used to apply paint and transparent finish materials. Sometimes used to apply coatings. Bristles may be synthetic (needed for water thinned paints) or natural, such as hog hair.

**Brushability** – Ease with which a paint or transparent finish material can be brushed.

**Brush marks** – Marks of a brush that remains in a dried coating, paint, or transparent finish film.

**Btu** – See British thermal unit.

**Buckling** – Wrinkling or ridging of a carpet after installation, caused by insufficient stretching, dimensional instability, or manufacturing defects.

**Build** – The apparent thickness or depth of a coating, paint, or transparent finish film after it has dried.

**Building brick** – See under brick masonry unit.

**Building drain** – The lowest part of a building's drainage system. It receives the discharge from soil, waste, and other drainage pipes inside the walls of a building and conveys it to a point 3 ft (900 mm) outside the building walls, where it joins with the building sewer.

**Building sewer** – The horizontal piping of a drainage system, which extends from the end of a building drain to a public sewer, private sewer, individual sewage disposal system, or other point of disposal. A building sewer begins at a point 3 ft (900 mm) outside the building wall, where the building drain ends. (Also called a house sewer.)

**Building storm drain** – A type of building drain used for conveying rainwater, surface water, groundwater, subsurface water, and cooling condensate; or a combined building sewer, extends to a point not less than 3 ft (900 mm) outside the building wall, where it joins with a storm sewer or combined storm and sewage sewer.

**Built environment** – The collection of buildings, facilities, transportation systems, and other structures and spaces created for the purpose of providing convenient places for work, play, living, and related human activities; contrasted with the natural environment.

**Bulked continuous filament (BFC)** – Continuous strands of synthetic fiber made into yarn without spinning; often extruded in modified cross section such as multi local, mushroom, or bean shape, or textured to increase bulk and covering power.

**Burling** – Removing surface defects such as knots, loose threads, and high spots to produce acceptable quality after weaving; also, filling in omissions in weaving.

**Burnishing** – Shiny or lustrous spots on a coating, paint, or transparent finish surface caused by rubbing.

**Butt-end joint** – Joint in which mill-cut or job-cut (exposed core) gypsum board ends or edges are butted together.

**Buttering** – Placing mortar on a masonry unit with a trowel.

**Calcimine** – Water-based paint generally consisting of animal glue, zinc white, and calcium carbonate or clay; now seldom used.

**Calcium chloride** – An accelerator added to concrete to hasten setting (not to be considered an antifreeze).

**Calendering** – A process for producing plastic film or sheeting by passing the material between revolving heated rolls.

**Call** – In surveying, a statement or mention of a course or distance.

**Cambium** – A thin layer of tissue that lies between a tree's bark and its wood. The cambium subdivides to form the new wood and bark cells of each year's growth.

**Cant** – A log slabbed on one or more sides.

**Cant strip** – A triangular filler between a roof and a parapet wall.

**Capacity insulation** – The ability of masonry to store heat as a result of its mass, density, and specific heat.

**Capillaries** – (1) Thin-walled tubes or vessels found in wood. (2) In concrete, channels that absorb water and are interrupted by entrained air bubbles.

**Carbon steel** – See under steel.

**Cardinal points** – The four major compass headings of north, east, south, and west.

**Carpet** – General designation of fabric constructions that serve as soft floor coverings, especially those that cover an entire floor and are fastened to it, as opposed to rugs. See also flocked carpet, fusion-bonded carpet, knitted carpet, needle-punched carpet, tufted carpet, and woven carpet.

**Carved carpet** – See sculptured under pile.

**Case hardening** – Hardening of the outer skin of an iron-based alloy by promoting surface absorption of carbon, nitrogen, or cyanide, generally accomplished by heating the alloy in contact with materials containing these elements and rapid cooling.

**Casting** – (1) In masonry and concrete, pouring a mix into a mold and permitting it to set to form the desired shaped object. (2) In metalwork, pouring molten metal into molds to form desired shapes. (3) In plastics, the shaping of plastic objects by pouring the material into molds and allowing it to harden without the use of pressure.

**Cast iron** – High-carbon iron made by melting pig iron with other iron-bearing materials and casting in sand or loam molds; characterized by hardness, brittleness, and high compressive and low tensile strengths.

**Catalyst** – (1) A substance that speeds up or slows down the rate of a chemical reaction without itself undergoing permanent change in composition. (2) A substance used to initiate the polymerization of monomers to form polymers.

**Caulking compound** – Semidrying or slow-drying plastic material used to seal joints or fill crevices such as those around windows and chimneys. Either elastomeric or acrylic joint sealants are generally used today where caulking compounds are called for. See also sealant, joint.

**Cavity wall** – A wall built of masonry units so arranged as to provide a continuous air space within the wall (with or without insulating material) and in which the inner and outer wythes of the wall are tied together with metal wall ties or continuous metal joint reinforcement.

**Cavity wall tie** – See under wall tie.

**CIB ratio** – The ratio of the weight of water absorbed by a clay masonry unit during immersion in cold water to the weight absorbed during immersion in boiling water. An identification of the probable resistance of clay brick to the action of freezing and thawing.

**Cellular plastic** – A plastic whose apparent density is decreased substantially by the presence of numerous cells distributed throughout its mass.

- Closed-cell plastic is cellular plastic in which there is a predominance of non-connecting cells.
- Open-cell plastic is a cellular plastic in which there is a predominance of interconnecting cells.

**Cellulose** – The principal constituent of wood that forms the framework of the wood cells.

**Cement** – A binding agent capable of uniting dissimilar materials into a composite whole. (See also Portland cement.)

**Centering** – Temporary formwork for the support of masonry arches or lintels during construction. Also called centers.

**Ceramic tile –** A thin surfacing unit having either a glazed or unglazed face made from clay or a mixture of clay and other ceramic materials and fired to a temperature sufficiently high to produce specific physical properties and characteristics.

**Ceramic tile finish –** All of the elements normally installed by a tile contractor, from the backing to the face of the tile. This may include just a tile-setting product, tile, and grout or, in addition, a mortar bed, reinforcement, and cleavage membrane. (Also called tile work.)

**Ceramic veneer –** Architectural terra cotta, characterized by large face dimensions and thick sections. An adhesion-type ceramic veneer is a thin section of ceramic veneer held in place without metal anchors by adhesion of mortar backing. An anchored-type ceramic veneer is a thicker section of ceramic veneer held in place by grout and wire anchors connected to backing.

**Cesspool –** A covered and lined underground pit used as a holding tank for domestic sewage and designed to retain the organic matter and solids, but to permit the liquids to seep through the bottom and sides. Cesspools are almost universally prohibited in this country and are not acceptable as a means of sewage disposal.

**Chain warp –** See under warp.

**Chalking –** Formation of a loose powder on the surface of a coating or paint after exposure to the elements.

**Chase –** A groove or continuous recess built in a masonry or concrete wall to accommodate pipes, ducts, or conduits.

**Check –** A lengthwise separation of wood, the greater part of which occurs across the annual growth rings. A check that passes entirely through a piece of wood is called a split.

**Checking – T**ype of coating, paint, or transparent finish failure in which many small cracks appear in the surface.

**Circuit vent –** A branch vent that serves two or more traps and extends from in front of the last fixture connection of a horizontal branch to a vent stack. (See also loop vent.)

**Circulation path –** An exterior or interior passageway from one place to another for pedestrians, including, but not limited to, walks, hallways, courtyards, stairways, and stair landings.

**Clad alloys –** Alloys having one or both surfaces of a metallurgically bonded coating, the composition of which may or may not be the same as that of the core, and which is applied for such purposes as corrosion protection, surface appearance, or brazing. (See also alclad sheet and alloy.)

**Cladding –** Bonding thin sheets of a coating metal with desirable properties (such as corrosion resistance or chemical inertness) over a less expensive metallic core not possessing these properties. Copper cladding over steel may be applied by hot dipping; stainless steel and aluminum cladding by hot rolling.

**Clay brick –** See under brick masonry unit.

**Cleavage (isolation) membrane –** A membrane such as saturated roofing felt, building paper, or 4 mil (0.1 mm) polyethylene film, installed between the backing and a mortar bed to permit independent movement of a tile finish.

**Closer –** The last masonry unit laid in a course.

**CMU –** See concrete masonry unit.

**Coarse aggregate –** See aggregate.

**Coating –** A mastic or liquid-applied surface finish, regardless of whether a protective film is formed or only decorative treatment results. There are two categories of coatings: coatings and special coatings.

- Materials called coatings are those that are usually applied in the shop or factory on metal, glass, porcelain, wood, and other materials. They include such products as Kynar coatings on metal, anodizing on aluminum, and liquid-applied colored finishes on wood doors and cabinets. Some coatings are virtually identical to paint, the major differences being that they are applied in a shop or factory and are usually sprayed on rather than being brushed or rolled on.
- Special coatings are relatively thick, high-performance architectural coatings, such as high-build glaze coatings; fire-retardant coatings; industrial coatings, such as those used in sewage disposal plants; and cementitious coatings. Special coatings are usually applied in the field.
- See also fire-retardant coating or paint, paints, and transparent finishes.

**Coke –** Processed form of bituminous coal used as a fuel, a reducing agent, and a source of carbon in making pig iron.

**Cold flow –** Permanent change in dimension due to stress over time without heat.

**Cold forming –** Forming thin sheets and strips to desired shapes at room temperature, generally with little change in the mechanical properties of the metal; includes roll, stretch, shear, and brake forming. (See also cold working.)

**Cold rolling –** See under cold working.

**Cold working –** See also cold forming and hot working.

- In aluminum, forming a metal product at room temperature by means of rolling, drawing, forging, or other mechanical methods of forming or shaping.
    - Cold rolling is the forming of sheet metal by rolling at room temperature metal that has been previously hot rolled to a thickness of about 0.125 in. (3.2 mm).
- In steel, shaping by cold drawing, cold reduction, or cold rolling at room temperature; generally accompanied by an increase in strength and hardness.
- Cold drawing is shaping by pulling through a die to reduce the cross- sectional area and impart the desired shape;

generally accompanied by an increase in strength, hardness, closer dimensional tolerances, and a smoother finish.

- Cold finishing is cold working that results in finished mill products.
- Cold reduction is cold rolling that drastically reduces sheet and strip thickness with each pass through the rolls; generally accompanied by an increase in hardness, stiffness, and strength and resulting in a smoother finish and improved flatness.
- Cold rolling is a gradual shaping between rolls to reduce the cross- sectional area or impart the desired shape; generally accompanied by an increase in strength and hardness.

**Collar joint –** Interior longitudinal vertical joint between two wythes of masonry.

**Colorant –** Concentrated color added to coatings and paints to make specific colors.

**Colorfast –** Fade resistant.

**Color uniformity –** Ability of a coating or paint to maintain a consistent color across its entire surface, particularly during weathering.

**Column –** A vertical structural member acting primarily in compression, whose horizontal dimension measured at right angles to its thickness does not exceed three times its thickness.

**Combination process –** A process used to retrieve additional alumina and soda from the red mud impurities of the Bayer process.

**Common alloy –** An alloy that does not increase in strength when heat-treated (non-heat treatable). Common alloys may be strengthened by strain hardening.

**Common brick –** See brick masonry unit.

**Common wall –** A wall that separates adjacent dwelling units within an apartment building or adjacent tenants in townhouses and other buildings; also called a party wall.

**Composite wall –** A multiple-wythe wall in which at least one of the wythes is dissimilar to the other wythe or wythes with respect to type or grade of masonry unit or mortar.

**Compounding –** The thorough mixing of a polymer or polymers with other ingredients such as fillers, plasticizers, catalysts, pigments, dyes, or curing agents.

**Compression molding –** Forming plastic in a mold by applying pressure and, usually, heat.

**Compressive strength –** A material's ability to resist compressive forces.

**Concrete –** A composite material made of Portland cement, water, and aggregates, and sometimes admixtures.

**Concrete block –** See concrete masonry unit.

**Concrete brick –** See under brick masonry unit.

**Concrete masonry unit (CMU) –** A masonry unit having Portland cement as its primary cementitious material.

- A decorative CMU is one of various available types of concrete masonry units with beveled face shell recesses or other articulation or texture.
- A faced CMU is one that has a special ceramic, glazed, plastic, polished, or ground face.
- A slump block is a CMU produced so that it will slump or sag before it hardens; for use in masonry wall construction.
- A split-face block is a solid or hollow CMU that is machine fractured (split) lengthwise after hardening to produce a rough, varying surface texture.

**Condensation –** The change of water from its gaseous form (water vapor) to liquid water; the liquid water so collected.

**Condensation polymerization –** A chemical reaction in which the molecules of two substances combine, giving off water or some other simple substance (see polymerization).

**Consistency –** A chemical reaction in which the molecules of two substances combine, giving off water or some other simple substance (see polymerization).

**Construction –** The method by which a carpet is made (loom or machine) and other identifying characteristics, including the number of pile rows per inch, pitch, wire height, number of shots, yam count and plies, total pile yarn weight, and pile yarn density.

**Construction joint –** (1) A joint placed in concrete to form a plane of weakness to prevent random cracks from forming due to drying shrinkage and temperature changes. (2)A prefabricated metal accessory intended to relieve shrinkage, temperature, or structural stresses in plaster, thus minimizing cracking.

**Contact adhesive –** See adhesive, drywall.

**Continuous casting –** A process in which molten metal is used directly to produce semi - finished products such as slabs or billets, bypassing ingot teaming, stripping, soaking, and rolling.

**Control joint –** A joint placed in concrete to form a plane of weakness to prevent random cracks from forming due to drying shrinkage and temperature changes. A prefabricated metal accessory intended to relieve shrinkage, temperature, or structural stresses in plaster, thus minimizing cracking.

**Coping –** Masonry units forming a finished cap on top of an exposed pier, wall, pilaster, chimney, etc., to protect the masonry below from penetration of water from above.

**Copolymer –** A polymer formed by the combination of two or more different monomers.

**Copper staining –** A stain usually caused by the corrosion products of copper screens, gutters, or downspouts washing down on a finished surface. Can be prevented by painting the copper or applying a transparent finish to it.

**Corbel –** A shelf or ledge formed by projecting successive courses of masonry out from the face of a wall.

**Core –** A shelf or ledge formed by projecting successive courses of masonry out from the face of a wall.

**Corner cracking –** Cracks occurring in the apex of inside corners of gypsum board surfaces, such as between adjacent walls or at walls and ceilings.

**Corner floating –** Gypsum board installation procedure that eliminates some mechanical fasteners at interior corners and permits sufficient movement of boards to eliminate corner cracking.

**Correction lines –** East-west reference lines used in the rectangular survey system, located at 24-mile intervals to the north and south of a base line.

**Corrosion –** Physical deterioration, decomposition, or loss of the cross section of a metal due to weathering, galvanic action, or direct chemical attack.

- Galvanic action is corrosion produced by electrolytic action between two dissimilar metals in the presence of an electrolyte.
- Direct chemical attack is corrosion caused by a chemical dissolving of the metal.
- Weathering is galvanic or chemical corrosion produced by atmospheric conditions.

**Coulomb –** A unit of electrical charge equal to the number of electrons conducted past a point in 1 second.

**Count –** A number identifying yam size or weight per unit of length (or length per unit of weight), depending on the carpet spinning system used (such as denier, woolen, worsted, cotton, or jute system).

**Course –** Compass direction from one reference point to the next for each leg of a metes and bounds survey.

- An angular course is a compass direction in degrees, minutes, and seconds, stated as a deviation eastward or westward from due north or south; used in metes and bounds descriptions and surveys.

- One of the continuous horizontal layers of masonry units, bonded with mortar. One course is equal to the thickness of the masonry units, bonded with mortar. One course is equal o the thickness of the masonry unit plus the thickness of one mortar joint.

**Coverage –** Area over which a given amount of coating, paint, or transparent finish will spread and hide the previous surface; usually expressed in sq ft/gal (m21L).

**Covering power –** See hiding power.

**Cracking –** Type of coating, paint, or transparent finish failure characterized by breaks in irregular lines wide enough to expose the underlying surface.

**Crazing –** Numerous hairline cracks in the surface of newly hardened concrete. Similar cracks in a paint or coating.

**Creep –** Same as cold flow.

**Crimping –** Method of texturing staple and continuous filament yam to produce irregular alignment of fibers in carpet and increase their bulk and covering power; also facilitates interlocking of fibers, which is necessary for spinning staple fibers into yam.

**Crook –** See warp.

**Crossband –** A layer of veneer in a plywood panel whose grain direction is at right angles to that of the face plies.

**Cross furring –** Furring members installed perpendicular to framing members.

**Cross grain –** See grain.

**Crosslinking –** A chemical reaction in which adjacent polymer molecules unite to form a strong three-dimensional network; usually occurs during the curing of thermosetting plastics.

**Cross slope –** The slope of a pedestrian way that is perpendicular to the direction of travel. (See also running slope.)

**Crown, joint –** The maximum height to which joint compound is applied over a gypsum board joint.

**Cryolite sodium –** Aluminum fluoride used with alumina in the final electrolytic reduction of aluminum. Found naturally in

Greenland; generally produced synthetically from alum, soda, and hydrofluoric acid.

**Cubing** – The assembling of concrete masonry units into cubes after curing for storage and delivery. A cube normally contains six layers of 15 to 18 blocks (8 X 8 X 16 in. [200 X 200 X 400 mm]) or an equivalent volume of other size units.

**Cue** – A device that alerts a user to an upcoming condition; includes audible, visual, and textural signals. (See also detectable warning.)

- An audible cue is a sound or a verbal alert.
- A tactile cue is one mat can be detected by touch.
- A visual cue is one that can be seen.

**Cup** – See warp.

**Curb ramp** – A short ramp cutting through a curb or built into it.

**Cure** – To change the properties of a polymeric system into a final, more stable condition by the use of heat, radiation, or reaction with chemical additives. Sometimes referred to as set.

**Curing** – The hardening of a concrete masonry unit (CMU).

- Atmospheric pressure steam curing is a method of curing CMUs, using steam at atmospheric pressure usually at temperatures of 120°F (48.89°C) to 180°F (82.2°C). Also called low-pressure steam curing.
- High-pressure steam curing is a method of curing CMUs, using saturated steam (365°F [185°C]) under pressure, usually 125 to 150 psi (87.88 to 105.46 Mg/m"). Also referred to as autoclave curing.
- Moist curing is a method of curing CMUs using moisture at atmospheric pressure and temperature of approximately 70°F (21.1 0c).
- The process of keeping concrete moist for an extended period after placement to ensure proper hydration and subsequent strength and quality.
- Final conversion or drying of a coating, paint, or transparent finish material.

**Curtain wall** – An exterior non-load-bearing wall. Such walls may be anchored to columns, spandrel beams, structural walls, or floors. (See also panel wall.)

**Cushioning** – Soft, resilient layer provided under carpet to increase underfoot comfort, to absorb pile-crushing forces, and to reduce impact sound transmission. Also called underlay or lining; see also padding.

**Cut and loop** – See multilevel loop.

**Cut pile** – A carpet face construction in which the pile is cut level so that it stands erect in a low, dense, plush, even surface.

**Cutting in –** Painting of an edge, such as wall color at the ceiling line or at the edge of woodwork.

**Cylinder test –** A laboratory test for compressive stress of a field sample of concrete (6 in. [152.4 mm] in diameter by 12 in. [305 mm] in length).

**Daily degree day –** The numerical difference between 65 ⊠F (18.3°C) and the average of all recorded temperatures on a given day that are lower than 65 ⊠F (l8.3°C).

**Damp course –** A course or layer of impervious material that prevents capillary entrance of moisture from the ground or a lower course. Often called damp check.

**Darby –** A tool used to level freshly placed concrete.

**Darbying –** Smoothing the surface of freshly placed concrete with a darby to level any raised spots and fill depressions.

**Dead load –** The weight of all permanent and stationary construction or equipment included in a building. (See also live load.)

**Decay –** The decomposition of wood substances by certain fungi.

**Decibel –** A logarithmic unit expressing the ratio between a sound being measured and a reference point.

**Decorative CMU –** See under concrete masonry unit.

**Degradation –** A permanent change in the physical or chemical properties of a plastic evidenced by impairment of these properties.

**Degree –** A unit of angular measure equal to the angle contained within two radii of a circle that describe an arc equal to 1/36oth of the circumference of the circle; also used to define an arc equal to 1/360th of the circumference of a circle.

**Degree days heating (DDH) –** The sum of the daily degree days when the temperature dropped below 65°F (l8.3°C).

**Delustered nylon –** Nylon on which the normally high sheen has been reduced by surface treatment.

**Denier –** System of yarn count used for synthetic carpet fibers: number of grams per 9000 meters of yarn length; one denier equals 4,464,528 yards per pound or 279,033 yards per ounce.

**Density –** See pile yarn density.

**Detectable warning –** A standardized surface texture applied to or built into walking surfaces or other elements to warn visually impaired people of hazards in the path of travel. (See also cue.)

**Deterioration –** See degradation.

**Dew point –** The temperature above freezing at which air becomes saturated and condensation occurs. (See also frost point.)

**Dimensional stability –** The ability of a material to retain its dimensions in service.

**Dimension lumber –** See under lumber.

**Direct chemical attack –** Corrosion caused by a chemical dissolving a metal.

**Disability –** A limitation or loss of use of a physical, mental, or sensory body part or function.

**Discontinuous construction –** A construction method used to separate a continuous path through which sound may be transmitted. Examples include the use of staggered studs, double walls, and the resilient mounting of surfaces.

**Dispersion –** The distribution of a finely divided solid in a liquid or a solid.

**Disposal field –** See absorption field.

**Distribution line –** Open joint or perforated pipe intended to permit soil absorption of effluent.

**Divider strips –** All-metal or plastic-top metal strips provided in a terrazzo finish to control cracking due to drying shrinkage, temperature variations, and minor structural movements; are also used for decorative purposes and convenience in placing a terrazzo topping.

**Drain –** A pipe that carries wastewater or waterborne wastes in a building drainage system.

**Drainage system –** That piping that conveys sewage, rainwater, or other liquid wastes up to a point of disposal, such as the mains of a public sewer system or a private septic disposal system. See also vent system and drain, waste, and vent (DWV) system.

**Drain, waste, and vent (DWV) system** – The collection of pipes that facilitates the removal of liquid and solid wastes and dissipates sewer gases.

**Drawing** – The process of pulling material through a die to reduce the size, to change the cross section or shape, or to harden the material.

**Dressed lumber** – Lumber that has been surfaced with a planing machine.

**Dressed size** – see size.

**Drier** – An ingredient included to speed the drying of coatings, paints, and trans- parent finishes.

**Drip** – A projection shaped to cause water to flow away from a lower surface, thus preventing it from running down the face of the lower surface.

**Drying** – The various stages of curing in a coating, paint, or transparent finish film.

- Dust-free is the stage of drying when particles of dust that settle on the surface do not stick to it.
- Tack-free is the stage of drying when the surface no longer feels sticky when lightly touched.
- Dry enough to handle is the stage of drying when the film has hardened sufficiently so that the object or surface may be used without marring.
- Dry enough to recoat is that stage of drying when the next coat can be applied.
- Dry enough to sand is the stage of drying when the film can be sanded without the sandpaper sticking or clogging.

**Drying oil** – A coating, paint, or transparent finish vehicle ingredient, such as linseed oil, which, when exposed to the air in a thin layer, oxidizes and hardens to a relatively tough elastic film.

**Dry lumber** – Under Product Standard PS 20-70, lumber with a moisture content of 19% or less.

**Dry rot** – A term that is loosely applied to many types of decay, which in the advanced state permit wood to be easily crushed to a dry powder. This term is a misnomer since all fungi require moisture.

**Drywall nail** – See nail, drywall.

**Drywall screw** – See screws, drywall.

**Dry well** – A covered and lined underground pit, similar to a seepage pit but intended to receive water free of organic matter, such as from roof drains, floor drains, or laundry tubs. Used as an auxiliary to a septic disposal system to avoid overloading the septic tank absorption system. (Also called leaching well or leaching pit.)

**Ductile –** Capable of being drawn out or hammered; able to undergo cold plastic deformation without breaking.

**Durability –** The ability of a coating, paint, or transparent finish to retain its desirable properties for a long time under expected service conditions.

**Dusting –** The appearance of a powdery material at the surface of a hardened concrete.

**Dye or dyestuff –** Colored material used to change the color of a coating or paint with little or no hiding of the underlying surface.

**Dyne –** A unit of force, which when acting on a mass of 1 gram accelerates it 1 centimeter per second.

**Echo –** A reflected sound loud enough and received late enough to be heard as distinct from the source.

**Economy brick –** See under brick masonry unit.

**Edge grain –** See under grain.

**Edges, gypsum board –** See gypsum board.

**Edging –** The finishing operation of rounding off the edge of a concrete slab to prevent chipping or damage.

**Efflorescence –** Deposit of soluble salts, usually white in color, appearing on the exposed surface of masonry, concrete, or plaster.

**Effluent –** Partially treated liquid sewage flowing from any part of a septic disposal system, septic tank, or absorption system.

**Eggshell finish –** Surface sheen midway between flat and semi-gloss.

**Elastic deformation –** Deformation caused by a stress small enough that when the stress is removed, the material returns to its original shape. (See also plastic deformation.)

**Elasticity –** The ability to recover the original size and shape after deformation.

**Elastic limit** – The amount of stress that, if exceeded, will cause a given material to deform or set permanently.

**Elastomer** – A material that at room temperature can be stretched repeatedly to at least twice its original length and that, upon release of the stress, will return instantly and with force to its approximate original length. A rubberlike substance.

**Electric induction furnace** – See under furnace, steel.

**Electrogalvanizing** – Electroplating with zinc to provide greater corrosion resistance.

**Electrolysis** – Also called galvanic corrosion, an electrochemical decomposition that results when dissimilar metals are each contacted by the same electrolyte, such as water. The process is similar to that which takes place in an automobile battery. One metal acts as a cathode, the other as an anode. When the electrolyte causes an electrical current to flow from one metal to the other, the anodic metal dissolves and hydrogen ions accumulate on the cathodic metal. Electrolysis can also take place in a single metal when one portion of it is cathodic and another portion is anodic if an electrolyte makes a bridge between the two portions.

**Electrolyte** – A nonmetallic substance in which electricity is conducted by the movement of ions.

**Electromotive force** – Something that moves or tends to move electricity.

**Electroplating** – A process that employs an electric current to coat a base metal (cathode) with another metal (anode) in an electrolytic solution.

**Emulsion** – Mixture of liquids (or a liquid and a solid) not soluble in each other, one liquid (or solid) being dispersed as minute particles in the other, base liquid, with the help of an emulsifying agent.

**Enamel** – A coating or paint capable of forming a very smooth, hard film, sometimes using varnish as the vehicle; may be flat, gloss, or semi-gloss.

**Enamel holdout** – Property of producing a tight film that prevents the penetration of subsequent enamel coats to underlying surfaces; prevents unequal absorption and uneven gloss.

**Ends, gypsum board** – See gypsum board.

**End wall** – The wall along the short dimension of a room.

**Engineered brick** – See under brick masonry unit.

**Engineered brick masonry –** Masonry in which the design is based on a rational, accepted structural engineering analysis

**Equilibrium moisture content –** The moisture content at which wood neither gains nor loses moisture when surrounded by air at a given relative humidity and temperature.

**Erosion –** Wearing away of a coating, paint, or transparent finish film caused by exposure.

**Etch –** A surface preparation for a coating, paint, or transparent finish by chemical means to improve adhesion.

**Evaporation –** The change of water from a liquid to a gas.

**Expandable plastic –** A plastic suitable for expansion into cellular form by thermal, chemical, or mechanical means.

**Expansion strips –** Double divider strips in a terrazzo finish separated by resilient material and provided generally for the same purpose as divider strips, but where a greater degree of structural movement is expected.

**Extender –** In plastics, a low-cost material used to dilute or extend high-cost resins without appreciably lessening the properties of the original resin. In coatings, paints, and transparent finishes, an inexpensive but compatible substance that can be added to a more valuable substance to increase the volume of material without substantially diminishing its desirable properties; in coatings and paints, extender pigments improve storage and application properties.

**Exterior wall –** Any outside wall of a building other than a party wall.

**External corner –** A projecting angle formed by abutting walls or a vertical surface and soffit (not to be confused with exterior, meaning exposed to the weather).

**Extrude –** To form lengths of shaped sections by forcing a plastic material through a shaped hole in a die.

**Extrusion –** In aluminum, a product formed by extruding. (a) An extrusion billet is a solid, wrought, semi -finished product intended for further extrusion into rods, bars, or shapes. (b) An extrusion ingot is a solid or hollow cylindrical casting used for extrusion into bars, rods, shapes, or tubes. In plastic, forcing plastic material through a shaped orifice to make rod, tubing, or sheeting.

**Faced CMU –** See concrete masonry unit.

**Faced wall –** A wall in which the facing and backing are of different materials and are bonded together to exert common action under load.

**Face shell –** The side wall of a hollow masonry unit or clay tile.

**Face size –** See under size.

**Facing –** A part of a wall that is used as a finished surface.

**Facing brick –** See under brick masonry unit.

**Factory and shop lumber –** See lumber.

**Fading –** Loss of color due to exposure to light, heat, or weathering.

**Fastener treatment –** Method of concealing gypsum board fasteners by successive applications of compound until a smooth surface is achieved.

**Featheredging (feathering) –** Tapering gypsum board joint compound to a very thin edge to ensure inconspicuous blending with adjacent gypsum board surfaces.

**Feather sanding –** Tapering the edge of a dried coating, paint, or transparent finish film with sandpaper.

**Ferritic steel –** See grain structure.

**Ferroalloys –** Iron-based alloys used in steelmaking as a source of desired alloying elements.

**Ferrous alloys –** Composite metals whose chief ingredient is iron (ferrum), metallurgically combined with one or more alloying elements.

**Fiber saturation point –** The stage in drying (or wetting) of wood at which the cell walls are saturated with water but the cell cavities are free of water, being approximately 30% moisture content in most species.

**Fiber, wood –** A comparatively long e/25 in. [1.016 mm] or less to 1/3 in. [8.47 mm]), narrow, tapering unit closed at both ends.

**Field –** In ceramic tile, the general area of the tile excluding trim. In gypsum board, the surface of the board exclusive of the perimeter. In masonry walls, the expanse of wall between openings, corners, etc., principally composed of stretchers. In resilient flooring, the area of a floor within the borders.

**Figure –** The pattern produced in a wood surface by annual growth rings, rays, knots, and deviations from the regular grain.

**Fill –** The sand, gravel, or compacted earth used to bring a subgrade up to a desired level.

**Filler –** (1) In plastics, a relatively inert material added to modify the strength, permanence, or working properties or to lower the cost of a resin. (2) In coatings, paints, and transparent finishes, a pigmented composition for filling the pores or irregularities in a surface in preparation for finishing.

**Filling –** See weft.

**Film –** In plastics, plastic sheeting having a nominal thickness not greater than 0.010 in. (0.254 mm). In coatings, paints, and transparent finishes, a thin application generally not thicker than 0.010 in. (0.254 mm).

**Fine aggregate –** See aggregate.

**Fineness modulus –** In plastics, plastic sheeting having a nominal thickness not greater than 0.010 in. (0.254 mm). In coatings, paints, and transparent finishes, a thin application generally not thicker than 0.010 in. (0.254 mm).

**Finish coat –** The final decorative plaster layer in either two-coat or three-coat work.

**Finished mill products –** Steel shapes that can be used directly in construction.

- Bars are hot-rolled or cold-drawn round, square, hexagonal, or multifaceted long shapes, generally larger than wire in cross section. Also hot- or cold-rolled rectangular flat shapes (flats) generally narrower than sheets and snip.
- Back plate is a cold-rolled, flat, carbon-steel product that is thinner than sheet and wider than strip, generally coated with zinc, tin, or terne metal.
- Foil is a cold-rolled flat product less than 0.005 in. (0.127 mm) thick.
- Plate is a hot-rolled flat product generally thicker than sheet and wider than strip.
- Sheet is a hot- or cold-rolled flat product generally thinner than plate and wider than strip.
- Strip is a hot-rolled or cold-rolled flat product generally narrower than sheet and thinner than plate.
- Structurals are hot-rolled steel shapes of special design (such as H beams, I beams, channels, angles, and tees) used in construction.
- Terneplate is backplate or sheet metal that has been coated with terne metal.
- Tinplate is backplate that has been coated with tin.
- Tubular products are hollow products of round, oval, square, rectangular, or multifaceted cross sections. In construction, round products are generally called pipe; square or rectangular products with thinner wall sections are called tube or tubing.
- Wire is a cold-finished product of round, square, or multifaceted cross section, generally smaller than bars; round wire is cold drawn, 0.005 in. (0.127 mm) to less than 1 in. (25 mm) in diameter; flat wire is cold rolled, generally narrower than bar.

**Fire brick –** See under brick masonry unit.

**Fire division wall –** A wall that subdivides a building to resist the spread of fire. It is not necessarily continuous through all stories to and above the roof. See also fire wall.

**Fireproofing –** A material or combination of materials built to protect structural members to increase their fire resistance.

**Fire-resistive material –** See noncombustible material.

**Fire-retardant coating or paint –** A coating or paint that will significantly (1) reduce the rate of flame spread, (2) resist ignition at high temperatures, and (3) insulate the underlying material to prolong the time required for the material to reach its ignition, melting, or structural weakening temperature.

**Firewall –** A wall that subdivides a building to resist the spread of fire and that extends continuously from the foundation through the roof. See also fire division wall.

**Fixture-unit –** A mathematical factor used by engineers to estimate the probable demand on a drainage or water supply system (volume, duration of flow, and intervals between operations) by various plumbing fixtures.

**Flaking –** Form of coating, paint, or transparent finish failure characterized by the detachment of small pieces of the film from the surface or previous coat; usually preceded by cracking or blistering.

**Flanking path –** A wall or floor and ceiling assembly that permits sound to be transmitted along its surface. Also: an opening that permits the direct transmission of sound through the air.

**Flashing –** In masonry construction, a thin, relatively impervious sheet material placed in mortar joints and across air spaces in masonry walls to collect water that may penetrate the wall and to direct it to the exterior.

- In masonry manufacture, the step during the burning process of clay masonry units that produces varying shades and colors in the units.
- In resilient flooring, the bending up of resilient sheet material against a wall or a projection, either temporarily for the purpose of fitting or permanently to form a one piece resilient base.

**Flash point –** Temperature at which a coating, paint, transparent finish, or solvent will ignite; the lower the flash point, the greater the hazard.

**Flash set –** Undesirable rapid setting of cement in concrete or mortar.

**Flat –** Dull, non-reflective; opposite of gloss.

**Flat applicator –** Rectangular flat pad with an attached handle that is used to paint shingles, shakes, and other special surfaces.

**Flat finish –** Finish having no gloss or luster.

**Flat grain –** See under grain.

**Flats –** Term applied to flat coatings and paints.

**Flatting agent –** Ingredient added to coatings and paint to reduce the gloss of the dried film.

**Flitch –** A portion of a log sawed on two or more sides and intended for manufacture into lumber or sliced or sawed veneer. A complete bundle of veneers laid together in sequence as they were sliced or sawed.

**Floating –** A concrete slab finishing operation that embeds aggregate, removes slight imperfections, humps, and voids to produce a level surface, and consolidates mortar at the surface. A condition in which a layer of water occurs between a mortar bed and a masonry unit, usually due to bleeding, causing the unit and the mortar to fail to bond with each other. In this condition, the unit is said to float. Separation of pigment colors on the surface of applied paint.

**Flocked carpet –** Single-level velvety pile carpet composed of short fibers embedded on an adhesive-coated backing.

**Floor brick –** See under brick masonry unit.

**Flow –** The ability of a coating, paint, or transparent finish to level out and spread into a smooth film; materials that have good flow usually level out uniformly and exhibit few brush or roller marks.

**Fluffing –** See shedding.

**Flux –** A mineral that, due to its affinity to the impurities in iron ores, is used in iron working and steelmaking to separate impurities in the form of molten slag.

- Basic flux is a mineral, such as limestone or dolomite, used in basic furnaces to make basic (low-phosphorus) steel.
- Neutral flux is a mineral (fluorspar) used to make slag more fluid.

**Foamed plastic –** See cellular plastic.

**Foil –** See under finished mill products.

**Footing –** The base of a foundation, column, or wall used to distribute the load over the sub-grade.

**Forging –** The working (shaping) of metal parts by forcing between shaped dies. (See also hot working.)

- Press forging is shaping by applying pressure in a press.
- Hammer forging is shaping by application of repeated blows, as in a forging hammer.

**Form –** A temporary structure erected to contain concrete during placing and initial hardening.

**Foundation wall –** A load-bearing wall below the floor nearest to exterior grade serving as a support for a wall, pier, column, floor, or other structural part of a building.

**Fractional section –** See under section.

**Frames –** Racks at the back of a jacquard loom, each holding pile yarn of a different color. In Wilton carpets, two to six frames may be used. The number is a measure of quality as well as an indication of the number of colors in the pattern, unless some of the yarns are buried in the backing.

**Freezing cycle day –** A day in which the air temperature passes either above or below 32°F (O°C). The average number of freezing cycle days in a year equals the difference between the mean number of days when the minimum temperature was 32°F (O°C) or below, and when the maximum temperature was 32°F (O°C) or below.

**Frequency –** The number of complete cycles of a vibration occurring in each see and measured in cycles per second (cps) and expressed in hertz (Hz).

**Frieze carpet –** See under pile.

**Frost point –** That temperature below freezing at which condensation occurs. (See also dew point.)

**Fungicide –** Agent that helps prevent mold or mildew growth on paint.

**Furnace, blast –** Tall, cylindrical masonry structure lined with refractory materials, used to smelt iron ores in combination with fluxes, coke, and air into pig iron.

**Furnace, steel –** Masonry or steel structure lined with refractory materials, used to melt pig iron, scrap metal, and sometimes agglomerated ores, ferroalloys, and fluxes into steel.

- A basic oxygen furnace is a suspended, tilting vessel that uses high-purity oxygen to oxidize impurities in hot pig iron and other iron-bearing materials to produce low phosphorus (basic) steel.
- An electric arc suspended furnace is a kettle that melts scrap metal, are, and sometimes ferroalloys with the heat of an electric arc to produce steels of controlled chemical composition. An electric induction furnace is a steel encased, insulated magnesia pot in which metal, scrap, and ferroalloys are melted with the heat of an electric current induced by windings of electric tubing; used chiefly to produce small quantities of high-grade steels such as alloy, stainless, and heat-resisting steels.
- An open hearth furnace is a masonry structure with a hearth exposed to the sweep of flames in which hot pig iron,

scrap metal, and fluxes are melted and oxidized by a mixture of fuel and air to produce basic or acid steel.

**Furring** – A method of finishing the interior face of a concrete or masonry wall to provide space for insulation, to prevent moisture penetration, or to provide a level, plumb, and straight surface for finishing. Furring consists of metal channels or studs or of wood snips or studs.

**Fusion-bonded carpet** – Carpet made by fusing carpet yarn and a backing, then cutting the substrates in two, making two pieces of carpet.

**Fuzzing** – Temporary condition on new carpet consisting of an irregular appearance caused by slack yarn twist, "snagging" of fibers, or breaking of yarn. Can be remedied by spot shearing.

**Galvanic corrosion** – See electrolysis.

**Galvanizing** – Zinc coating by electroplating or hot dipping, which produces a characteristic bright, spangled finish and protects the base metal from atmospheric corrosion.

**Gang grooved** – Plywood panels produced by passing them under a machine with grooving knives set at certain intervals.

**Gauge** – The distance between tufts across the width of knitted and tufted carpets, expressed in fractions of an inch.

**Glaze** – Used to describe several types of finishing materials.

- Glazing putty is a compound of creamy consistency applied to fill surface imperfections.
- A glazing stain is very thin, semitransparent, and usually pigmented with Vandyke brown or burnt sienna, applied over a previously stained, filled, or painted surface to soften or blend the original color without obscuring it.
- A glaze coat is a clear finish applied over previously coated surfaces to create a gloss finish.

**Glazing compound** – Dough-like material, consisting of vehicle and pigment, that retains its plasticity over a wide range of temperatures and for an extended period of time. Either elastomeric or acrylic joint sealants are generally used today where glazing compounds are called for. (See also sealant, joint.)

**Gloss** – Shiny, reflective surface quality; term sometimes used broadly to include coatings, paints, and transparent finishes with these surface properties.

**Glue line** – The line of glue visible on the edge of a plywood panel. Also applies to the layer of glue itself.

**Grade** – The designation of the quality of wood, steel, and other materials and products made from them, such as plywood.

**Graded aggregate –** An aggregate containing particles of uniformly graduated size from the finest fine aggregate size to the maximum size of coarse aggregate.

**Graded sand –** A sand containing particles of uniformly graduated size from very fine up to 1/4 in. (6.4 mm).

**Grain –** The direction, size, arrangement, appearance or quality of the fibers in wood. Cross grained wood is sawed with the fibers not parallel with the longitudinal axis of the piece. This grain may be diagonal, in a spiral pattern, or a combination of both.

- Diagonal-grained wood is sawn at an angle with the bark of the tree such that the annual growth rings are at an angle with the axis of the piece.
- Edge-grained wood is sawn parallel with the pith of a log and at nearly right angles to the annual growth rings, making an angle of 45 to 90 degrees with the wide surface of the piece. Also called quarter-sawn wood and vertical-grained wood.
- Flat-grained wood is sawn parallel with the pith of the log and nearly tangent to the annual growth rings, making an angle of less than 45 degrees with the surface of the piece. Also called plain- sawn wood.
- Open-grained wood is a common designation for wood with large pores, such as oak, ash, chestnut, and walnut.

**Graining –** Simulating the grain of wood by means of specially prepared colors or stains and the use of graining tools or special brushing techniques.

**Grain raising –** Swelling and standing up of wood grain caused by absorbed water or solvents.

**Grain structure –** The microscopic internal crystalline structure (size and distribution of particles) of a metal that affects its properties, known as austenitic, ferritic and martensitic.

- Austenitic steels are tough, strong, and nonmagnetic. Austenitic stainless steels have a chromium content of up to 25% and a nickel content of up to 22% and can be hardened by cold working.
- Ferritic steels are soft, ductile, and strongly magnetic. Ferritic stainless steels usually have a chromium content of 12 to 27% and are not harden able by heat treatment.
- Martensitic steels can be made very hard and tough by heat treatment and rapid cooling. Martensitic stainless steels have a chromium content of 4 to 12%.

**Great circle –** A line described on a sphere by a plane bisecting the sphere into equal parts. The equator is a great circle, as are pairs of opposing meridians.

**Green concrete –** Freshly placed concrete.

**Green lumber –** Under Product Standard PS 20-70, lumber with a moisture content of more than 19%. Unseasoned lumber that has not been exposed to air or kiln drying.

**Greenwich Meridian –** The Meridian Line is an imaginary line which runs from the North Pole to the South Pole. By international convention it runs through "the primary transit" instrument (main telescope) at the Royal Observatory in Greenwich.

- It is known at Zero Longitude and it is the line from which all other lines of longitude are measured. This includes the line that runs 180° away from Greenwich also known as the International Date Line.

**Grin –** Condition in which the backing shows through sparsely spaced pile tufts. A carpet may be grinned (bent back) deliberately to reveal its construction.

**Gross cross-sectional area –** In masonry, the total area of a section perpendicular to the direction of the load, including areas within cores, cellular spaces, and other openings in the material.

**Ground coat –** Base coat in an antiquing system; applied before graining colors, glazing, or other finish coat.

**Grounds –** Nailing strips placed in concrete and masonry walls as a means of attaching trim, furring, cabinetry, or equipment.

**Grout, masonry –** Mortar of a consistency that will flow or pour easily without segregation of the ingredients. A liquid mixture of cement, water, and sand of pouring consistency.

**Grout, tile –** A formulation used to fill the joints between tiles; may be cementitious, resinous, or a combination of both.

**Hard-burned –** Clay products that have been fired at high temperatures. They have relatively low absorptions and high compressive strengths.

**Hardness –** Cohesion of particles on the surface of a coating, paint, or transparent finish as determined by the ability to resist scratching or indentation.

**Hardwood –** The botanical group of trees that is broad-leaved and deciduous. The term does not refer to the actual hardness of the wood.

**Header –** A masonry unit that overlaps two or more adjacent wythes of masonry to provide structural bond. (Also called bonder.)

**Header course –** A continuous bonding course of header brick.

**Head joint –** The vertical mortar joint between ends of masonry units.

**Heartwood –** The wood that extends from the pith to the sapwood, the cells of which no longer participate in the growth process of the tree. Heartwood may be impregnated with gums, resins, and other materials, which usually make it darker and more decay resistant than sapwood.

**Heat capacity –** The amount of heat required to raise the temperature of 1 cu ft of a material 1°F (0.5556°C).

**Heat-set nylon –** Nylon fiber that has been heat-treated to retain a desired shape.

**Heat sink –** A material or system that collects and stores heat.

**Heat-treatable alloys –** Aluminum alloys capable of gaining strength by being heat treated. The alloying elements show increasingly solid solubility in aluminum with increasing temperature, resulting in pronounced strengthening.

**Heat treatment –** Of aluminum (see solution heat treatment):

- Annealing is a heat treatment process in which an alloy is heated to a temperature between 600°F (315.56°C) and 800°F (426.67°C) and then slowly cooled to relieve internal stresses and return the alloy to its softest and most ductile condition.(2) Of steel: Controlled heating and cooling of steels in the solid state for the purpose of obtaining certain desirable mechanical or physical properties.
- Annealing is heating metal to high temperatures (1350°F [732.2°C] to 1600°F [871.1 0c] for steel).

**Gusset plate –** Wood or metal plate used as a means of joining coplanar structural members in trusses. Gusset plates lap the butt joints between members.

**Gypsum board –** A panel consisting of a noncombustible core of calcined gypsum, surfaced on both sides with a covering material specifically designed for various uses with respect to performance, application, location, and appearance.

- Wallboard is a class of gypsum board used primarily as an interior finished surface.
- Lath is a class of gypsum board used as a base for gypsum plaster.
- Backing boards are gypsum boards that serve as a base to which gypsum wallboard or tile is applied.
- Sheathing is a class of gypsum board used as a base for exterior finishes.
- Edges are gypsum board extremities that are paperbound and run the long dimension of the board as manufactured.
- Ends are gypsum board extremities that are mill- or job-cut, exposing the gypsum core, and run the short dimension of the board as manufactured.

**Hardboard –** A dense panel board manufactured of wood fibers with the natural lignin in the wood reactivated to serve as a binder for the wood fibers.

**Hertz (Hz) –** The unit of frequency of a periodic process equal to one cycle per second.

**Hiding power –** Ability of a coating or paint to obscure the surface to which it is applied, generally expressed as the number of square feet that can be covered by I gal of material or the number of gallons required to cover 1000 sq ft. Also called covering power.

**High-density plywood –** See under plywood.

**High-early-strength cement** – Cement used to produce a concrete that develops strength more rapidly than normal.

**High-low loop** – See multilevel loop.

**High polymer** – A polymer of high molecular weight.

**High-pressure laminate** – A laminate molded and cured at pressures not lower than 1000 psi (703.07 mg/m-) and usually between 1200 psi (843.68 mg/m") and 2000 psi (1406.14 mg/rn-).

**High-pressure steam curing** – See under curing.

**Hollow brick** – See under brick masonry unit.

**Hollow masonry unit** – See masonry unit.

**Hollow wall** – A wall built of masonry units arranged to provide an air space within the wall between the facing and backing wythes.

**Horizontal application** – Applying gypsum board with the edges perpendicular to supporting members such as studs, joists, channels, or furring strips. (See also vertical application.)

**Hot-dip process** – Coating a metal with another metal by immersing it in a bath of the molten coating metal. The coating metals most commonly used on steel is zinc, terne metal and aluminum.

**Hot rolling** – See rolling and hot working.

**Hot working** – Forming metal at elevated temperatures at which metals can be more easily worked.

1. For aluminum alloys:

   (a) Hot working temperatures are usually in the 300°F (148.9°C) to 400°F (204.4 0c) range. (b) Hot rolling is the shaping of aluminum plate by rolling heated slabs of metal. Hot rolling is usually used for work down to about 0.125 in. (3.175 mm) thick.

2. For steel: Shaping hot plastic metal by hot rolling, extruding, or forging.

   (a) Hot working temperatures are above 1500°F (815.6°C). Hot working is generally accompanied by increases in strength, hardness, and toughness. (b) Hot forming is the forming of a hot plastic metal into desired shapes, with little change in the mechanical properties of the metal. (c) Extruding is shaping lengths of hot metal by forcing them through a die of the desired profile. (d) Forging is shaping hot metal between dies with compression force or impact. (e) Hot rolling is gradual shaping by squeezing hot metals between rolls.

**House sewer –** (See building sewer.)

**Hydration –** The chemical reaction of water and cement that produces a hardened concrete.

**Hz –** See hertz.

**Impact Insulation Class (ITC) –** A single-number rating developed by the Federal Housing Administration to estimate the impact sound isolation performance of floor and ceiling assemblies.

**Noise Rating (INR) Impact –** A single-number rating used to compare and evaluate the ability of floor and ceiling assemblies to isolate impact sound transmission (see sound isolation).

**Impact sound pressure level (ISPL) –** The sound level in decibels measured in the receiving room resulting from the transmission of sound produced by a standard tapping machine through an adjacent floor and ceiling assembly.

**Incident sound impervious soil –** A tight, cohesive soil, such as clay, that does not allow the ready passage of water. A sound striking a surface, as contrasted with a sound reflected from the surface. The angle of incidence equals the angle of reflection.

**Individual sewage disposal system –** A combination of a sewage treatment plant (package plant or septic tank) and method of effluent disposal (soil absorption system or stream discharge) serving a single dwelling.

**Inert –** A combination of a sewage treatment plant (package plant or septic tank) and method of effluent disposal (soil absorption system or stream discharge) serving a single dwelling.

**Ingot –** (1) A mass of aluminum cast into a convenient shape for storage or transportation, to be later re-melted for casting or finishing by rolling, forging, or another process. (2) A cast pig iron or steel shape made by pouring hot metal into a mold.

**Inhibitor –** A substance that prevents or retards a chemical reaction; inhibitors are often added to plastic resins to prolong their storage life.

**Injection molding –** Forming plastic by fusing it in a chamber with heat and pressure and then forcing part of the mass into a cooler chamber, where it solidifies.

**Insolation (incident solar radiation) –** The solar radiation that strikes a surface.

**Intercoat adhesion –** Adhesion between two coats of paint.

**Internal corner –** An enclosed angle of less than 180 degrees formed by abutting walls or the juncture of walls and the ceiling (not to be confused with interior, meaning protected from the weather).

**Isolation –** See sound isolation.

**Isolation joint –** A joint placed to separate a concrete slab into individual panels or from adjacent surfaces.

**Isolation membrane –** In tile floors, see cleavage (isolation) membrane. In a terrazzo finish, a membrane such as asphalt-saturated roofing felt, building paper, or polyethylene film installed between the subfloor and the terrazzo under bed to prevent bonding and permit independent movement of each.

**Jacquard –** Mechanism for a Wilton loom that uses punched cards to produce the desired color design.

**Jaspe carpet –** See under pile.

**Joint –** See mortar joint.

**Joint beading –** See ridging.

**Joint compound –** A material used for finishing joints in gypsum board.

**Joint crown –** See crown, joint.

**Joint reinforcement –** Steel wire, bar, or fabricated reinforcement that is placed in horizontal mortar joints.

**Joints –** See control joint, construction joint, and isolation joint.

**Joint tape –** Paper or paper-faced cotton tape used over joints between wallboard to conceal the joints and provide a smooth surface for painting.

**Joint treatment –** Method of reinforcing and concealing gypsum board joints with tape and successive layers of joint compound.

**Joist –** One of a series of parallel beams used to support floor, ceiling, and roof loads. Joists are supported in turn by bigger beams, girders, or bearing walls.

**Joists and planks** – See under lumber.

**Jumbo brick** – See under brick masonry unit.

**Jute** – Strong, durable yarn spun from fibers of the jute plant, native to India and the Far East; used in the backings of many carpets.

**Kiln drying** – See under seasoning.

**Knitted carpet** – Carpet made on a knitting machine by looping together backing, stitching, and pile yarns with three sets of needles, as in hand knitting.

**Knot** – The portion of a branch or limb that has been surrounded by subsequent growth of wood.

**Kraftcord** – Tightly twisted yam made from wood pulp fiber, used as an alternative for cotton or jute in carpet backing.

**Lacquer** – Coating that dries quickly by evaporation of its volatile solvent and forms a film from its nonvolatile constituent, usually nitrocellulose; may be pigmented or clear.

**Laitance** – A soft, weak layer of mortar appearing on a horizontal surface of concrete due to segregation or bleeding.

**Laminate** – A product made by bonding together two or more layers of materials.

**Laminated wood** – A piece of wood built up of laminations that have been joined with glue, mechanical fastenings or both.

**Laminating adhesive** – See adhesive, drywall.

**Langley** – The measure of isolation; equal to 1 calorie per square centimeter or 3.69 Btus per square foot.

**Lap** – To lay or place one coat so that its edge extends over and covers the edge of a previous coat.

**Lateral** – A branch of an absorption field, consisting of either. The length of the distribution line between overflow pipes or The length of the distribution line between the tee or cross fitting and the farthest point in a closed-loop field.

**Lateral support of walls –** Means whereby walls are braced either horizontally by columns, pilasters, or cross walls or vertically by floor and roof construction.

**Latex –** A water suspension of fine particles of rubber or rubber-like plastics.

**Latex paint –** A paint containing latex and thinned with water.

**Lath, gypsum –** See gypsum board.

**Latitude –** The position of a point on the earth's surface north or south of the equator, stated as an angular measure (degrees, minutes, and seconds) of the meridian arc contained between that point and the equator.

**Leaching pit –** See dry well.

**Leaching well –** See dry well.

**Lead –** The section of a masonry wall built up and racked back on successive courses. A line is attached to leads as a guide for building a wall between them.

**Legal description –** A written, legally recorded identification of the location and boundaries of a parcel of land. A legal description may be based on a metes and bounds surveyor the rectangular survey system, or it may make reference to a recorded plat or survey.

**Leveling –** Ability of a film to flow out free from ripples, pockmarks, and brush marks after application.

**Level loop pile –** A woven or tufted carpet style in which the tufts are in loop form and of the same height.

**Level tip shear –** Randomly patterned cut and loop pile carpet.

**Lifting –** Softening and penetration of a previous film by solvents in the paint being applied over it, resulting in raising and wrinkling.

**Light-fastness –** Ability to resist fading.

**Light framing lumber –** See lumber.

**Lignin –** The second most abundant continuant of wood, making up 12 to 28% in most species. It encrusts the cell walls and cements the cells together.

**Linear polymer –** A polymer that is arranged in a long, continuous chain with a minimum number of side chains or branches.

**Lining felt –** A mineral fiber or asphalt felt specifically manufactured for use under resilient flooring.

**Lintel –** A structural member used to carry the load over an opening in a wall.

**Lip –** When related to barrier-free design, an abrupt vertical change in level.

**Live load –** The total of all moving and variable loads that may be placed on or in a building. (See also dead load.)

**Longitude –** The position of a point on the earth's surface east or west of the Greenwich meridian, stated as an angular measure (degrees, minutes, and seconds) of the arc on the equator contained between a meridian passing through that point and the Greenwich meridian.

**Long oil –** Varnish or paint vehicle with more than 55% of the resin consisting of oil or fatty acid.

**Loom –** Machine on which carpet is woven, as distinguished from other machines on which carpets may be tufted, flocked, or punched.

**Loomed carpet –** See woven carpet.

**Loop pile –** A woven or tufted carpet style in which the pile surface consists of uncut loops; also called round wire.

**Loop vent –** A branch vent that serves two or more traps and extends from in front of the last fixture connection of a horizontal branch to the stack vent. (See also circuit vent.)

**Loudness –** A subjective response to sound, indicating the magnitude of the hearing sensation, depending on the listener's ear.

**Lumber –** The wood product of a saw and planning mill not further manufactured than by sawing, re-sawing, and passing lengthwise through a standard planning machine, cross-cut to length, and worked.

- Beams and stringers are large pieces of lumber measuring 5 in. (127 mrn) or more in thickness and 8 in. (203.2 mrn) or more in width. These are graded with respect to their strength in bending when loaded on the narrow face.

- Boards are lumber up to 2 in. (50 mrn) thick and 2 in. (50 mrn) or more in width.
- Dimension lumber is lumber 2 to 4 in. (50 to 100 mrn) thick and 2 in. (50 mrn) or more in width. Factory and shop lumber is intended to be cut again for use in further manufacture.
- Joists and planks are pieces of lumber 2 to 4 in. (50 to 100 mrn) in nominal thickness and 4 in. (100 mrn) or more in width. These are graded with respect to strength in bending when loaded either on the narrow face, as a joist, or on the wide face, as a plank. Light framing is lumber 2 to 4 in. (50 to 100 mm) thick and 2 to 4 in. (50 to 100 mm) wide.
- Matched lumber is lumber that has been edge dressed and shaped to make a close tongue-and-groove joint at the edges or ends when laid edge to edge or end to end.
- Patterned lumber is lumber that is shaped to a pattern or to a molded form in addition to being dressed, matched, ship lapped, or any combination of these.
- Posts and timbers are lumber that is approximately square, 5 in. (127 mm) and thicker, and having a width not more than 2 in. (50.8 mm) greater than its thickness.
- Stress grade lumber is the same as structural lumber.
- Structural lumber is lumber that has been machine rated or visually graded into grades with assigned working stresses. Includes most yard lumber grades, except boards.
- Yard lumber is intended for general building purposes; includes boards, dimension lumber, and timbers.

**Machinability** – The ability to be milled, sawed, tapped, drilled, and reamed without excessive tool wear, with ease of chip metal removal and surface finishing.

**Main** – The principal artery of a drainage or water supply system to which branches may be connected. It is usually the lowest horizontal piping. In a drainage system the main is the building drain; in a water system it is the distributing main, whether located in the basement or on the top floor.

**Mainstreaming** – A process that seeks to integrate physically handicapped persons into society by: (1) equipping them with the personal devices and adaptive skills needed to function effectively in the built environment and (2)removing physical barriers that prevent them from functioning like able-bodied individuals.

**Main vent** – The principal artery of a vent system to which vent branches may be connected. It may be either a vertical pipe that collects one or more branch vents or a horizontal pipe to which a number of vent stacks are connected before they go through the roof.

**Major arch** – See under arch.

**Malleability** – The ability to be shaped without fracture by either hot or cold working

**Marine varnish** – Varnish specially designed for immersion in water and exposure to a marine atmosphere.

**Marl** – A soil or rock containing calcium carbonate (limestone).

**Martensitic steel** – See under grain structure.

**Masking** – The effect produced by ambient sound that seems to diminish the loudness of transmitted noise. Temporary covering of areas not to be painted.

**Masking tape** – A strip of paper or cloth tape, easily removable and used temporarily to cover areas that are not to be painted.

**Masonry bonded hollow wall** – A hollow wall in which the facing and backup are bonded together with solid masonry units.

**Masonry cement** – A packaged pre-mixture of Portland cement, lime, and other ingredients to which sand and water are added in the field to make masonry cement mortar.

**Masonry unit** – A manufactured building unit of burned clay, shale, concrete, stone, glass, gypsum or other material.

- A hollow masonry unit is one whose net cross-sectional area in any plane parallel to the bearing surface is less than 75% of the gross cross-sectional area.
- A modular masonry unit is one whose nominal dimensions are based on a 4 in. (100 mm) module.
- A solid masonry unit is one whose net cross-sectional area in every plane parallel to the bearing surface is 75% or more of the gross cross-sectional area.

**Mastic** – Heavy-bodied paste-like coating of high build often applied with a trowel.

**Matched lumber** – See under lumber.

**Matrix, terrazzo** – Topping mortar consisting of binders, and sometimes pigments and inert fillers that fills the spaces between chips and binds them into a homogeneous mass.

**Medium-density plywood** – See plywood.

**Meridian** – Imaginary north-south line on the earth's surface described by a great circle arc from the North Pole to the South Pole. All points on a meridian are of the same longitude. (See also great circle.) The Greenwich meridian, also called the prime meridian, is the meridian passing through the Royal Observatory at Greenwich, England. It is designated as the starting line (zero degrees) for measuring east and west longitude. A principal meridian is a meridian of specified longitude, used in the rectangular survey system, serving as the main north-south reference line for a particular state or area. Guide meridians are north-to- south reference lines located at 24-mile intervals east and west of a principal meridian.

**Metallics** – Class of paints that include metal flakes.

**Metes and bounds** – A system of land survey and description based on starting from a known reference point and tracing the boundary lines around an area.

**Mil** – One one-thousandth of an inch (0.0254 mm).

**Mildewcide** – See fungicide.

**Mildew resistance** – Ability of a coating, paint, or transparent finish to resist the growth of molds and mildew; mildew is particularly prevalent in moist, humid, and warm climates.

**Mild steel** – See under steel.

**Millwork** – Lumber that is shaped to a pattern or to a molded form in addition to being dressed, matched, ship lapped, or any combination of these. Millwork includes most finished wood products such as doors, windows, interior trim, and stairways, but not flooring or siding products.

**Mineral spirits** – Common solvent for coatings, paints, and transparent finishes; derived from the distillation of petroleum.

**Minor arch** – See under arch.

**Minute** – A unit of angular measure equal to 1/60th of a degree.

**Mod acrylic** – See under acrylic.

**Modifier** – An ingredient added to a plastic to improve or modify its properties.

**Modular masonry unit** – See masonry unit.

**Modulus of elasticity** – The ratio of stresses lower than the elastic limit to their respective strains.

**Moist curing** – See under curing.

**Moisture content of a concrete masonry unit** – The amount of water contained in a unit, expressed as a percentage of the total absorption (e.g., a concrete masonry unit at 40% moisture content contains 40% of the water it can absorb).

**Moisture content of wood** – The amount of water contained in wood at the time it is tested, expressed as a percentage of the weight of the wood when oven-dry.

**Monolithic concrete monomer** – Concrete placed in one continuous pour without construction joints. A relatively simple compound that can react to form a polymer.

**Monument** – A permanent reference point for land surveying whose location is recorded; either a man-made marker or a natural landmark.

**Mores que** – Multicolored yarn made by twisting together two or more strands of different shades or colors.

**Mortar** – Substance used to join masonry units, tile, stone, and other materials.

Mortar bed, tile – A 3/4-in. (19.1-mm)-to 1-1/4-in. (31.8-mm)-thick bed of Portland cement and sand mortar onto which a layer of neat Portland cement (water- cement paste) is applied to receive tile. Also called thickbed.

**Mortar joint** – The joint between masonry units.

A tooled joint is one that is compressed and shaped with a special concave or V-shaped tool.

A troweled joint is one finished with a trowel to form a struck joint or a weathered joint.

In a raked joint the mortar is raked out to a specified depth while the mortar is still green.

**Mortar, masonry** – A plastic mixture of one or more cementitious materials, sand, and water.

**Mortar, tile** – A mixture of Portland cement and other ingredients used to install tile. Also see adhesive, tile.

- A leveling or setting-type mortar is a mixture of Portland cement, sand, and sometimes lime, used as a bed in which tile is installed (setting bed), or as a coat to produce a plumb and level surface (leveling coat) so that subsequent coats can be applied in a uniform thickness.
- A bonding-type mortar is anyone of a variety of formulations used to bond tile to a backing or mortar bed. Formulations may be mainly cementitious, such as commercial cement mortar; resinous, such as epoxy mortar; or a combination of both, as in latex Portland cement mortar.

**Multilevel loop** – A carpet style in which the yams are looped at several levels; also called highlow loop and cut and loop.

**Nail, drywall** – A nail suitable for gypsum board application. Such nails are typically bright, coated, or chemically treated low-carbon steel nails with flat, thin, slightly filleted and countersunk heads approximately 1/4 in. (6.4 mm) in diameter and medium or long diamond points. Annularly threaded nails (GWB- 54) and smooth or deformed shank nails should conform to ASTM C514.

**Nail gluing** – A method of gluing wood in which the nails hold the wood members until the glue sets.

**Nail popping** – Surface defect in gypsum board resulting in a conspicuous protrusion of joint compound directly over a nail head.

**Nail spotting –** See fastener treatment.

**Nap –** Length of fibers on a paint roller cover.

**Natural gray yarn –** Unbleached and undyed yam spun from a blend of black, brown, or gray wools.

**Natural resin –** See under resin.

**Neat cement –** A mixture of cement and water (no aggregates).

**Neat Portland cement –** Unsanded mixture of Portland cement and water used as a bond coat in conventional thick bed installation of tile.

**Needle-punched carpet –** Carpet made by punching loose, unspun fibers through a woven sheet, which results in a pileless carpet similar to a heavy felt; usually consists entirely of synthetic fibers.

**Net cross-sectional area –** The gross cross-sectional area of a section minus the area of cores, cellular spaces and other voids it contains.

**Noise –** Unwanted sound.

**Noise reduction –** Reducing the level of unwanted sound by means of acoustical treatment.

**Noise reduction coefficient (NRC) –** A single-number index of the noise-reducing efficiency of acoustical materials. Found by averaging a material's sound absorption coefficients at 250, 500, 1000, and 2000 cycles per second.

**Nominal dimension –** A dimension greater than the actual dimension that is used to identify the size of a material. See also size.

- In masonry, the nominal dimension is greater than the actual dimension by the amount of the thickness of a mortar joint, but not more than 1/2 in. (12.7 mm).
- In wood, the nominal dimension (also called nominal size) is greater than the actual dimension by an amount roughly equivalent to the size lost due to wood shrinkage during drying, plus the amount planed off, to square and smooth the piece.

**Nominal size –** See nominal dimension; size.

**Noncombustible material** – A material that will neither ignite nor actively support combustion when exposed to fire in air at a temperature of 1200°F (648.9°C).

**Nondrying oil** – Oil that does not readily oxidize and harden when exposed to air.

**Non-heat-treatable alloy** – An alloy that is not capable of gaining strength by heat treatment and that depends on the initial strength of the alloy or cold working for additional strength. Also called a common alloy.

**Non-load-bearing wall** – A wall that supports no vertical load other than its own weight. (See also bearing wall.)

**Nonvolatile vehicle** – Liquid portion of coatings, paints, and transparent finishes except for their volatile thinners and water.

**Normal Portland cement** – Portland cement, Type I.

**Norman brick** – See under brick masonry unit.

**Octave** – The interval between two sounds with a frequency ratio of 2: 1.

**Ohm** – A measure of electrical resistance equal to that of a circuit that permits 1 volt to cause 1 amp to flow through it.

**Oil color** – Single pigment dispersion in linseed oil used for tinting coatings and paints.

**Oil paint** – See under paint.

**Oil stains** – May be penetrating or non-penetrating.

- Penetrating oil stains contain dyes and resins that penetrate a surface;
- Non-penetrating oil stains contain larger amounts of pigments and are usually opaque or translucent.

**Oil varnish** – See under transparent finish.

**Olefins** – Long-chain synthetic polymers composed of at least 85% by weight of ethylene, propylene, or other olefin units.

**One-package (one-part) formulation** – Coating or paint formulated to contain all the necessary ingredients in one package and generally not requiring any field additions except pigment and thinner.

**Opacity** – Degree of obstruction to the passage of visible light.

**Opaque coating** – A coating that hides the previous surface or coating.

**Open-grained** – See under grain.

**Open hearth furnace** – See under furnace, steel.

**Oven-dry wood** – Wood that has been dried in an oven to consistent moisture content and, for all practical purposes, no longer holds any water.

**Overlaid plywood** – See under plywood.

**Oxidation** – The chemical combination of a substance with oxygen.

**Package dyeing** – Placing spun and wound yarn on large, perforated forms and forcing the dye through the perforations.

**Padding** – Cellular rubber, felted animal hair, jute fibers, or plastic foams in sheet form, used as cushioning under carpet. (See also cushioning.)

**Paint** – A liquid, pigmented material applied in the field and producing an opaque film. Primers may, however, be applied by hand or machine in a factory or shop, but are part of the paint system and are therefore also called paint. In addition, all parts of a paint system are called paint, collectively and individually. Such parts include primers, emulsions, enamels, opaque stains, sealers, fillers, and other applied materials used as prime, intermediate, or finish coats. (See also coating and transparent finish.)

- An emulsion is a paint with a vehicle consisting of an oil, oleo resinous varnish, or resin binder dispersed in water (see also emulsion).
- Latex paint is paint with latex resin as the chief binder.
- Oil paint is paint with drying oil or oil varnish as the basic vehicle ingredient.
- A paste is paint with sufficiently concentrated pigment to permit substantial thinning before use.
- Water-based paint is paint with a vehicle that is water emulsioner, water dispersion, or that has ingredients that react chemically with water.

**Paint remover** – Compound that softens old paint and transparent finishes and permits scraping off the loosened material.

**Paint system** - Collectively, the several coats that are necessary to produce a complete paint coating. Materials that are used in the various coats are called paint.

**Panel wall –** An exterior non-load-bearing wall in skeleton frame construction wholly supported at each story. (See also curtain wall.)

**Parallel –** An imaginary east-west line on the earth's surface, consisting of a circle on which all points are equidistant from one of the poles. All points on a parallel are at the same latitude.

**Parapet wall –** That part of a wall entirely above the roof line.

**Parging –** (1)The application of mortar to the back of the facing material or the face of the backing material within a masonry wall; the mortar so applied. Also called back-plastering, back parging, or pargeting. (2)The application of Portland cement mortar or plaster to the exterior face of masonry, often below or near the ground; the material so applied.

**Particleboard –** A composition board consisting of distinct particles of wood bonded together with a synthetic resin or other binder.

**Partition –** An interior wall, one story or less in height.

**Party wall** – A wall used for joint service by adjoining buildings. See also common wall.

**Pattern bond –** Patterns formed by exposed faces of masonry units and their joints.

**Patterned lumber** – See under lumber.

**Paving brick –** See under brick masonry unit.

**Peeling** – Detachment of a dried coating, paint, or transparent finish film in relatively large pieces, usually caused by moisture or grease under the finish.

**Perceived noise level (PndB) –** A single-number rating of aircraft noise in decibels, used to describe the acceptability or noisiness of aircraft sound. PNdB is calculated from measured interior and exterior noise levels and correlates well with subjective responses to various kinds of aircraft noise.

**Perforated wall –** A wall that contains a considerable number of relatively small openings. Often called a pierced wall or screen wall.

**Perimeter In gypsum board work –** The surface (as opposed to the edges) of a gypsum board panel near the edges and ends.

**Pervious soil –** Usually a granular soil, such as sand or gravel that allows water to pass readily through it.

**Physically handicapped person –** An individual who has a physical impairment, including impaired sensory, manual, or speaking abilities, that results in a functional limitation in gaining access to and using a building or facility.

**Pickling –** Removing the oxide scale formed on hot metal as it air cools by dipping it in a solution of sulfuric or hydrochloric acid.

**Piece dyeing –** Immersing an entire carpet in a dye bath to produce single-color or multicolor pattern effects. (See also resist printing.)

**Pier –** An isolated column of masonry.

**Pig –** A pig iron ingot.

**Pig iron –** High-carbon crude iron from a blast furnace used as the main raw material for ironworking and steelmaking.

Basic pig iron is a high-phosphorus iron used in basic steelmaking furnaces.

**Pigment –** Fine, solid particles suspended in the vehicle of a coating or paint that provide color (hiding power) as well as other properties.

**Pilaster –** A thickened wall section or column built as an integral part of a wall.

**Pile –** The raised yarn tufts of woven, tufted, and knitted carpets that provide the wearing surface and desired color, design, or texture.

- In flocked carpets, the upstanding, nonwoven fibers.
- Cut loop pile is a pile surface in which tufts have been cut to reveal the fiber ends.
- AJrieze carpet is a rough, nubby-textured carpet using tightly twisted yarns; same as twist carpet.
- Jaspe is a carpet surface characterized by irregular stripes produced by varying textures or shades of the same color.
- Multilevel carpet has a texture or design created by different heights of tufts of either cut or uncut loop.
- Plush carpet has a cut pile surface that does not show any yarn texture.
- Sculptured (carved) carpet has surface designs created by combinations of cut and loop pile and variations in pile height.
- Shag carpet has a surface consisting of long, twisted loops.
- Stria (striped) carpet has a striped surface effect obtained by loosely twisting two strands of one shade of yarn with one strand of a lighter or darker shade.
- Twist carpet is the same as frieze carpet.
- Uncut loop is pile in which the yarns are continuous from tuft to tuft, forming visible loops.

**Pile crushing –** Bending of pile due to foot traffic or the pressure of furniture.

**Pile height –** The height of pile measured from the top surface of the backing to the top surface of the pile. Also called pile wire height.

**Pile setting –** Brushing after shampooing to restore damp pile to its original height.

**Pile yarn density –** The weight of pile yarn per unit of volume in carpet, usually stated in ounces per cubic yard (grams per cubic meter).

**Pilling –** Appearance defect associated with some staple fibers in which balls of tangled fibers are formed on the carpet surface, which are not removed readily by vacuuming or foot traffic; pills can be removed by periodic clipping.

**Pipe –** See under finished mill products.

**Pitch –** The number of tufts or pile warp yarns in a 27 in. (685.8 mm) width of woven carpet.

**Pitch pocket –** An opening extending parallel to the annual growth rings of a tree. These contain or have contained either solid or liquid pitch.

**Pith –** The small, soft core occurring in the center of the growth rings of a tree, branch, twig, or log.

**Placing –** The act of putting concrete in position (sometimes incorrectly called pouring).

**Plain masonry –** Masonry without reinforcement, or reinforced only to resist shrinkage or temperature changes.

**Plain-sawn wood –** See under grain.

**Plaster –** All elements of a gypsum or Portland cement plaster membrane, such as the several coats of plaster, metal reinforcement, accessories, and backing paper, when required.

**Plaster mix –** Mortar consisting of properly proportioned quantities of cementitious materials, aggregate, water, and sometimes pigments, plasticizers, and other admixtures.

**Plastic –** Material that contains as an essential ingredient an organic substance of large molecular weight, or a synthetic or processed substance. A plastic is solid in its finished state but at some stage in its manufacture can be shaped by flow (see polymer).

**Plastic deformation –** Deformation caused by a stress exceeding the elastic limit of a material so that it does not return to its original shape when the stress is removed. (See also elastic deformation.)

**Plasticizer –** In plastics, a material added to increase the workability and flexibility of a resin. In coatings, paints, and transparent finishes, a substance added in the liquid state to impart flexibility to a hardened film.

**Plat –** A map of surveyed land showing the location and the boundaries and dimensions of a parcel.

- A recorded plat is a plat that is recorded at an appropriate government office, usually the county recorder's office. In addition to location notes and a boundary line layout, a recorded plat may contain information such as restrictions, easements, approvals by zoning boards and planning commission, and lot and block numbers for a subdivision.

**Plate –** See under finished mill products.

**Plumbing fixtures –** Devices or appliances that are supplied with water and receive or discharge liquids or wastes.

**Ply –** When preceded by a number, the number of single strands used in a finished yarn.

**Plywood –** A cross banded assembly made of layers of veneer or of veneer in combination with a core of lumber, particleboard, or another composition core, all joined with an adhesive.

- Standard plywood is hardwood plywood produced to meet governing industry standards. Also, un-sanded interior softwood plywood for sheathing and flooring.
- High-density overlaid plywood is overlaid plywood in which the overlay sheet contains 40% resin by weight. Medium-density overlaid plywood is overlaid plywood in which the overlay sheet contains 20% resin by weight.
- In overlaid plywood the face veneer is bonded on one or both sides with paper, resin impregnated paper, or metal.
- Specialty plywood is hardwood plywood that is not necessarily manufactured to meet industry standards.

**P.O.B. (place of beginning) –** The starting point of a metes and bounds description or survey.

**Pointing –** Troweling mortar into a joint after a masonry unit has been laid.

**Polymer –** A chemical compound formed by the reaction of simple molecules to form more complex molecules of higher molecular weight.

**Polymerization –** A chemical reaction in which the molecules of a monomer are linked together to form large molecules whose molecular weight is a multiple of that of the original substance.

**Polypropylene –** See olefins.

**Polyurethane** – See resin; transparent finish.

**Polyvinyl acetate** – See under resin.

**Ponding** – A curing method used on flat concrete surfaces whereby a small earth dam or other water-retaining material is placed around the perimeter of the surface and the enclosed area is flooded with water.

**Portland blast furnace cement** – Cement made by grinding not more than 65% of granulated blast furnace slag with at least 35% of Portland cement.

**Portland cement** – A hydraulic cement produced by pulverizing clinker consisting essentially of hydraulic calcium silicates and usually containing one or more of the forms of calcium sulfate as an interground addition.

- Types I and IA Portland cement are used in general construction when the special properties of other types are not required.
- Types II and IIA Portland cement are used in general construction where moderate heat of hydration is required.
- Types III and IIIA Portland cement are used when a high early strength is required.
- Type IV Portland cement is used when low heat of hydration is required.
- Type V Portland cement is used when high sulfate resistance is required.

**Portland-pozzolan cement** – Cement made by blending not more than 50% pozzolan (a material consisting of siliceous or siliceous and aluminous material) with at least 50% of Portland cement.

**Post-forming** – The forming of laminates that have been cured into simple shapes by heat and pressure.

**Posts and timbers** – See under lumber.

**Potable water** – Water of sufficient quality, either through treatment or natural phenomena, to be drinkable.

**Potential difference** – The voltage difference between two points.

**Pot life** – Time period after mixing reactive components, in a two-component coating, paint, or transparent finish system, during which material can be satisfactorily used.

**Pots** – Carbon-lined vessels used in the reduction processing of aluminum. Molten aluminum is collected and siphoned off from the bottom of pots.

**Precast concrete** – Concrete components that are cast and cured off-site or on-site in a location other than where they will be finally placed.

**Prefabricated brick masonry** – Masonry panels fabricated other than in their final location in the structure. Also known as preassembled, panelized, and sectionalized brick masonry.

**Preframed panels** – Panels fabricated with precut lumber and plywood.

**Preservative** – A substance that will prevent, for a finite time that varies with quantity, the action of wood-destroying fungi, insects of various kinds, and other destructive life in wood that has been properly impregnated with that substance.

**Pressure gluing** – A method of gluing that places the wood members under high pressure until the glue sets.

**Pre-stressed concrete** – Concrete that has been subjected to compressive stresses before external loads have been applied by the pre-stretching (or stressing) of high- strength steel reinforcement within the concrete. This pre-stressing may be done by pre-tensioning (stretching the steel before the concrete is placed around it) or by post-tensioning (stretching the steel after the concrete has been cured).

**Prime meridian** – See under meridian.

**Primer, paint** – First of several coats, intended to prepare a surface for the succeeding coats; sometimes a special product, but may be same as the finish coat.

**Primer, resilient flooring** – A brushable solvent-based asphaltic preparation recommended as a first coat over porous or dusty concrete floors and panel underlayment; intended to seal the pores and improve the bond with asphaltic adhesives used for the installation of asphalt and vinyl composition tile.

**Primer-sealer** – Product formulated to possess properties of both a primer and a sealer.

**Principal meridian** – See under meridian.

**Print dyeing** – Screen printing a pattern on carpet by successive applications of pre- metalized dyes, which are driven into the pile construction by an electromagnetic charge.

**Puddling** – The compacting or consolidating of concrete with a rod or other tool.

**Putty** – Dough-like material consisting of pigment and vehicle; used for sealing glass in sash or frames and for filling imperfections in wood and metal surfaces; does not retain its plasticity for extended periods, as does a glazing compound or joint sealant. Both elastomeric and acrylic joint sealants are superior to putty and are generally used today where putty is called for. (See also sealant, joint.)

**Quarter-sawn wood** – See under grain.

**Quenching** – See under heat treatment.

**Quoin** – A right-angled masonry comer that is usually projected when of the same material as the surrounding material, but may be flush with the surrounding masonry when of a different material. A typical example of a quoin consists of squared stones set into a rubble stone or brick wall. Quoins are often larger than the surrounding masonry units.

**Ramp** – When related to accessibility for handicapped persons, a walking surface in an accessible space that has a running slope greater than 1:20. The maximum slope is limited by the applicable code or law.

**Random shear** – A carpet style created by shearing only the higher loops of either level loop or multilevel loop carpet.

**Range lines** – North-south reference lines used in the rectangular survey system, located at 6-mile intervals between guide meridians.

**Rays** – Strips of cellulose extending radially within a tree. These store food and transport it horizontally in the tree.

**Ready-mixed concrete** – Concrete mixed at a plant or in trucks en route to the job and delivered ready for placing.

**Recorded plat** – See under plat.

**Rectangular survey system** – A land survey system based on geographical coordinates of longitude and latitude; originally established by acts of Congress to survey the lands of public domain and now used in most states. Also called Government Survey System.

**Red mud** – Solid impurities collected by either filtering or gravity settling during the Bayer process of aluminum refining.

**Reduction** – (An electrolytic process used to separate aluminum from aluminum oxide. Separation of iron from its oxide by smelting ores in a blast furnace.

**Refining of steel** – Melting pig iron and other iron-bearing materials in steel furnaces to achieve desired contents of residual and alloying elements.

**Reflection** – The return from surfaces of sound not absorbed on contact with the surfaces or transmitted through the material contacted.

**Refractories –** When related to steel production, nonmetallic materials with superior heat and impact resistance used for lining furnaces, flues, and vessels for ironworking and steelmaking.

**Reinforced masonry –** Masonry containing embedded steel so that the two materials act together to resist applied forces.

**Reinforced plastic –** A plastic material whose strength and, to a lesser degree, stiffness have been upgraded by the addition of high-strength fillers such as glass fiber.

**Reinforcing bars –** Steel placed in concrete or masonry to take tensile, compressive, and shear stresses.

**Relative humidity –** The amount of water vapor in air stated as a percentage. The ratio of the amount of water in air at a given temperature and atmospheric pressure to the amount that same air can contain when it is saturated.

**Relief vent –** A vent whose primary function is to provide circulation of air between drainage and vent systems.

**Relieving arch –** See under arch.

**Repeat –** The distance along the length of a carpet from one point in a figure or pattern to the same point at which it again occurs.

**Residual elements –** Nonferrous elements (such as carbon, sulfur, phosphorus, manganese, and silicon) that occur naturally in raw materials and are controlled in steelmaking.

**Resin –** In plastics, the essential ingredients of a plastic mix before final processing and fabrication of the plastic object. In coatings, paints, and transparent finishes, a mixture of organic or synthetic compounds with no sharply defined melting point, no tendency to crystallize, soluble in certain organic solvents but not in water. It is the main ingredient of most coatings, paints, and transparent finishes, binds the other ingredients together, and aids adhesion to the surface. Includes acrylic, alkyd, epoxy, nitrocellulose, polyurethane, polyvinyl acetate, silicone, styrene butadiene, and vinyl.

- A natural resin may be a fossil of ancient origin, such as amber, or an extract of certain pine trees, such as rosin, copal, and damar.
- A synthetic resin is a manmade substance exhibiting properties similar to those of natural resins; typical synthetic resins used in coatings, paints, and transparent finishes include alkyd, acrylic, latex, phenolic, urea, and others.

**Resist printing –** Placing a dye-resist agent on carpet before piece dyeing so that the pile will absorb color according to a predetermined design.

**Resonance –** The sympathetic vibration, resounding, or ringing of such things as enclosures, room surfaces, and panels when they are excited at their natural frequencies.

**Retaining wall –** A wall that is subjected to lateral pressure other than wind pressure, such as a wall built to support a bank of earth.

**Retarder –** An admixture added to concrete to retard its set.

**Retempering –** Restoring workability to mortar that has stiffened due to evaporation by adding water and remixing.

**Retentivity –** See water retention.

**Reverberation –** The continuing travel of sound waves between reflective surfaces after the original source has stopped transmitting.

**Reverberation time (T) –** The time in seconds required for a sound to diminish 60 decibels (dB) after the source has stopped transmitting.

**Ridging –** A surface defect in a gypsum board surface resulting in conspicuous wrinkling of the joint tape at treated joints.

**Riser In plumbing systems –** A water supply pipe that extends vertically one full story or more to convey water to branches or fixtures.

**Roller –** Paint applicator having a revolving cylinder covered with lambs wool, fabric, foamed plastic, or other material.

**Rolling –** Shaping plate and sheet metal, blooms, and billets by passing them through steel rollers.(See also cold working and hot working.)

**Roman brick –** See under brick masonry unit.

**Room acoustics –** A branch of architectural acoustics dealing with both acoustical correction and noise reduction. (See also acoustics.)

**Rosin –** Natural resin obtained from various pine trees; an ingredient of varnishes and some manmade resins.

**Rotary-cut veneer –** See under veneer.

**Rough-in –** The installation of those parts of a plumbing system that can be completed before the plumbing fixtures are installed. This includes drainage, water supply, and vent piping and the necessary fixture supports. Also, the plumbing system parts so installed.

**Round wire** – A pile wire that does not cut the pile loop; or woven carpet with an uncut loop pile.

**Rowlock** – A brick unit laid on its face edge. Usually laid in a wall with its long dimension perpendicular to the wall face. Also spelled rolok.

**Running slope** – The slope of a pedestrian way that is parallel to the direction of travel. (See also cross slope.)

**Rust preventive paint or primer** – First coat of paint applied directly to iron or steel structures to slow down or prevent rusting.

**Sabin** – The measure of sound absorption of a surface, equivalent to 1 sq ft (0.093 m 2) of a perfectly absorptive surface.

**Sags** – Excessive flow, causing runs or sagging in a coating, paint, or transparent finish film during application; usually caused by applying too heavy a coat or thinning too much.

**Salamander** – A portable stove used to heat the surrounding air.

**Sand finish** – See texture.

**Sanding surfacer** – Heavily pigmented finishing material used for building a surface to a smooth condition; it is sanded after drying.

**Sandwich panel** – A composite structural panel made of two thin, strong, hard facings bonded firmly to a core of relatively lightweight, weaker material with insulating properties.

**Sapwood** – The living wood of pale color near the outside of a tree.

**Satin finish** – See semi-gloss.

**Saturated air** – Air that contains 100% of the amount of water vapor it can contain. (See also relative humidity.)

**Saturated molecule** – A molecule that will not unite readily with another element or compound.

**Saturation coefficient** – See cm ratio.

**Sawed veneer** – See under veneer.

**Scaling** – The breaking away of a hardened concrete surface (to a depth of about 1/16 in. [1.6 mm] to 3/16 in. [4.76 mm]), usually occurring at an early age of the concrete.

**Scarf jointing** – A joint in which the ends of plywood panels are beveled and glued together.

**Scoring** – Partial cutting of concrete flat work for the control of shrinkage cracking. Also used to denote the roughening of a slab to develop a mechanical bond.

**Scrap metal** – Source of iron for ironworking and steelmaking, consisting of rolled product croppings, rejects, and obsolete equipment from steel mills and foundries and waste ferrous material from industrial and consumer products.

**Scratch coat** – The first plaster layer in three-coat work, which embeds the reinforcement and provides a suitably rigid and roughened (scratched) surface for the following coat.

**SCR brick** – See under brick masonry unit.

**Screed** – A wood or metal template to which a concrete surface is leveled.

**Screeding** – Striking off excess concrete in the finishing operation of concrete slab work.

**Screws, drywall** – Screws developed for gypsum board application, usually with self- tapping, self-threading points, special-contour flat heads, and deep Phillips recesses for use with a power screwdriver.

- Type S drywall screws are used for sheet metal studs and furring.
- Type W drywall screws are used for wood framing and furring.
- Type G drywall screws are used for attaching gypsum

**Scribing** – A method of transferring the profile of an obstruction, projection, or material edge to a piece of material, such as resilient flooring or wood trim, so that it can be accurately cut and fitted.

**Scrim** – Rough, loosely woven fabric often used as a secondary backing on tufted carpets.

**Scrubbability** – Ability of a coating, paint, or transparent finish film to withstand scrubbing and cleaning with water, soap, and other household cleaning agents.

**Sculptured carpet** – See under pile.

**Scum –** A mass of sewage matter that floats on the surface of the sewage in a septic tank.

**Scum clear space –** In a septic tank, the distance between the bottom of the scum mat and the bottom of the outlet device (tee, ell, or baffle).

**Sealant, joint –** Anyone of a number of plastic materials, including rubber, formulated to fill and seal stationary and moving joints. See also caulking compound, glazing compound, and putty, which are types of joint sealants.

**Sealer –** In paint and coatings, a formulation intended to prevent excessive absorption of a finish coat of coating, paint, or transparent finish into a porous surface or to prevent bleeding through the finish coat. In resilient flooring, a solution of equal parts of wax-free shellac and denatured alcohol; recommended as a first coat over existing wood strip floors from which the finish has been removed; intended to seal wood pores, prevent excessive moisture absorption, and provide a dimensionally stable base for direct application of lining felt or resilient flooring.

**Seasoning –** Removal of moisture from green wood.

- Air drying is seasoning by exposure to air, usually in a yard.
- Kiln drying is seasoning in a kiln (oven) under controlled conditions of heat, humidity, and air circulation.

**Second –** A unit of angular measure equal to l/60th of a minute.

**Section –** An area of land used in the rectangular survey system, approximately 1 mile square, bounded by section lines. The rectangular survey system provides for the further subdivision of sections into halves, quarters, and quarter-quarters. A fractional section is an adjusted section of land generally containing less (sometimes more) than 1 sq mi. The deficiency (or excess) may be the result of the convergence of meridians, the presence of bodies of water, or uncertainties in surveying.

**Section lines –** North-south reference lines used in the rectangular survey system, parallel to the nearest range line to the east, and east-west lines parallel to the nearest township line to the south; these lines divide townships into 36 approximately equal squares called sections.

**Seeds –** Small, undesirable particles or granules other than dust found in a coating, paint, or transparent finish.

**Seepage bed –** See absorption bed.

**Seepage pit –** A covered underground pit with a concrete or masonry lining designed to permit partially treated sewage to seep into the surrounding soil. Also called dry well in some parts of the country.

**Segregation –** Separation of the heavier coarse aggregate from the mortar, or of water from the other ingredients of a concrete mix, during handling or placing.

**Self-cleaning** – Controlled chalking of a paint film so that dirt does not adhere to the surface.

**Selvage** – The finished long edge of woven carpet that will not unravel and will not require binding or serging.

**Semi-gloss** – Degree of surface reflectance midway between gloss and eggshell; also coatings and paints displaying these properties.

**Semitransparent** – Degree of hiding greater than transparent but less than opaque.

**Separated construction** – See discontinuous construction.

**Septic (sewage) disposal system** – A system for the treatment and disposal of sewage by means of a septic tank and a soil absorption system.

**Septic tank** – A watertight, covered receptacle that receives the discharge of sewage from a building sewer and is designed and constructed to separate solids from liquids, to digest organic matter during a period of retention, to store digested solids through a period of retention, and to allow the clarified liquids to discharge for final disposal or additional treatment.

**Serging** – A method of finishing a cut long edge of carpet to prevent unraveling; distinguished from finishing a cut end, which may require binding.

**Serial distribution** – A combination of several absorption trenches, seepage pits, or absorption beds arranged in sequence so that each is forced to utilize the total effective absorption area before liquid flows into the succeeding component.

**Service temperature** – The maximum temperature at which a material can be continuously employed without noticeable reduction in strength or other properties.

**Setting bed** – See mortar bed, tile.

**Settling** – Coating, paint, or transparent finish material separation in which pigments and other solids accumulate at the bottom of the container.

**Sewage** – The liquid and solid waste matter carried off by sewers. It contains organic (animal or vegetable) matter in suspension or solution, as well as liquids containing chemicals in solution.

**Sewer** – An underground conduit for carrying off sewage and rainwater.

**Sewerage –** A system of sewers; the removal and disposal of liquid and solid wastes by sewers.

**Sewer brick** – See under brick masonry unit.

**Shading –** Bending or crushing a pile surface so that the fibers reflect light unevenly. This is not a defect but rather an inherent characteristic of some pile fabrics.

**Shake –** A separation along the grain in a tree, the greater part of which occurs between the annual growth rings. A wood shingle-like roofing material.

**Shake painter** – See flat applicator.

**Shale** – Laminated clay or silt com-pressed by earth overburden. Unlike slate, shale splits along its bedding planes.

**Shearing** – A carpet finishing operation that removes stray fibers and fuzz from loop pile and produces a smooth, level surface on cut loop pile.

**Shear wall –** A wall that resists horizontal forces applied in the plane of the wall.

Sh**eathing, gypsum** – See under gypsum board.

**Shedding** – A normal temporary condition of dislodged, loose short fibers in new carpet after initial exposure to traffic and sweeping.

**Sheen** – Degree of luster of a dried coating, paint, or transparent finish film.

**Sheen uniformity** – Even distribution of luster over the entire surface of an applied finish.

**Sheet** – See under finished mill products.

**Sheeting** – A form of plastic in which the thickness is very small in proportion to the length and width; usually refers to a product with a thickness greater than 0.010 in. (0.254 mm) (see also film).

**Sheet lamination In multi-ply gypsum board construction –** Method of applying adhesive to the entire surface to be bonded. (See also strip lamination.)

**Shellac –** A transparent finish material made from resins dissolved in alcohol.

**Shooting –** See sprouting.

**Short circuit –** Related to sound control, a bypassing connection or transmission path that tends to nullify or reduce the sound-isolating performance of a construction assembly.

**Shot –** See weft.

- Decrease in initial volume due to removal of moisture from fresh concrete or green lumber.
- May also refer to a decrease in volume due to subsequent decreases in temperature or moisture content in concrete.

**Side wall –** The wall along the long dimension of a room.

**Signage –** Verbal, symbolic, and pictorial information.

**Silica –** Silicon dioxide (Si02), occurring as quartz, a major constituent of sand, sandstone, and quartzite.

**Silicone –** Any of a number of polymeric organic silicon compounds used in paint, sealants, roof membranes, and water repellents. (See also resin.)

**Siphon breaker –** See atmospheric vacuum breaker.

**Size –** Water-based formulation, with glue or starch binders, intended as a sealer over existing wall paint or plaster; now seldom used. The size of lumber.

- The actual size of lumber is its measured size after seasoning and dressing,
- The dressed size of lumber is its size after surfacing.
- The face size of lumber is the exposed width of a piece of lumber when installed.
- The nominal size of a piece of lumber is its approximate rough-sawn commercial size by which lumber is known and sold.

**Skein dyeing –** Immersing batches of yarn (skeins) in vats of hot dye.

**Skin –** Tough covering that forms on liquid coating, paint, and transparent finish materials when left exposed to air.

**Slab –** In concrete, a flat, thin (as compared with its other dimensions) structure. A structural slab is a suspended, self-supporting, reinforced concrete floor or roof slab.

- A slab on grade is a non-suspended, ground-supported concrete slab, usually but not always having some temperature reinforcement.

- An edge-supported slab on grade rests atop the perimeter foundation wall.
- A floating slab on grade terminates at the inside face of the perimeter foundation wall and is said to "float" independently of the foundation wall.
- A monolithic slab on grade is a combination slab and foundation wall formed into one integral mass of concrete. Also called a thickened- edge slab.
- In wood, the outside piece cut from a log in squaring it.

**Slabbed** – To have removed an outer slab from a log.

**Slag** – A glass-like waste product, generally from an ironworking or steelmaking furnace. Molten mass composed of fluxes in combination with unwanted elements, which floats to the surface of the hot metal in the furnace and thus can be removed.

**Slag cement** – See Portland blast furnace cement.

**Sliced veneer** – See under veneer.

**Sloshing** – Attempting to fill vertical joints after units are laid by throwing mortar into the joint with a trowel from above.

**Sludge** – The accumulated solids that settle out of sewage, forming a semi liquid mass on the bottom of a septic tank.

**Sludge clear space in a septic tank** – The distance between the top of the sludge and the bottom of the outlet device.

**Slump** – A measure of the consistency of a concrete mix (in inches).

**Slump block** – See under concrete masonry units.

**Slump test** – A method of measuring slump by filling a conical mold, removing it, and measuring the sag or slump of the sample.

**Smelting** – Melting of iron-bearing materials in a blast furnace to separate iron from impurities with which it is chemically combined or mechanically mixed.

**Soap** – A brick or tile of normal face dimensions having a nominal 2 in. (50 mm) thickness.

**Soft-burned clay** – Clay products that have been fired at low temperature ranges. They have relatively high absorptions and low compressive strengths.

**Softening range –** The range of temperature in which a plastic changes from a rigid to a soft state, sometimes referred to as softening point.

**Softness –** Film property displaying low resistance to scratching or indentation; opposite of hardness.

**Soft temper –** The state of maximum workability of aluminum obtained by annealing.

**Softwood –** The botanical group of trees that have needle- or scale-like leaves and are evergreen for the most part. Some exceptions are cypress, larch, and tamarack. This term does not relate to the actual hardness of the wood.

**Soil absorption field –** See absorption field.

**Soil absorption system –** Any system that utilizes the soil for subsurface absorption of treated sewage, such as an absorption trench, absorption bed, or seepage pit.

**Soil pipe –** A pipe that conveys the discharge of water closets, urinals, or fixtures having functions similar to those of a building drain or building sewer (with or without the discharge from other fixtures).

**Solar screen –** A perforated masonry wall used as a sunshade.

**Soldier –** Masonry unit set vertically on end with face showing on the masonry surface.

**Solid masonry unit –** See under masonry unit.

**Solid masonry wall –** A wall built of solid or hollow masonry units laid continuously, with joints between units completely filled with mortar.

**Solution dyeing –** Adding dye or colored pigments to synthetic material while in liquid solution before extrusion into fiber.

**Solution heat treatment –** The first temperature-raising step in the thermal treating of a heat treatable aluminum alloy. Also called heat treatment.

**Solvent –** The volatile portion of the vehicle of a coating, paint, or transparent finish, such as turpentine or mineral spirits, which evaporates during the drying process.

**Solvent-based** – Adhesives and primers consisting of cementitious binders and fillers dissolved in a volatile hydrocarbon carrier such as alcohol or cutback.

**Solvent-thinned** – Formulation of a coating, paint, or transparent finish in which the binder is dissolved in the thinner (as in oil paint), rather than emulsified (as in latex paint).

**Sound** – A vibration in an elastic medium in a frequency range capable of producing the sensation of hearing.

**Sound attenuation** – See attenuation.

**Sound isolation** – Materials or methods of construction designed to resist the transmission of airborne and structure-borne sound through walls, floors, and ceilings; the effect of such materials or methods.

**Sound pressure** – The instantaneous pressure at a point as a result of the sound vibration minus the static pressure at that point; the change in pressure resulting from sound vibration. It is measured in dynes per square centimeter (cm-), A sound pressure of 1 dyne/ern? is about that of conversational speech at close range and is approximately equal to 1 millionth of atmospheric pressure.

**Sound pressure level (SPL)** – Sound pressure measured on the decibel scale; the ratio in decibels between a measured pressure and a reference pressure.

**Sound transmission** – The passage of sound through a material or assembly.

- Airborne sound transmission is the transmission of sound through the air as a medium rather than through a solid, such as the structure of a building. Airborne sound is produced when a surface is caused to vibrate, thus producing alternating air pressures adjacent to the surface. The alternating pressures then radiate through the air in waves of higher and lower pressures.
- Structure-borne sound transmission is the transmission of sound through a solid or assembly of solids, such as a wall or the structure of a building. It occurs when the vibrations from equipment, or the impact of footsteps or dropped objects come in contact with a solid.

**Sound transmission class (STC)** – A single-number rating for evaluating the efficiency of assemblies in isolating airborne sound transmission (see sound isolation). The higher the STC rating, the more efficient the assembly.

**Space dyeing** – Alternating bands of color applied to yarn by rollers at predetermined intervals before tufting.

**Spackling Material** – Used as crack filler for preparing surfaces before painting.

**Spall** – A small fragment removed from the face of concrete or of a masonry unit by a blow or by action of the elements.

**Spandrel wall –** That part of a panel curtain wall above the head of a window; in a multistory building, includes the panel below the sill of the window in the story above. Very durable varnish designed for service on exterior surfaces.

**Spatter –** Small particles or drips of liquid coating, paint, or transparent finish materials thrown or expelled when applying these materials.

**Specialty plywood –** See under plywood.

**Split-face block –** See under concrete masonry unit.

**Spot priming –** Method for protecting localized spots. The only areas primed are those that require additional protection due to rusting or peeling of the former coat of paint or transparent finish.

**Spreading rate –** Measure of the area that can be covered by a unit volume of coating, paint, or transparent finish material, generally expressed as square feet per gallon (m21L).

**Springwood –** The portion of the annual growth ring of a tree that is formed during the early part of the season's growth. This is usually less dense and weaker mechanically than summerwood.

**Sprouting –** Temporary condition on new carpets in which strands of yarn work loose and project above the pile. Can be remedied by careful clipping or spot shearing.

**Stabilizer –** A material added to prevent or retard degradation of a plastic when exposed to sunlight or other environmental conditions.

**Stack –** (1) A structure or part thereof that contains a flue or flues for the discharge of gases. (2) The vertical main of a system of soil, waste, or vent piping.

**Stack vent –** The extension of a soil or waste stack above the highest horizontal drain connected to the stack. It is sometimes called a waste vent or soil vent.

**Stain –** A discoloration of wood that may be caused by such diverse agencies as microorganisms, metals, or chemicals. A penetrating formulation intended primarily for wood surfaces.

- An opaque stain is classified as paint; a transparent stain is a transparent finish material. An opaque stain is a stain that hides the substrate and previous surface finish materials.
- A transparent stain changes the color of a wood without obscuring the grain; depending on the amount of pigment, transparent stains may be more or less transparent and may leave little or no surface film.

**Staple fibers-** Relatively short natural (wool) or synthetic fibers ranging from about 11/2 in. (38 rnm) to 7 in. (180 rnm) long, which are spun into yarn.

**Steam curing –** See under curing.

**Steel –** Iron-based alloy containing manganese, carbon residual, and often other alloying elements, characterized by its strength and toughness; distinguished from gray cast iron by its ability to be shaped by hot working or cold working as initially cast.

- Alloy steel is steel in which residual elements exceed the limits prescribed for carbon steel or to which alloying elements are added within specified ranges.
- Carbon steel is steel in which the residual elements are controlled but to which alloying elements are not usually added.
- Heat-resisting steel is a low-chromium steel with at least 4% chromium which retains its essential mechanical properties at elevated temperatures.
- High-strength low-alloy steel is steel with less than 1 % of an alloying element, manufactured to high standards for strength, ductility, and partial chemical specifications.
- Mild steel is carbon steel with carbon content between 0.15 and 0.25%.
- Stainless steel is steel that contains at least 10% chromium. It has excellent corrosion resistance, strength, and chemical inertness at high and low temperatures.

**Stock dyeing –** Dyeing raw fibers before they are carded (combed) or spun.

**Storm sewer –** A sewer used for conveying rainwater, surface water, condensate, cooling water, or similar liquid wastes, exclusive of sewage and industrial waste.

**Story –** That portion of a building included between the upper surface of a floor and the upper surface of the floor directly above, except that the topmost story is that portion of a building included between the upper surface of the topmost floor and the ceiling or roof above. Where a finished floor level directly above a basement or cellar is more than 6 ft (1800 mm) above grade, such a basement or cellar is considered a story.

**Story pole –** Marked pole for measuring vertical masonry courses during construction.

**Strain –** The change in cross-sectional area of a body produced by stress. Measured in inches per inch (millimeter per millimeter) of length.

**Strain hardening –** A method of strengthening non-heat-treatable aluminum alloys by either cold rolling or other physical or mechanical working.

**Strand caster –** A machine that continuously casts steel slabs and billets.

**Streaking –** Irregular occurrence of lines or streaks of various lengths and colors in an applied film; usually caused by some form of contamination.

**Strength –** A term used to describe all the properties of wood that enable it to resist forces or loads.

**Stress –** The intensity of a mechanical force acting on a body; either tensile, compressive, shear, or the combination of compressive and tension forces known as bending, or the twisting force, torsion. Tensile, compressive, and shear forces are measured by dividing the total force by the area over which the force acts (force per unit of area), such as pound per square inch (kilogram per square meter), for example.

- In wood, the allowable unit, or working, stress is the stress used in designing wood members. It is appropriate to the species and grade of the wood.
- Values for each type of stress are obtained by multiplying the basic stress for that species by the strength ratio assigned to each grade.
- Most codes include the allowable working stress for each grade. In wood, the basic stress is the design stress for a clear wood specimen free from strength-reducing features such as knots, checks, and cross grain.
- Such a specimen is assumed to have all the factors appropriate to the nature of structural lumber and the conditions under which it is used, except those that are accounted for in the strength ratio.

**Stretcher –** Masonry unit laid with its length horizontal and parallel with the face of the masonry and with its smallest dimension vertical.

**Stretching forming –** The stretching of metal for the purpose of flattening it or for forming it to a pre-determined shape.

**Stria (striped) –** See under pile.

**Stringer –** See under lumber.

**Strip –** See under finished mill products.

**Strip lamination –** In multi-ply gypsum board construction, a method of applying adhesive in parallel strips spaced 16 in. (406 mm) to 24 in. (610 mm) apart. (See also sheet lamination.)

**Strip reinforcing –** In single-ply gypsum board construction, an installation procedure in which strips of gypsum board are applied to the framing members to reinforce gypsum board joints and provide a base for adhesive application.

**Struck joint –** See mortar joint.

**Structural clay tile –** Hollow masonry units composed of burned clay, shale, fire clay, or mixtures of these.

- End-construction tile is designed to be laid with the axis of its cells vertical.
- Facing tile is made for exterior and interior use with its face exposed.
- Side-construction tile is intended for placement with the axis of its cells horizontal.

**Structural lumber** – See under lumber.

**Structurals** – See under finished mill products.

**Stucco** – Portland cement, water, sand, and possibly a small quantity of lime (Portland cement plaster), along with, perhaps, other aggregates; used on exterior surfaces.

**Stucco finish** – A factory-prepared mix of stucco for application as finish coats.

**Stud adhesive** – See adhesive, drywall.

**Stuffer yarn** – See under warp.

**Styrene butadiene** – See under resin.

**Subfloor** – The structural material or surface that supports a finish floor and floor loads and serves as a working platform during construction.

**Subgrade** – An earth surface on which another material, such as concrete, is placed.

**Sublimation** – The transition of ice directly into water vapor.

**Substrate** – Surface to be covered with a coating, paint, or transparent finish.

**Suction** – The initial rate of water absorption by a clay masonry unit. (See absorption rate.)

**Summerwood** – The portion of the annual growth ring of a tree that is formed after springwood formation has ceased. It is usually denser and stronger mechanically than springwood.

**Sump** – A tank or pit that receives sewage or other liquid waste, located below the normal grade of a building's gravity sewer system, and that must be emptied by mechanical means.

**Sump pump** – A mechanical device used for pumping out sewage, liquid, or industrial wastes from locations below a building's gravity drain.

**Surfacer** – Pigmented formulation for filling minor irregularities before a finish coat of paint is applied; usually applied over a primer and sanded for smoothness.

**Survey** – The measure and marking of land, accompanied by maps and field notes that describe the measures and marks made in the field.

**Surveying** – The process of making a survey.

**Swale** – A low, flat depression in the exterior grade, used to drain away storm water.

**System, paint** – See paint system.

**Tack rag** – Piece of loosely woven cloth that has been dipped into varnish oil and wrung out. When it becomes tacky or sticky, it is used to wipe a surface to remove small particles of dust.

**Tactile** – Describes an object that can be perceived with the sense of touch.

**Tactile cue** – See under cue.

**Taping in gypsum board construction** – Applying joint tape over embedding compound in the process of joint treatment.

**Temper designation** – Designation (following an alloy designation number) that denotes the temper of an aluminum alloy.

**Tempering** – See heat treatment.

**Terne** – A lead-tin alloy usually consisting of 4 parts lead and 1 part tin.

**Terneplate** – See under finished mill products.

**Terazzo** – A floor topping made of marble or other stone chips set in cement mortar, ground smooth and polished.

**Terazzo finish** – All elements installed by a terrazzo contractor from subfloor to finished surface, such as a sand bed, isolation membrane, under bed, and topping.

**Texture** – In wood, a term often used interchangeably with grain. It refers to the structure of wood.

**Texture paint –** A paint that may be manipulated by brush, roller, trowel, or another tool to produce various effects.

**Thermal mass –** The heat storage capacity of a material.

**Thermoplastic** – A plastic that can be repeatedly softened by heating and hardened by cooling.

**Thermoset –** A plastic that, after curing, forms a permanently hardened product that cannot be softened again by reheating.

**Thickbed –** See mortar bed, tile.

**Thinners –** Solvents used to thin coating, paint, or transparent finish materials.

**Thin-set –** In terrazzo, a method of installing relatively thin toppings ct/4 in. [6.4 mm] to 1/2 in. [12.7 mm] thick) directly over a suitable subfloor; generally possible with resinous binders only. In tile, a method of bonding tile with a thin layer ct/16 in. [1.6 mm] to 1/4 in. [6.4 mm] thick) of special mortar or adhesive to a suitable backing or to a properly cured mortar bed.

**Thixotropy –** Property of a material that causes it to change from a thick, pasty consistency to a fluid consistency upon agitation, brushing, or rolling.

**Three-coat work –** Application of plaster in three separate layers (scratch, brown, and finish coats), totaling at least 718 in. (22.2 mm) in thickness.

**Tie –** See wall tie.

**Tinplate** – See under finished mill products.

**Tint base –** Basic paint in a custom color system to which colorants are added to make a wide range of colors.

**Tone-on-tone –** Carpet pattern made by using two or more shades of the same hue.

**Tooled joint –** See mortar joint.

**Toothing –** Projecting brick or concrete masonry unit in alternate courses to provide for bond with adjoining masonry that will be laid later.

**Topping in terazzo finishes –** A decorative wear layer consisting of marble chips embedded in a suitable matrix and requiring grinding, polishing, or washing to form finished terrazzo.

**Touch-up –** Ability of a coating, paint, or transparent finish film to be spot repaired (usually within a few months of the initial application) without showing color or gloss differences. The repair of a coating, paint, or transparent finish film by selectively adding finishing material to damaged or missed areas after the earlier coats have dried.

**Toughness –** Maximum ability of a material to absorb energy without breaking, as from a sudden shock or impact.

**Township –** An area of land used in the rectangular survey system, approximately 6 miles square, bounded by range lines and township lines.

**Township lines –** East-west reference lines used in the rectangular survey system, located at 6-mile intervals between correction lines.

**Transfer molding –** Forming plastic by fusing it in one chamber with heat and then forcing it into another chamber, where it solidifies; commonly used with thermosetting plastics.

**Transmission loss –** The decrease in or attenuation of sound energy, expressed in decibels, of airborne sound as it passes through building construction.

**Transparent finish –** A system of materials that are applied as liquids or by hand in the field or in a factory or shop to form a finish through which the substrate or previous finish is visible.

- Lacquer is a transparent finish material that is employed mostly as a shop or factory finish on furniture and casework. It is not usable over existing finish films. In fact, it is an effective paint remover.
- Polyurethane is a hard, highly abrasion-resistant and chemical- resistant transparent finish, often used as a floor finish and as a bar-top finish. Some manufacturers call their polyurethanes varnishes; others call them lacquers. In fact, although they have some characteristics of each, they are neither. Polyurethanes are available in both oil-modified and moist-curing formulations. See also resin.
- Shellac is a fast-drying, transparent finish material consisting of lac resins, produced by the lac insect, dissolved in alcohol. Shellac has a relatively short shelf life.
- Spar varnish is an exterior, weather-resistant, transparent finish material based generally on long-oil phenolic resin; the term originated from the use of this material on spars of ships.
- Varnish is a finish material that dries to a transparent or translucent film when exposed to air. Varnish is a mixture of resin, drying oil, drier, and a solvent.

**Transparent finish system –** The several coats and materials necessary to produce a transparent finish. The various materials may include dyes, bleaches, or stains to change the color of substrates such as wood, and undercoats and finish coats of one of the materials listed under transparent finish or another transparent finish material, such as oil.

**Trap –** A fitting or device designed to provide, when properly vented, a liquid seal that will prevent the back passage of air without materially affecting the flow of sewage or wastewater through it.

**Trimmer arch –** See under arch.

**Troweled joint –** See mortar joint.

**Troweling –** A concrete slab finishing operation that produces a smooth, hard surface.

**Tubular steel products –** See under finished mill products.

**Tuck pointing –** Refilling defective mortar joints that have been cut out in existing masonry.

**Tufted carpet –** Carpet made by inserting the pile yarns through a pre-woven fabric backing on a machine with hundreds of needles (similar to a huge sewing machine).

**Tufts –** Surface loops of pile fabric.

**Turpentine –** Colorless liquid used as thinner for oil paints and varnishes, distilled from products of the pine tree.

**Twist –** See pile, warp.

**Two-coat work –** Application of plaster in two layers (base coat and finish coat), totaling at least 5/8 in. (15.9 mm) in thickness.

**Two-package (two-part) formulation –** Coating, paint, or transparent finish material formulated in two separate packages and requiring that the two ingredients be mixed before characteristic properties can be obtained and the material can be applied.

**Under bed –** Layer of nonstructural Portland cement mortar sometimes used over a subfloor to provide a suitable base for Portland cement terrazzo and to minimize cracking.

**Undercoat –** Primer or intermediate coat in a multicoated system.

**Underlay –** See cushioning.

**Underlayment –** A mastic or panel board material installed over a subfloor to provide a suitable base for resilient flooring when the subfloor does not possess the necessary properties for direct application of the flooring.

**Uniformity –** In coating, paint, or transparent finish: not varying in gloss, sheen, color, hiding, or other property.

**Unsaturated molecule –** A molecule that is capable of uniting with certain other elements or compounds without creating any side products.

**Vacuum forming –** Shaping a heated plastic sheet by causing it to flow in the direction of reduced air pressure.

**Vehicle –** Liquid portion of a coating, paint, or transparent finish, including ingredients dissolved in it.

**Velvet carpet –** See woven carpet.

**Veneer –** (1) A single-facing withe of masonry units or similar materials attached to a wall for the purpose of providing ornamentation, protection, or insulation, but not bonded or attached to intentionally exert common action under load. (2) A thin sheet of wood.

- Rotary- cut veneer is veneer cut in a continuous strip by rotating a log against the edge of a knife in a lathe.
- Sawed veneer is veneer produced by sawing.
- Sliced veneer is veneer that is sliced by moving a log or flitch against a large knife.

**Veneered wall –** A wall having a face of masonry units or other weather-resisting materials attached to the backing, but not so bonded as to intentionally exert common action under load.

**Veneer wall tie** – See wall tie.

**Vent stack –** A vertical vent pipe installed primarily for the purpose of providing circulation of air to and from a part of a drainage system.

**Vent system –** A collection of pipes installed to provide a flow of air to or from a drainage system, or to provide circulation of air within such a system to protect trap seals from siphonage and backpressure.

**Vertical application –** Gypsum boards applied with the edges parallel to supporting members and borders. (See also horizontal application.)

**Vertical grain –** See under grain.

**Vibrating –** A mechanical method of compacting concrete.

**Vibrator –** A mechanical device that vibrates at a speed of 3000 to 10,000 revolutions per minute and is inserted into wet concrete or applied to its forms to compact concrete.

**Vinyl** – A polymer derived from ethylene; used in paint, coatings, and fabric. (See also resin.)

**Vinyl foam cushioning** – Carpet cushioning made from a combination of foamed synthetic materials.

**Visual cue** – See under cue.

**Voids** – Air spaces between pieces of aggregate within a cement paste.

**Volt** – The potential difference between two points in a wire carrying a current of 1 ampere when the power dissipated is 1 watt; equivalent to the potential difference across 1 ohm of resistance when 1 ampere is flowing through it.

**Voltage** – Electrical pressure, measured in volts and comparable to pounds per square inch (psi) in a fluid medium. Reference to 120 and 240 nominal voltages includes typical operating ranges of 115 to 125 and 230 to 250, respectively. Same as potential difference.

**Wallboard, gypsum** – See under gypsum board.

**Wall tie** – A header (bonder) or metal anchor that connects wythes of masonry to each other or to other materials.

- A cavity wall tie is a rigid, corrosion-resistant metal tie that bonds two wythes of a cavity wall. It is usually steel, 3/16 in. (4.76 mm) in diameter, and formed in a Z shape or a rectangle.
- A veneer wall tie is a strip or piece of bent metal used to tie a facing veneer to the backing; sometimes in two pieces to permit movement.

**Wane** – Bark or lack of wood, from any cause, on the edge or comer of a piece of lumber.

**Warp** - In wood: variation from a true or plane surface.

- Bow is distortion of a board in which the face is convex or concave longitudinally.
- Crook is distortion of a board in which the edge is convex or concave.
- Cup is distortion of a board in which the face is convex or concave transversely.
- Twist is distortion caused by the turning of the edges of a board so that the four comers of any face are no longer in the same plane.
- In carpet: backing yams running lengthwise in the carpet.
- In chain warp, zigzag warp yarn works over and under the shot yams of the carpet, binding the backing yarns together.
- Pile warp is lengthwise pile yams in Wilton woven carpets that form part of the backing.
- Stuffer warp is yam that runs lengthwise in a carpet but does not intertwine with any filling (weft shot) yam; serves to give weight, thickness, and stability to the fabric.

**Washability –** Ability of a coating, paint, or transparent finish to be easily cleaned without wearing away during cleaning.

**Water absorption –** See absorption rate.

**Water-cement ratio –** The ratio, by weight, of water to cement, or the amount of water, in gallons, used per 94 lb sack of cement to make concrete. It is an index of strength, durability, water tightness, and consistency.

**Water hammer –** Pounding noises and vibration that sometimes develop in a piping system when its air chambers become filled with water or have been omitted entirely; the problem may also be due to worn washers in faucets.

**Waterproofing –** Prevention of moisture flow through concrete or masonry due to water pressure; an impervious liquid or sheet material used to waterproof.

**Water retention –** A property of mortar that prevents the loss of water to masonry units having high suction. It also prevents bleeding or water gain when mortar is in contact with units having low suction. Also called water retentivity.

**Water spotting –** Coating, paint, or transparent finish appearance defect caused by water droplets.

**Water supply system in a building –** Consists of the water service pipe, water distributing pipes, branches to plumbing fixtures and appliances, and necessary fittings and control valves.

**Watt –** In acoustics, a unit of sound power equal to 1 X 10 7 dynes per centimeter per second, which is the basic expression of the flow of sound energy. In electricity, a unit of electrical power equal to the work done by a current of 1 ampere under the pressure of 1 volt.

**Wattage –** The amount of electrical power measured in watts; a single unit combining the effect of both voltage (pressure) and rate of flow (amperage) by multiplying these quantities (volts times amperes equal's watts).

**Watt-hour –** Unit of energy consumed, consisting of watts multiplied by time in hours; the result is often expressed in thousands of watt-hours, called kilowatt- hours.

**Weathering –** Corrosion (galvanic or chemical) produced by atmospheric conditions. Effect of exposure to weather on a coating, paint, or transparent finish film, raw wood, and other materials.

**Weathering index –** The product of the average annual number of freezing cycle days and the average annual winter rainfall.

**Weaving –** Process of forming carpet on a loom by interlacing the warp and weft yarns.

**Weep holes –** Openings placed in mortar joints of facing materials at the level of a flashing to divert to the exterior any moisture collected on the flashing.

**Weft –** Backing yarns that run across the width of a carpet. In woven carpets, the weft shot (filling) yarns and the warp chain (binder) yarns interlock and bind the pile tufts to the backing. In tufted carpets, pile yarns that run across the carpet are also considered weft yarns.

**Welding –** Creating a metallurgical bond between metals with heat and sometimes with the use of pressure and filler metal.

- Arc welding employs an electric arc as the source of heat.
- Gas welding employs a fuel gas (acetylene, hydrogen) and oxygen as the sources of heat. Shielded welding is a process in which gases or fusible granular materials are used to shield the weld area from the damaging effects of oxygen and nitrogen in the air.
- Shielded metal-arc welding is arc welding in which a flux-coated metal electrode is consumed to form a pool of filler metal and a gas shield around the weld area. Also known as manual metal-arc welding and stick electrode welding.
- Inert gas-shielded arc welding is arc welding in which shielding is provided by an inert gas envelope (such as argon, helium, a combination of argon and helium, or carbon dioxide) from an external supply. Filler metal is supplied either by a consumable metal electrode, as in inert-gas- shielded metal arc welding (MIO), or by a separate filler rod used with a non-consumable tungsten electrode, as in inert gas-shielded tungsten arc welding (TIO).
- Submerged arc welding is arc welding in which the weld area is shielded by a fusible granular material that melts to protect the weld area. Filler metal is obtained from either a consumable electrode or a separate filler rod.

**White lead –** Oldest white pigment, chemically known as lead sulfate or lead carbonate.

**Wilton carpet –** See woven carpet.

**Winter rainfall –** The sum in inches of the mean monthly corrected precipitation occurring between the first killing frost in the fall and the last killing frost in the spring.

**Wire, steel –** See under finished mill products.

**Wires (pile wire, gauge wire, standing wire) –** Metal strips over which the pile tufts are formed in woven carpets. (See also round wire.)

**Woolen yarn –** Soft, bulky yarn spun from both long and short wool fibers that are not combed straight but lie in all directions so that they will interlock to produce a felt-like texture.

**Workability –** Relative ease or difficulty with which concrete can be placed and worked into its final position within forms and around reinforcing bars. However, workability is contingent on the absence of segregation of the concrete. If the aggregate segregates, workability is considered to diminish (or terminate), regardless of how easily the concrete flows into place.

**Working stress –** See stress.

**Worsted yarn –** Strong, dense yarn made from long staple fibers that are combed to align the fibers and remove extremely short fibers.

**Woven carpet –** Carpet made by simultaneously interweaving backing and pile yarns on one of several types of looms from which the carpets derive their names.

- Axminster carpet is carpet made on an Axminster loom, which is capable of intricate color designs, usually with a level cut-pile surface.
- Loomed carpet is carpet made on a modified upholstery loom with a characteristic dense, low-level loop pile, generally bonded to cellular rubber cushioning.
- Velvet carpet is carpet made on a simple loom, usually of a solid color or moresque, with cut or loop pile of either soft or hard- twisted yarns.
- Wilton carpet is carpet made on a loom employing a jacquard mechanism, which selects two or more colored yarns to create the pile pattern.

**Wrinkling –** Development of ridges and furrows in a coating, paint, or transparent finish film when it dries.

**Wrought aluminum products –** Products formed by rolling, drawing, extruding, or forging.

- A bar is a solid section that is long in relation to its cross-sectional dimensions and has a completely symmetrical cross section that is square or rectangular (excluding flattened wire) with sharp or rounded corners or edges, or is a regular hexagon or octagon. An aluminum bar has a width or greatest distance between parallel faces of % in. (9.5 mm) or more.
- An extruded section is a rod, bar, tube, or any other shape produced by the extrusion process.
- Foil is a solid sheet section rolled to a thickness of less than 0.006 in. (0.1524 mm).
- Forging stock is a rod, bar, or other section suitable for subsequent change in cross section by forging.
- A pipe is a tube having certain standardized combinations of outside diameters and wall thicknesses.
- A plate is a solid section rolled to a thickness of 0.250 in. (6.4 mm) or more in rectangular form and with either sheared or sawed edges.
- A rod is a solid, round aluminum section % in. (9.5 mm) or greater in diameter, whose length is greater than its diameter.
- A sheet is a solid section rolled to a thickness ranging from 0.006 in. (0.1524 mm) to 0.249 in. (6.3246 mm) inclusive, supplied with sheared, slit, or sawed edges.
- Structural shapes are solid shapes used as load-bearing members. They include angles, channels, W shapes, tees, zees, and others. A tube is a hollow product whose cross section is completely symmetrical and is round, square, rectangular, hexagonal, octagonal, or elliptical, with sharp or rounded comers, and whose wall is of uniform thickness except as affected by comer radii.
- A wire is a solid section that is long in relation to its cross- sectional diameter, having a completely symmetrical cross section that is square or rectangular (excluding flattened wire) with sharp or rounded comers or edges, or is round or a rectangular hexagon or octagon, and whose diameter, width, or greatest distance between parallel faces is less than % in. (9.5 rom).

**Wrought iron –** Relatively pure iron mechanically mixed with a small amount of iron- silicate slag; characterized by good corrosion resistance, weldability, toughness, and high ductility.

**Wrought steel products –** Products formed by rolling, drawing, extruding, or forging. (See also finished mill products.)

**Wythe –** A continuous vertical section of masonry one unit in thickness. Also called withe and tier.Yard lumber – See under lumber.

**Yellowing –** Development of a yellow color or cast in white, pastel, colored, or clear finishes.

1. Describe the type of screws used with Gypsum installation and light-gage steel?

a. Type W screws
b. Type U screws
c. Type R screws
d. Type S screws

2. The self-weight of the structural members normally provides the largest portion of the _____ load of a building.

a. Dead
b. Live
c. Wind
d. Heavy

3. Which of following roof styles is described: roof characterized by two slopes on each of its four sides with the lower slope being steeper than the upper slope?

a. Salt Box
b. Side-gabled
c. Mansard
d. Pavilion-hipped

4. Identify the correct definition of Ductility.

a. Ductility is similar to the concept of support, except that connection refers to
b. A system of forces composed of two equal forces of opposite direction, offset by
c. Bending deformation, i.e., deformation by increasing curvature.
d. Ductility generally refers to the amount of inelastic deformation which a

5. Which of the following is not true concerning trusses?

a. The trusses are often used as visual or spatial elements.
b. Trusses are also used for heavily loaded long spans requiring more structural
c. Trusses are never used as repetitive lightweight members, such as steel "bar
d. Trusses are not limited to planar assemblies, and can be arranged as

6. Match the definition below with the correct term: ______ occurs in loosely packed saturated sand when seismic shaking compacts the sand, resulting in increased pressure in the surrounding water. The pressure in the water can rise to the point where it carries all the stress in the soil, so the sand grains carry no net pressure and can flow past one another.

a. Dissipation
b. Liquefaction
c. Saturation
d. Indemnification

7. Match the definition below with the correct term: One who has contracted to be responsible for another, especially one who assumes responsibilities or debts in the event of default.

a. Surety

b. Privity

c. Compensation

d. Quittance

8. Identifiy the acronym: CSI

a. Construction Science Institute

b. Construction Specifications Institute

c. Construction SPEX Institute

d. Construction Source Institute

9. Match the definition below with the correct term: Term used to define portable and fixed, hand operated fire fighting equipment for use in buildings. The term not only includes water, carbon dioxide, foam and dry powder fire extinguishers but fire hose reels, internal fire hydrants, fire service hose and nozzles.

a. FSPR

b. ASHRAE

c. FEXT

d. FRSA

10. What distance is required between masonary veneer and sheathing?

a. .5 inch

b. 1 inch

c. 1.5 inch

d. 2 inch

11. According to Walker's Estimating Guide, if a 1/2" x 14' x 42' plywood installation requires approximately 250 8d common wire nails per 100 sq. Ft, the total weight of nails required is ___ lbs.

between 9.6 and 12.6

between 12.6 and 15.5

between 15.6 and 18.6

12. According to the Principals and Practices of Heavy Construction, column forms designed for a 3' high column to be poured at the rate of 10' per hour at a temperature of 60F must be designed for a maximum pressure of _____ ( assume the normal weight of concrete at 150 lbs per cubic ft.).

450 psf

1800 psf

1650 psf

1950 psf

13. The handling and erection of 208,000 lbs of W 18x35 steel beams requires the following labor:

- Labor type: Foreman / Number of Men: 1 / Rate per man per hr.: $23.75
- Labor Type: Iron Workers / Number of Men: 7 / Rate per man per hr.: $18.90
- Labor Type: Crane Operator / Number of Men:1/ Rate per man pr hr.: $19.85

The crew can erect 11 tons of steel per 8 hr. Day. Measure beam lengths from grid center lines and make no deductions for columns, The total labor cost for handling and erecting all the W 18 X 35 steel beams is :

Between $12,901 and $14,600

Between $14,601 and $16,300

Between $16,301 and $18,000

Greater than $18,000

14. According to Walker's Estimating Guide, the total number of 3 3/4" X 8" X 2 1/4" standard brick needed to build an 85 lineal foot long brick wall, two brick thick, 7' high with 1/4" end mortar joint and 5/8" bed mortar joint is _______ ( do not allow for waste )

7,240

7,540

8,730

10,860

15. According to the Builder's Guide to accounting, the main objective in tracking job costs is:

To project future profits

To accurately determine the most profitable job

To accurately track expenses by job

To accurately project future overhead expense

16. A strength test shall be the average of the strengths of ________ cylinders made from the same sample of concrete and tested at ____ days or at test age designated for determination of f'c.

a. 3, 28

b. 1, 56

c. 4, 56

d. 2, 28

17. Beams, girders, or slabs supported by columns or walls shall not be cast or erected until concrete in the vertical support members is no longer plastic.

True

False

18. A standard hook has a ___ degree bend plus 12 db (bar diameters) extension at the free end of bar

a. 180

b. 90

c. 45

d. 30

19. The minimum clear spacing between parallel bars in a layer shall be db, but not less than _______ inch.

a. 1

b. ½

c. ¾

d. 1/4

20. All nonprestressed bars shall be enclosed by lateral ties, at least No. 3 in size for longitudinal bars No. ___ or smaller, and at least No. 4 in size for No. 11, No. 14, No. 18 and bundled longitudinal bars.

a. 8

b. 10

c. 11

d. 12

21. Except for _________ steel, steel reinforcement with rust, mill scale, or a combination of both shall be considered satisfactory, provided the minimum dimensions (including height of deformations) and weight of a hand-wire-brushed test specimen comply with applicable ASTM specifications referenced in 3.5

a. Prestressing

b. Anchor bolt

c. Structural

d. Tie wire

22. When total quantity of a given class of concrete is less than _________ cubic yards, strength tests are not required when evidence of satisfactory strength is submitted to and approved by the building official.

a. 20

b. 75

c. 50

d. 10

23. Tolerance for longitudinal location of bends and ends of reinforcement shall be +/- ______ inches

a. 2

b. 3

c. 1

d. 1/2

24. Concrete in an area represented by core tests shall be considered structurally ________ if the average of three cores is equal to at least 85 percent of f'c and if no single core is less than ______ percent of f'c.

a. Adequate, 85

b. Adequate, 75

c. Inadequate, 75

d. Adequate, 85

25. Form supports for prestressed concrete members shall not be removed until sufficient ________ has been applied to enable prestressed members to carry their dead load and anticipated construction loads.

a. Prestressing

b. Post tensioning

c. Curing

d. Force

26. In reference to removal of forms, shores, and reshoring, sufficient strength shall be demonstrated by ________ _________ considering proposed loads, strength of forming and shoring system, and concrete strength data.

a. Compressive strength

b. Construction schedule

c. Contractors math

d. Structural analysis

27. In reference to cold weather requirements all concrete materials and all reinforcement, forms, fillers, and ground with which concrete is to come in contact shall be free from ______.

a. Ice

b. Frost

c. Both a and b

d. Snow

28. Conduits, pipes, and sleeves shall be permitted to be considered as replacing structurally in compression the displaced concrete provided they are of uncoated or galvanized iron or ______ not thinner than standard schedule 40 steel pipe.

a. Pvc

b. Steel

c. Aluminum

d. Tin

29. Samples for strength tests of each class of concrete placed each day shall be taken not less than once a day, nor less than once for each _______ cubic yards of concrete.

a. 170

b. 150

c. 100

d. 75

30. What is the minimum cover (in inches) for reinforcement in concrete cast against and permanently exposed to earth?

a. 2

b. 3

c. 1

d. 1/2

31. In reference to conduits and pipes embedded in concrete, conduit/pipe shall not be larger in outside dimension than _____ the overall thickness of slab, wall, or beam in which they are embedded.

a. 1/3

b. 1/2

c. 1/4

d. 3/4

32. Procedures for protecting and curing concrete shall be improved when strength of field-cured cylinders at test age designated for determination of f'c is less than _____ percent of that of companion __________-cured cylinders.

a. 90, field

b. 50, field

c. 75, laboratory

d. 85, laboratory

33. Concrete (other than high-early strength) shall be maintained above _____ degrees F and in a moist condition for at least the first _____ days after placement, except when cured in accordance with 5.11.3

a. 32, 2

b. 40, 3

c. 40, 7

d. 50, 7

34. Water shall be _______ from place of deposit before concrete is placed unless a _______ is to be used or unless otherwise permitted by the building official.

a. Removed, pump

b. Added, pump

c. Removed, tremie

d. Added, tremie

35. For the strength level of an individual class of concrete to be considered satisfactory, no individual strength test can fall below f'c by more than _______ psi when f'c is 5000 psi or less.

a. 500

b. 100

c. 1000

d. 250

36. Clear spacing between spirals shall not exceed ___ in., nor be less than ___ in.

a. 1, 2

b. 3,1

c. 2,1

d. 1,3

37. What is the minimum cover (in inches) for primary reinforcement in a concrete beam not exposed to weather or in contact with the ground?

a. 1 ½

b. 2

c. 1

d. 3/4

38. For cast-in-place construction, size of spirals shall not be less than ____ in. diameter.

a. 1/2

b. 3/8

c. 1/4

d. 3/4

39. During hot weather, proper attention shall be given to ingredients, production methods, handling, placing, protection, and curing to prevent excessive concrete temperatures or water evaporation that could impair required _______ or serviceability of the member or structure.

a. Life

b. Strength

c. Durability

d. Aesthetics

40. For bundled bars, minimum concrete cover shall be equal to the equivalent diameter of the bundle, but need not be greater than ____ in.; except for concrete cast against and permanently exposed to earth, where minimum cover shall be 3 inches.

a. 2

b. 1

c. 3/4

d. 3

41. In spirally reinforced or tied reinforced compression members, clear distance between longitudinal bars shall be not less than 1.5db nor less than ______ in.

a. 1 ½

b. 2

c. ½

d. 1

42. Bars larger than No. _____ shall not be bundled in beams.

a. 12

b. 10

c. 8

d. 11

43. Reinforcement partially embedded in concrete shall not be field ________, except as shown on the design drawings or permitted by the engineer.

a. Bent

b. Modified

c. Cut

d. Welded

44. What is the tolerance on minimum concrete cover for an 8 inch thick reinforced concrete wall?

a. -1/2 inch

b. -3/4 inch

c. -3/8 inch

d. -1/4 inch

45. High-early-strength concrete shall be maintained above _______ degrees F and in a moist condition for at least the first _____ days, except when cured in accordance with 5.11.3

a. 50, 3

b. 50, 7

c. 40, 7

d. 40, 3

46. There are a multitude of tasks for both contractor and architect in designing and building a masonry veneer steel stud wall system. Which of the following tasks is not part of the architect's role?

a. Detailing transitions

b. Planning on-site material sequencing

c. Documenting air leakage performance

d. Verifying material compatibilities

47. Air barriers restrict airflow in and out of the wall, minimize leakage, and minimize condensation.

True

False

48. What should an architect consider when selecting an air barrier for a masonry veneer steel stud wall system?

a. Will it comply with water resistive testing to ASTM E331?
b. Will it comply with air leakage testing to ASTM E2357?
c. Does the system comply with NFPA 285?
d. All of the above

49. Aside from R-value, what is the key characteristic of continuous insulation?

a. Water resistance
b. Light weight
c. Easy to install
d. Wind resistance

50. In Zones 5 through 8, where is the vapor retarder placed?

a. Inboard of the insulation
b. High vapor pressure side
c. Low vapor pressure side
d. Both A and B

51. Vapor generally flows from a low vapor pressure to a high vapor pressure.

True
False

52. What level of permeance do Class III vapor retarders have?

a. ≤ 0.1 perm
b. > 1.0 perm
c. > 0.1 perm, ≤ 1.0 perm
d. < 1.0 perm

53. What part of the masonry veneer steel stud wall system acts as the rain screen?

a. Air barrier
b. Water resistive barrier
c. Continuous insulation
d. Masonry

54. A well-designed water drainage system involves

a. protected drainage pathways.

b. redundancies.

c. air circulation.

d. All of the above

e. Both A and B

55. What type of masonry veneer anchor is NOT approved for commercial construction?

a. Barrel style with air and water sealing washers

b. Bracket style

c. Corrugated style

d. Barrel style

56. Every climate zone north of Miami requires some form of continuous insulation.

True

False

57. Which of the following statements refers to water resistance standard ASTM E331?

a. The wall being tested is subjected to thousands of cycles of water testing.

b. The wall sample is water tested after the wall has undergone air pressure cycle testing in the same test frame.

c. The goal with water testing is to flex the wall back and forth.

d. Wall systems are NEVER tested beyond the mandatory 15 minutes.

58. Which test limits floor-to-floor fire spread at the joint between the wall and the floor/ceiling assembly?

a. ASTM E119

b. ASTM E2307

c. NFPA 285

d. ASTM C794

59. In a masonry veneer steel stud wall system, passing the NFPA 285 test is largely dependent on

a. the location of the opening.

b. the head and jamb details.

c. the brick used.

d. None of the above

60. Complete wall systems that provide all of the components necessary to make a masonry veneer steel stud wall system work can be specified using a performance specification Section 01 83 16 Exterior Envelope Performance Requirements.

True

False

61. Slab-on-grade requirements now include:

a. R-5 added to R-value for heated slab

b. R-10 for 2' in climate zones 4 and 5

c. R-10 for 4' in climate zones 6 through 8

d. all of the above

62. Maximum fenestration U-factor is ?

a. 0.30 in all climate zones

b. 0.30 in climate zones 2-4 and 0.32 in climate zones 5-8

c. 0.40 in climate zone 2, 0.35 in climate zones 3-4, and 0.32 in climate zones 5-8

d. subject to NFRC requirements

63.There are new requirements for R-3 or better pipe insulation on most types of hot-water pipes.

True

False

64. 2012 IECC Section 401.3 Mandatory Requirement certificate on panel box must include...?

a. Major component R-values

b. FSC certifications

c. U-factor, SHGC of Windows

d. both answers a & c

65. Under 2012 IECC Lighting equipment: 75% of lamps must be high-efficacy lamps, or 75% of lighting fixtures must be only high-efficacy lamps.?

True

False

66. Under the 2012 IECC, blower-door testing requirements are not mandatory.

True

False

67. 2012 IECC blower-door test requirements mandate...?

a. only the 2009 threshold of 7 ach50

b. 5 ach50 for climate zones 1 and 2, and 3 ach50 for homes in all other zones

c. 3 ach50

d. 5 ach50

68. Under 2012 IECC, whole-house mechanical ventilation systems are required...

a. in all homes

b. in climate zones 5-8

c. in climate zones 3-8, and some homes in climate zones 1-2

d. in certain homes taking the prescriptive path

e. they're not required in IECC

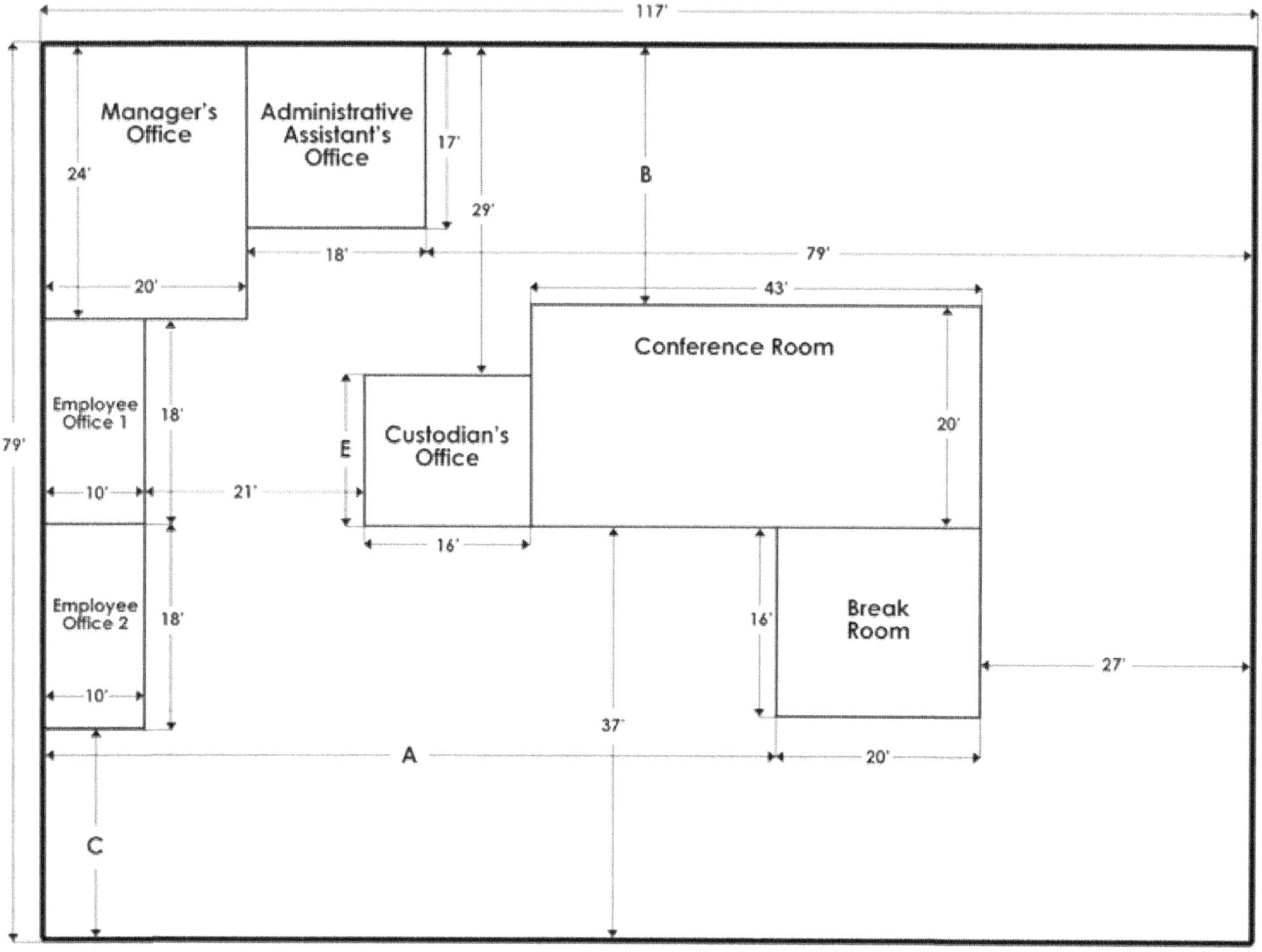


69. What is the distance ("A") from the left edge of the property to the break room?

a. 47'

b. 67'

c: 70'. To find the unknown distance ("A"), subtract the known widths from the total width of the property. The total width of the property is 117'. The other known widths are 20' and 27'. To find A, subtract 20' and 27' from 117'. A + 20' + 27' = 117'. A = 117' - 20' - 27' = 70'.

d. 19'

e. N



FLORIDA CONSTRUCTIONSCHOOL.org

70. What is the distance ("B") from the top edge of the property to the conference room?

a. 57′

b: 22′. To find the unknown length ("B"), subtract the known lengths from the total length of the property. The total length of the property is 79′. The known lengths are 37′ and 20′. To find B, subtract 37′ and 20′ from 79′. B + 20′ + 37′ = 79′. B = 79′ - 20′ - 37′ = 22′.

c. 27′

d. 59′

e. N

71. What is the distance ("C") from the bottom of the property to the employee office?

a: 19′. To find the unknown length ("C"), subtract the known lengths from the total length of the property. The total length of the property is 79′. The known lengths are 18′, 18′, and 24′. To find C, subtract 18′, 18′, and 24′ from 79′. C + 18′ + 18′ + 24′ = 79′. C = 79′ - 18′ - 18′ - 24′ = 19′.

b. 60′

c. 10′

d. 18′

e. N

72. What is the area of the manager's office?

a. 44 ft2

b: 480 ft2. To find the area of the manager's office, multiply the length of the office by the width of the office. The length of the office is 24′. The width of the office is 20′. Area of the manager's office = 24′ - 20′ = 480 ft2.

c. 360 ft2

d. 576 ft2

e. N

73. Provided a modification to a fire protection system is small, no approval is needed by the building or fire official

True

False

74. Every automatic sprinkler system must be monitored except

a. One and two family dwellings

b. Systems with fewer than 6 sprinkler heads

c. Jurisdictions that do not require Central Station Service as outlined in NFPA 72

d. Both A & B

e. All of the Above

f. None of the above, they always have to be monitored

75. A system designed to alert individuals of the potential threat from hazardous materials is referred to as a

a. Fire alarm system

b. Threat level assessment system

c. Emergency alarm system

d. Class D system

76. A Supervising Station is

a. A Central Station as defined in NFPA 72

b. A Remote Station as defined in NFPA 72

c. A facility that receives signals and at which personnel are in attendance at all times to respond to these signals

d. A constantly attended station with trained personnel available to respond immediately to the emergency

77. Which of the following is not a mandatory requirement to be included on shop drawings?

a. Battery Calculations

b. The name of the Authority Having Jurisdiction

c. Floor plans

d. Detailed information from manufacturer's data sheets identifying the equipment being installed

78. Because fire alarm designs are dictated by code, they do not have to comply with the guidelines for accessibility.

True

False

79. Because of new types of construction and the advent of zoning and zoned reporting, there is no longer a need for any of the fire alarm equipment to be red in color.

True

False

80. When a building is fully sprinklered with an approved supervised sprinkler system, there is no requirement for a smoke detector to be installed above the control equipment.

aTrue

False

81. Protective Covers installed on alarm boxes must always be provided with a local annunciator to indicate when the cover has been tampered with or dislodged.

True

False

82. Fire alarm systems required by Chapter 9, or by the Florida Fire Prevention Code must be monitored by an approved Central Station in accordance with NFPA 72

True

False

# TRADES RESIDENTIAL CONTRACTOR EXAM

1. Describe the type of screws used with Gypsum installation and light-gage steel?

a. Type W screws

b. Type U screws

c. Type R screws

d. Type S screws

2. The self-weight of the structural members normally provides the largest portion of the _____ load of a building.

a. Dead

b. Live

c. Wind

d. Heavy

3. Which of following roof styles is described: roof characterized by two slopes on each of its four sides with the lower slope being steeper than the upper slope?

a. Salt Box

b. Side-gabled

c. Mansard

d. Pavilion-hipped

4. Identify the correct definition of Ductility.

a. Ductility is similar to the concept of support, except that connection refers to

b. A system of forces composed of two equal forces of opposite direction, offset by

c. Bending deformation, i.e., deformation by increasing curvature.

c. Ductility generally refers to the amount of inelastic deformation which a

5. Which of the following is not true concerning trusses?

a. The trusses are often used as visual or spatial elements.

b. Trusses are also used for heavily loaded long spans requiring more structural

c. Trusses are never used as repetitive lightweight members, such as steel "bar

d. Trusses are not limited to planar assemblies, and can be arranged as

6. Match the definition below with the correct term: _______ occurs in loosely packed saturated sand when seismic shaking compacts the sand, resulting in increased pressure in the surrounding water. The pressure in the water can rise to the point where it carries all the stress in the soil, so the sand grains carry no net pressure and can flow past one another.

a. Dissipation

b. Liquefaction

c. Saturation

d. Indemnification

7. Match the definition below with the correct term: One who has contracted to be responsible for another, especially one who assumes responsibilities or debts in the event of default.

a. Surety

b. Privity

c. Compensation

d. Quittance

8. Identifiy the acronym: CSI

a. Construction Science Institute

b. Construction Specifications Institute

c. Construction SPEX Institute

d. Construction Source Institute

9. Match the definition below with the correct term:

Term used to define portable and fixed, hand operated fire fighting equipment for use in buildings. The term not only includes water, carbon dioxide, foam and dry powder fire extinguishers but fire hose reels, internal fire hydrants, fire service hose and nozzles.

a. FSPR

b. ASHRAE

c. FEXT

d. FRSA

10. What distance is required between masonary veneer and sheathing?

a. .5 inch

b. 1 inch

c. 1.5 inch

d. 2 inch

11. According to Walker's Estimating Guide, if a 1/2" x 14' x 42' plywood installation requires approximately 250 8d common wire nails per 100 sq. Ft, the total weight of nails required is ___ lbs.

between 9.6 and 12.6

between 12.6 and 15.5

between 15.6 and 18.6

between 18.6 and 21.6

*Explanation*

14x42x250 / 100 / 135 = 10.8

*Reference*

Walker's p. 6.24

12. According to the Principals and Practices of Heavy Construction, column forms designed for a 3' high column to be poured at the rate of 10' per hour at a temperature of 60F must be designed for a maximum pressure of _____ ( assume the normal weight of concrete at 150 lbs per cubic ft.).

450 psf

1800 psf

1650 psf

1950 psf

*Reference*

Principles and Practices, 5th ed. Table 6-2

13. The handling and erection of 208,000 lbs of W 18x35 steel beams requires the following labor:

Labor type: Foreman / Number of Men: 1 / Rate per man per hr.: $23.75

Labor Type:Iron Workers / Number of Men: 7 / Rate per man per hr.: $18.90

Labor Type: Crane Operator / Number of Men:1 / Rate per man pr hr.: $19.85

The crew can erect 11 tons of steel per 8 hr. Day. Measure beam lengths from grid center lines and make no deductions for columns, The total labor cost for handling and erecting all the W 18 X 35 steel beams is :

Between $12,901 and $14,600

Between $14,601 and $16,300

Between $16,301 and $18,000

Greater than $18,000

*Explanation*

208,000 / 2000 = 104 tons/11=9.45 days x 8 = 75.6 crew hours. $23.75 + ( 7 x 18.90 = 132.3) + 19.85 = $175.9 crew hour cost. 75.6 x $175.9 = $13,298

14. According to Walker's Estimating Guide, the total number of 3 3/4" X 8" X 2 1/4" standard brick needed to build an 85 lineal foot long brick wall, two brick thick, 7' high with 1/4" end mortar joint and 5/8" bed mortar joint is _______ ( do not allow for waste )

7,240

7,540

8,730

10,860

### Explanation

7 x 85 = 595 sq. ft. of wall. From Table, 12.17 bricks required per 100 sq. ft. wall area. 12.17 x 595 = 7241.15

### Reference

Walkers table Chapter 4, Number of Standard Brick

15. According to the Builder's Guide to accounting, the main objective in tracking job costs is:

To project future profits

To accurately determine the most profitable job

To accurately track expenses by job

To accurately project future overhead expense

### Concrete

16. A strength test shall be the average of the strengths of ________ cylinders made from the same sample of concrete and tested at _____ days or at test age designated for determination of f'c.

a. 3, 28

b. 1, 56

c. 4, 56

d. 2, 28

17. Beams, girders, or slabs supported by columns or walls shall not be cast or erected until concrete in the vertical support members is no longer plastic.

True

False

18. A standard hook has a ____ degree bend plus 12 db (bar diameters) extension at the free end of bar

a. 180

b. 90

c. 45

d. 30

19. The minimum clear spacing between parallel bars in a layer shall be db, but not less than _______ inch.

a. 1

b. 1/2

c. 3/4

d. 1/4

20. All nonprestressed bars shall be enclosed by lateral ties, at least No. 3 in size for longitudinal bars No. ___ or smaller, and at least No. 4 in size for No. 11, No. 14, No. 18 and bundled longitudinal bars.

a. 8

b. 10

c. 11

d. 12

21. Except for ________ steel, steel reinforcement with rust, mill scale, or a combination of both shall be considered satisfactory, provided the minimum dimensions (including height of deformations) and weight of a hand-wire-brushed test specimen comply with applicable ASTM specifications referenced in 3.5

a. Prestressing

b. Anchor bolt

c. Structural

d. Tie wire

22. When total quantity of a given class of concrete is less than ________ cubic yards, strength tests are not required when evidence of satisfactory strength is submitted to and approved by the building official.

a. 20

b. 75

c. 50

d. 10

23. Tolerance for longitudinal location of bends and ends of reinforcement shall be +/- _____ inches

a. 2

b. 3

c. 1

d. 1/2

24. Concrete in an area represented by core tests shall be considered structurally ________ if the average of three cores is equal to at least 85 percent of f'c and if no single core is less than ______ percent of f'c.

a. Adequate, 85

b. Adequate, 75

c. Inadequate, 75

d. Adequate, 85

25. Form supports for prestressed concrete members shall not be removed until sufficient ________ has been applied to enable prestressed members to carry their dead load and anticipated construction loads.

a. Prestressing

b. Post tensioning

c. Curing

d. Force

26. In reference to removal of forms, shores, and reshoring, sufficient strength shall be demonstrated by __________ __________ considering proposed loads, strength of forming and shoring system, and concrete strength data.

a. Compressive strength

b. Construction schedule

c. Contractors math

d. Structural analysis

27. In reference to cold weather requirements all concrete materials and all reinforcement, forms, fillers, and ground with which concrete is to come in contact shall be free from _______.

a. Ice

b. Frost

c. Both a and b

d. Snow

28. Conduits, pipes, and sleeves shall be permitted to be considered as replacing structurally in compression the displaced concrete provided they are of uncoated or galvanized iron or _______ not thinner than standard schedule 40 steel pipe.

a. Pvc

b. Steel

c. Aluminum

d. Tin

29. Samples for strength tests of each class of concrete placed each day shall be taken not less than once a day, nor less than once for each ________ cubic yards of concrete.

a. 170

b. 150

c. 100

d. 75

30. What is the minimum cover (in inches) for reinforcement in concrete cast against and permanently exposed to earth?

a. 2

b. 3

c. 1

d. 1/2

31. In reference to conduits and pipes embedded in concrete, conduit/pipe shall not be larger in outside dimension than _____ the overall thickness of slab, wall, or beam in which they are embedded.

a. 1/3

b. 1/2

c. 1/4

d. 3/4

32. Procedures for protecting and curing concrete shall be improved when strength of field-cured cylinders at test age designated for determination of f'c is less than _____ percent of that of companion _________-cured cylinders.

a. 90, field

b. 50, field

c. 75, laboratory

d. 85, laboratory

33. Concrete (other than high-early strength) shall be maintained above _____ degrees F and in a moist condition for at least the first _____ days after placement, except when cured in accordance with 5.11.3

a. 32, 2

b. 40, 3

c. 40, 7

d. 50, 7

34. Water shall be ______ from place of deposit before concrete is placed unless a ______ is to be used or unless otherwise permitted by the building official.

a. Removed, pump

b. Added, pump

c. Removed, tremie

d. Added, tremie

35. For the strength level of an individual class of concrete to be considered satisfactory, no individual strength test can fall below f'c by more than ______ psi when f'c is 5000 psi or less.

a. 500

b. 100

c. 1000

d. 250

36. Clear spacing between spirals shall not exceed ___ in., nor be less than ___ in.

a. 1, 2

b. 3,1

c. 2,1

d. 1,3

37. What is the minimum cover (in inches) for primary reinforcement in a concrete beam not exposed to weather or in contact with the ground?

a. 1 1/2

b. 2

c. 1

d. 3/4

38. For cast-in-place construction, size of spirals shall not be less than ____ in. diameter.

a. 1/2

b. 3/8

c. 1/4

d. 3/4

39. During hot weather, proper attention shall be given to ingredients, production methods, handling, placing, protection, and curing to prevent excessive concrete temperatures or water evaporation that could impair required _______ or serviceability of the member or structure.

a. Life

b. Strength

c. Durability

d. Aesthetics

40. For bundled bars, minimum concrete cover shall be equal to the equivalent diameter of the bundle, but need not be greater than ____ in.; except for concrete cast against and permanently exposed to earth, where minimum cover shall be 3 inches.

a. 2

b. 1

c. 3/4

d. 3

41. In spirally reinforced or tied reinforced compression members, clear distance between longitudinal bars shall be not less than 1.5db nor less than ______ in.

a. 1 1/2

b. 2

c. ½

d. 1

42. Bars larger than No. ____ shall not be bundled in beams.

a. 12

b. 10

c. 8

d. 11

43. Reinforcement partially embedded in concrete shall not be field _______, except as shown on the design drawings or permitted by the engineer.

a. Bent

b. Modified

c. Cut

d. Welded

44. What is the tolerance on minimum concrete cover for an 8 inch thick reinforced concrete wall?

a. -1/2 inch

b. -3/4 inch

c. -3/8 inch

d. -1/4 inch

41. High-early-strength concrete shall be maintained above ______ degrees F and in a moist condition for at least the first _____ days, except when cured in accordance with 5.11.3

a. 50, 3

s. 50, 7

c. 40, 7

d. 40, 3

*WALLS VAPOR*

42. There are a multitude of tasks for both contractor and architect in designing and building a masonry veneer steel stud wall system. Which of the following tasks is not part of the architect's role?

a. Detailing transitions

b. Planning on-site material sequencing

c. Documenting air leakage performance

d. Verifying material compatibilities

43. Air barriers restrict airflow in and out of the wall, minimize leakage, and minimize condensation.

True

False

44. What should an architect consider when selecting an air barrier for a masonry veneer steel stud wall system?

a. Will it comply with water resistive testing to ASTM E331?

b. Will it comply with air leakage testing to ASTM E2357?

c. Does the system comply with NFPA 285?

d. All of the above

45. Aside from R-value, what is the key characteristic of continuous insulation?

a. Water resistance

b. Light weight

c. Easy to install

d. Wind resistance

46. In Zones 5 through 8, where is the vapor retarder placed?

a. Inboard of the insulation

b. High vapor pressure side

c. Low vapor pressure side

d. Both A and B

47. Vapor generally flows from a low vapor pressure to a high vapor pressure.

True

False

48. What level of permeance do Class III vapor retarders have?

a. ≤ 0.1 perm

b. > 1.0 perm

c. > 0.1 perm, ≤ 1.0 perm

d. < 1.0 perm

49. What part of the masonry veneer steel stud wall system acts as the rain screen?

a. Air barrier

b. Water resistive barrier

c. Continuous insulation

d. Masonry

50. A well-designed water drainage system involves

a. protected drainage pathways.

b. redundancies.

c. air circulation.

d. All of the above

e. Both A and B

51. What type of masonry veneer anchor is NOT approved for commercial construction?

a. Barrel style with air and water sealing washers

b. Bracket style

c. Corrugated style

d. Barrel style

52. Every climate zone north of Miami requires some form of continuous insulation.

True

False

53. Which of the following statements refers to water resistance standard ASTM E331?

a. The wall being tested is subjected to thousands of cycles of water testing.

b. The wall sample is water tested after the wall has undergone air pressure cycle testing in the same test frame.

c. The goal with water testing is to flex the wall back and forth.

d. Wall systems are NEVER tested beyond the mandatory 15 minutes.

54. Which test limits floor-to-floor fire spread at the joint between the wall and the floor/ceiling assembly?

a. ASTM E119

b. ASTM E2307

c. NFPA 285

d. ASTM C794

55. In a masonry veneer steel stud wall system, passing the NFPA 285 test is largely dependent on

a. the location of the opening.

b. the head and jamb details.

c. the brick used.

d. None of the above

56. Complete wall systems that provide all of the components necessary to make a masonry veneer steel stud wall system work can be specified using a performance specification Section 01 83 16 Exterior Envelope Performance Requirements.

True

False

### *Energy Answers*

57. Slab-on-grade requirements now include:

a. R-5 added to R-value for heated slab

b. R-10 for 2′ in climate zones 4 and 5

c. R-10 for 4′ in climate zones 6 through 8

d. all of the above

Highlighting the increased importance and attention paid to the building envelope, for slabs with a floor surface <12″ below grade, an R-10 (typically 2″) insulation is required in climate zones 4 and above. Slab edge insulation must extend downward from top of slab a minimum of 24″ (zones 4 and 5) or 48″ (zones 6,7, and 8). Insulation can be vertical or extend horizontally under the slab or out from the building. Insulation extending outward must be under 10″ of soil or pavement. For heated slabs, an additional R-5 is required, with an insulation depth of the footing or 2 feet, whichever is less, in zones 1-3.

58. Maximum fenestration U-factor is ?

a. 0.30 in all climate zones

b. 0.30 in climate zones 2-4 and 0.32 in climate zones 5-8

c. 0.40 in climate zone 2, 0.35 in climate zones 3-4, and 0.32 in climate zones 5-8

d. subject to NFRC requirements

2012 IECC made major changes to fenestration requirements, so builders will have to assess new maximum U-factor and solar heat-gain coefficients (SHGC) for their particular climate zone. Marine climate zones have special exemptions noted in the code. Prescriptive requirements are found in Table 402.1.1 of the 2012 IECC.

59.There are new requirements for R-3 or better pipe insulation on most types of hot-water pipes.

True

False

Requirements for pipe insulation mean reduction of temperature change in the water between heating point and delivery point. Insulation keeps the water in the pipes hotter with less initial energy input, thus saving energy and reducing operating costs. Owing to its increased focus on DHW distribution, the 2012 IECC requires piping associated with service hot water systems to be insulated to a minimum of R-3.

60. 2012 IECC Section 401.3 Mandatory Requirement certificate on panel box must include...?

a. Major component R-values

b. FSC certifications

c. U-factor, SHGC of Windows

d. both answers a & c

This required certificate must appear on the breaker panel, in the attic next to the attic insulation card, or inside a kitchen cabinet, and must include major component (insulation installed in or on ceiling, roof, walls, foundation and ducts outside conditioned spaces) R-values, U-factor and SHGC of windows, equipment efficiencies, duct and envelope testing results, and a load calculation summary. Appendix 1A contains a sample certificate for reference.

61. Under 2012 IECC Lighting equipment: 75% of lamps must be high-efficacy lamps, or 75% of lighting fixtures must be only high-efficacy lamps.?

True

False

The 2012 IECC raises the requirement of high-efficacy lamps to a 75% minimum, up from the 50% requirement found in 2009's IECC. High-efficacy lamps may be a compact fluorescent lamp (CFL), a T8 or smaller linear fluorescent lamp, or any lamp meeting minimum efficiency requirements. 2012 minimum efficiency requirements are: 60 lumens per watt for lamps over 40 watts, 50 lumens per watt for lamps 15 watts to 40 watts, and 40 lumens per watt for lamps rated at 15 watts or less. Refer to section R404.1 (2012 IECC) for further details.

62. Under the 2012 IECC, blower-door testing requirements are not mandatory.

True

False

Per section R402.4.1.2 of 2012 IECC, which also provides mandated maximum acceptable air leakage rates, every new home must pass a blower-door test. The 2009 IECC allowed builders to either follow a checklist of air tightness requirements or have the home tested with a blower door. 2012 does away with that option, and mandates both an air-sealing checklist (Table R402.4.1.1) and a blower-door test.

63. 2012 IECC blower-door test requirements mandate...?

a. only the 2009 threshold of 7 ach50

b. 5 ach50 for climate zones 1 and 2, and 3 ach50 for homes in all other zones

c. 3 ach50

d. 5 ach50

For more details, see the DOE Building Technologies Program Air Leakage Guide

64. Under 2012 IECC, whole-house mechanical ventilation systems are required...

a. in all homes

b. in climate zones 5-8

c. in climate zones 3-8, and some homes in climate zones 1-2

d. in certain homes taking the prescriptive path

e. they're not required in IECC

The 2012 IECC does not have specific requirements in and of itself for mechanical ventilation; rather, it refers the builder to IRC or IMC approved means. Fan efficacy is laid out by the 2012 IECC, and can be found in Table R403.5.1. Nevertheless, in areas complying with the 2012 IRC, any new home with a blower-door test result of less than 5.0 ach50 must include a whole-house ventilation system (2012 IRC M1507.3). Since the 2012 IECC prescribes air leakage of 3 or less ach50, excluding climate zones 1 and 2, if effectively mandates whole-house ventilation.

## ADMINISTRATION NO ANSWERS GIVEN-FILL THESE IN

65. This chapter "Administration" is largely concerned with maintaining "due process of law" in enforcing the building performance criteria contained in the body of the code.

True

False

66. The purpose of this code is to establish the minimum requirements to safe guard the public health, safety and general welfare through structural strength, means of egress facilities, stability, sanitation, adequate light and ventilation, energy conservation, and safety to life and property from fire and other hazards attributed to the built environment and to provide safety to fire fighters and emergency responders during emergency operations.

True

False

67. The provisions of the Florida Building Code,________ shall apply to the installation, alteration, repair and replacement of plumbing systems, including equipment, appliances, fixtures, fittings and appurtenances, and where connected to a water or sew age system and all aspects of a medical gas system.

Plumbing

Mechanical

Fuel Gas

68. FACBC is abbreviated as ______________________________.

Florida Access Code for Building Construction

Florida Accessibility Code for Building Construction

69. FFPC is abbreviated as ______________________________.

Florida Fuel Prevention Code

Florida Fire Prevention Code

70. (Section 102.7) ______________of an existing manufactured building does not constitute an alteration.

Allocation

Relocation

71. (Section 105.1.2) The work performed in accordance with an annual permit must be inspected by the________, so it is necessary to know the location of such work and when it was performed.

Resident of Florida

Resident of Texas

Building official

72. Section 104 talks about _______________________.

Permits

Construction documents

Duties and powers of the building official

73. The construction documents shall be pre pared by a design professional as required by the statutes.

True

False

74. Shop drawings for the fire protection system(s) should be submitted to indicate conformance with this code and the construction documents and should be approved prior to the start of system installation.

True

False

75. The examination of the documents by the building official may not include the following minimum criteria and documents: a floor plan; site plan; foundation plan; floor/roof framing; and all exterior elevations.

True

False

76. ____________________ refers to the ability of the temporary structure to resist anticipated live, environmental and dead loads.

Structural strength

Concrete strength

77. The building official is authorized to issue a permit for temporary structures and temporary uses. Such permits are limited to time of service, but shall not be permitted for more than _________days.

90

120

180

78. A permit will not be issued until fees authorized under Section 553.80, Florida Statutes, have been paid. Nor shall an amendment to a permit be released until the additional fee, if any, due to an increase in the estimated cost of the building, structure, electrical, plumbing, and mechanical or gas systems has been paid.

True

False

79. The _____________function is one of the most important aspects of building department operations. This section authorizes the building official to inspect the work for which a permit has been issued and re quires that the work to be inspected remain accessible to the building official until inspected and approved.

Inspection

Section utilities

80. Sheathing inspection is to be done either as a part of dry-in inspection or done separately at the request of the contractor after all roof and wall sheathing and fasteners are complete.

True

False

81. Threshold building" means any building which is greater than _____________in height, or which has an assembly occupancy classification as de fined in the Florida Building Code.

Three stories or 40 feet

Three stories or 50 feet

Three stories or 60 feet

82. Upon receipt of a violation notice from the building official, all construction activities identified in the notice must immediately cease, except as expressly permitted to correct the violation.

True

False

83. Section 114 talks about ________________.

Unsafe Structures and Equipment Reserved.

Stop Work Order

84. The building official is authorized to, in writing, suspend or revoke a certificate of occupancy or completion issued under the provisions of this code wherever the certificate is issued in error, or on the basis of incorrect information supplied, or where it is determined that the building or structure or portion thereof is in violation of any ordinance or regulation or any of the provisions of this code.(Section110)

True

False

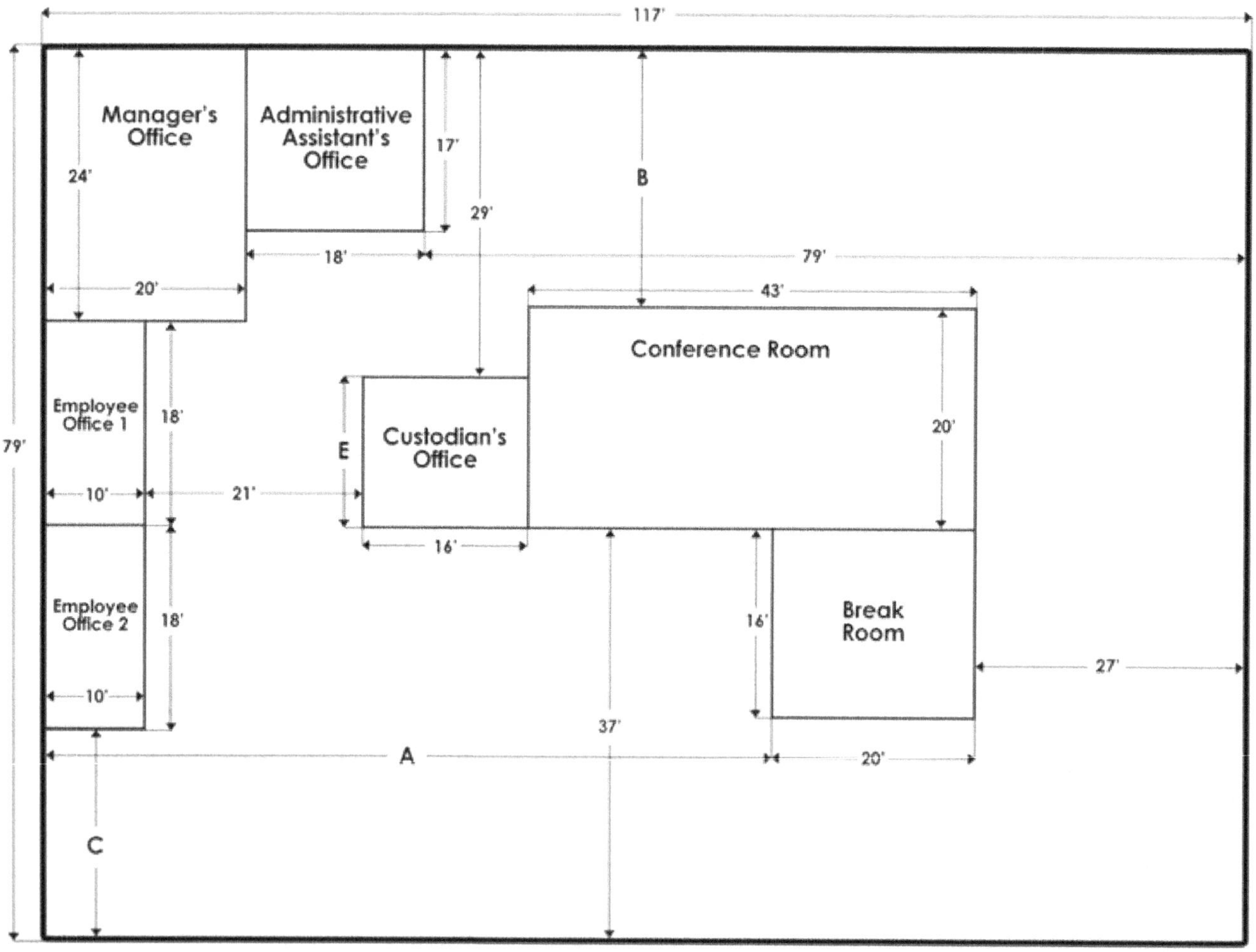


*Graphic Arithmetic*

85. What is the distance ("A") from the left edge of the property to the break room?

a. 47′

b. 67′

c. 70′

d. 19′

e. N

To find the unknown distance ("A"), subtract the known widths from the total width of the property. The total width of the property is 117′. The other known widths are 20′ and 27′. To find A, subtract 20′ and 27′ from 117′. A + 20′ + 27′ = 117′. A = 117′ - 20′ - 27′ = 70′.

86. What is the distance ("B") from the top edge of the property to the conference room?

a. 57′

b. 22′

c. 27′

d. 59′

e. N

To find the unknown length ("B"), subtract the known lengths from the total length of the property. The total length of the property is 79′. The known lengths are 37′ and 20′. To find B, subtract 37′ and 20′ from 79′. B + 20′ + 37′ = 79′. B = 79′ - 20′ - 37′ = 22′.

87. What is the distance ("C") from the bottom of the property to the employee office?

a. 19′

b. 60′

c. 10′

d. 18′

e. N

To find the unknown length ("C"), subtract the known lengths from the total length of the property. The total length of the property is 79′. The known lengths are 18′, 18′, and 24′. To find C, subtract 18′, 18′, and 24′ from 79′. C + 18′ + 18′ + 24′ = 79′. C = 79′ - 18′ - 18′ - 24′ = 19′.

88. What is the area of the manager's office?

a. 44 ft2

b. 480 ft2

c. 360 ft2

d. 576 ft2

e. N

To find the area of the manager's office, multiply the length of the office by the width of the office. The length of the office is 24′. The width of the office is 20′. Area of the manager's office = 24′ - 20′ = 480 ft2.

89. Provided a modification to a fire protection system is small, no approval is needed by the building or fire official

True

False

90. Every automatic sprinkler system must be monitored except

a. One and two family dwellings

b. Systems with fewer than 6 sprinkler heads

c. Jurisdictions that do not require Central Station Service as outlined in NFPA 72

d. Both A & B

e. All of the Above

f. None of the above, they always have to be monitored

91. A system designed to alert individuals of the potential threat from hazardous materials is referred to as a

a. Fire alarm system

b. Threat level assessment system

c. Emergency alarm system

d. Class D system

92. A Supervising Station is

a. A Central Station as defined in NFPA 72

b. A Remote Station as defined in NFPA 72

c. A facility that receives signals and at which personnel are in attendance at all times to respond to these signals

d. A constantly attended station with trained personnel available to respond immediately to the emergency

93. Which of the following is not a mandatory requirement to be included on shop drawings?

a. Battery Calculations

b. The name of the Authority Having Jurisdiction

c. Floor plans

d. Detailed information from manufacturer's data sheets identifying the equipment being installed

94. Because fire alarm designs are dictated by code, they do not have to comply with the guidelines for accessibility.

True

False

95. Because of new types of construction and the advent of zoning and zoned reporting, there is no longer a need for any of the fire alarm equipment to be red in color.

True

False

96. When a building is fully sprinklered with an approved supervised sprinkler system, there is no requirement for a smoke detector to be installed above the control equipment.

True

False

97. Protective Covers installed on alarm boxes must always be provided with a local annunciator to indicate when the cover has been tampered with or dislodged.

True

False

98. Fire alarm systems required by Chapter 9, or by the Florida Fire Prevention Code must be monitored by an approved Central Station in accordance with NFPA 72

True

False

# BUSINESS & FINANCE QUICK GUIDE

## ESTABLISHING THE CONTRACTING BUSINESS — CONTENT AREA A 11%

### *Determining the Business Organizational Structure*

Business structure laws and regulations

Fiduciary responsibilities of officers and directors

Open vs. closed corporations

Organizational charts and chain of responsibilities

State and local licensure requirements

Tax advantages and/or liabilities for various business structures

### *Develop the Business Plan*

Core Skill- Knowledge of accounting practices

Local marketplace

Scope of contractor license

### *Establish Relationships with Other Professionals*

Accountant specialization

Attorney specialization

Insurance types and limitations

Underwriting requirements for bonding

### *Acquire Fixed Assets*

Advantages/disadvantages of business location

Advantages/disadvantages of lease vs. purchase

### *Obtain Insurance*

Core Skill- Knowledge of accounting practices

Advantages/disadvantages of various types of insurance

Coverages and limitations of insurance

## MANAGING ADMINISTRATIVE DUTIES — CONTENT AREA B 26%

### *Develop the Business*

Availability of staffing for business operation

Income sources

Markets and market share

### *Determine Outsourced Services*

### *Determine Business Overhead*

FICA

Advertising costs (business cards, dues, printing, etc.)

Communication costs (cell phones, land lines, etc.)

Cost of sales (travel expenses)

Federal unemployment (FUTA)
General liability rates
Lease expenses
Loan financing expenses (interest, etc.)
Medicare rates
Rent costs
State unemployment (SUTA)
Utility costs
Worker's compensation

### *Preparing Bids/Proposals*

Accounting principles
AIA documents
Business projections/goals current status
Company overhead
Contract documents
Contract law
Cost of financing projects
Costs associated with growth
General conditions costs of projects
How to review contracts
How to write offer
Insurances associated with labor rates
Labor productivity
Statute of frauds
Taxes associated with labor rates
Components of valid contract

### *Purchase Materials/Supplies*

Depreciative costs
Fundamentals of Uniform Commercial Code
Inventory system operation (FIFO, etc.)
Invoice approval systems
Negotiating skills
Purchasing systems
Receiving systems
State sales tax laws
Statute of frauds
Vendors in area

### *Prepare Invoices/Draw Requests*

Core Skill- Knowledge of basic math skills

Calculation of percentage of work completed

Contract/subcontract documents

How to prepare invoices/draw requests

Lien laws

### *Develop a Safety Program*

Drug testing regulations

MSDS sheets

OSHA regulations

### *Maintain Insurance*

General terms and definitions used in policies

Insurance policies

Limits of insurance

Various types of insurance

Various types of risk

### *Managing Contracts Knowledge of contract law*

Contract scope

Job completion schedules

Mediation and arbitration processes

Local building code requirements

Tort law

Risk management

## MANAGING TRADE OPERATIONS CONTENT AREA C 10%

### *Schedule Trade Operations*

Critical path method (CPM)

Delivery times

Knowledge of manufacturing times

Knowledge of requests for information (RFI)

Knowledge of sequencing trades

Knowledge of submittals/approval/fabrication process

### *Maintain OSHA/Safety Records*

Knowledge of document/record retainage requirements

Knowledge penalties for non-compliance with OSHA

### *Purchase/Order Materials & Supplies*

Core Skill- Knowledge of accounting skills

Core Skill- Knowledge of basic math skills

Knowledge of job schedules

Knowledge of negotiation skills

Knowledge of organizational skills

Knowledge of plan reading skills

Knowledge of quality control

Knowledge of quantity take-offs

Knowledge of terms and abbreviations on invoices

Knowledge of types of building materials

### *Leasing/Purchasing Equipment*

Knowledge of cost of operation of equipment

Knowledge of depreciation

Knowledge of equipment operation

Knowledge of forecasted use of purchased equipment

Knowledge of interest costs for financing

Knowledge of maintenance

Knowledge of salvage resale values

Knowledge of support equipment required for equipment

Knowledge of tax credits associated with purchases

Knowledge of training needs for equipment

Knowledge of transportation costs for equipment

### *Manage Material/Tool/Equipment Inventory*

Knowledge of equipment maintenance procedures

Knowledge of inventory methods

## 4. CONDUCTING ACCOUNTING FUNCTIONS — CONTENT AREA D 32%

### *Manage Accounts Receivable*

Core Skill- Knowledge of accounting principles

Core Skill- Knowledge of basic math skills

Knowledge of computer skills

Knowledge of lien laws

### *Manage Accounts Payable*

Knowledge of accounting principles

Knowledge of basic math skills

Knowledge of computer skills

Knowledge of how to calculate discounts

Knowledge of lien laws

### *Manage Cash Flow*

Core Skill- Knowledge of accounting

Knowledge of banking

Knowledge of basic math skills

Knowledge of financial ratios

### *File Tax Forms & Returns*

Core Skill- Knowledge of accounting principles

Core Skill- Knowledge of basic math

Knowledge of federal tax laws

Knowledge of property tax laws

Knowledge of record keeping requirements

Knowledge of sales tax laws

Knowledge of state tax laws

### *Track Job Costs*

Core Skill- Knowledge of accounting principles

Core Skill- Knowledge of basic math

### *Calculate Employee Payroll*

Core Skill- Knowledge of accounting

Core Skill- Knowledge of state & federal tax laws

Core Skill- Knowledge of basic math

Knowledge of employment laws

Knowledge of employment/labor laws

Knowledge of hierarchy of garnishments

## 5. MANAGING HUMAN RESOURCES — CONTENT AREA E 6%

### *Hire New Employees*

Knowledge of employment laws

Knowledge of discrimination laws

Knowledge of interviewing skills

Knowledge of required forms for new hires

Knowledge of background checks

### *Develop Human Resource Policies & Procedures*

Knowledge of employment/labor laws

Knowledge of OSHA

Knowledge of chain of custody (drug tests)

Knowledge of insurance regulations

### *Evaluate Employees*

Knowledge of employment/labor laws

# 6. COMPLYING WITH GOVERNMENT REGULATIONS — CONTENT AREA F 15%

### *1. Comply with Federal Laws & Regulations*

Knowledge of FEMA (immigration components)

Knowledge of OSHA

Knowledge of tax laws

Knowledge of National Pollution Discharge Elimination System (NPDES)

Knowledge of environmental laws

### *2. Comply with State Laws& Regulations*

Knowledge of Chapter 455 F.S.(Business & Professional Regulation)

Knowledge of Chapter 713 F.S. (Liens)

Knowledge of 61G4 F.A.C.

Knowledge of Worker's Compensation Laws/DOR Sales/Use Tax

Knowledge of Chapter 489, Part 1 F.S (Construction Contracting)

Knowledge of required continuing education

Knowledge of CEU credit records

Knowledge of license holder responsibilities

## BUSINESS STRUCTURE LAWS AND REGULATIONS

Starting a Business: A Step by Step Plan

Name your business, DBA 'Doing Business As'... starts with a name search.

When starting a new business, there are many important decisions to make and many rules and procedures that must be addressed. While there is no single source for all filing requirements, the following steps have been developed to assist you in starting your business.

### *Step 1*

It is helpful to begin with a business plan. A business plan is a blueprint of every aspect of your business. Sales, Marketing, Advertising, Promotion and Location are just some of the categories to consider when creating a plan. Go to the U.S. Small Business Administration website to find a tutorial on how to create a business plan.

### *Step 2*

Decide a location. If you would like help deciding on a location for your business, real estate professionals and the Chamber of Commerce provides site selection services for businesses.

### *Step 3*

Choose a business structure. Select a business entity type from the following list for a brief overview of the principal types of legal business structures available in Louisiana. Private legal and tax advisors should be consulted before making a determination as to the type of business entity to form.

- Corporation
- Limited Liability Company
- Limited Partnership
- General Partnership
- Limited Liability Partnership
- Sole Proprietorship

See more and descriptions of business entity in the following section 'business plan'.

### *Step 4*

Your next step will be to file your tax and employer identification documents.

### *Step 5*

Most businesses require licenses or permits in order to operate.

**Following info from:** http://www.stateofflorida.com/corporations.aspx

**Here are the steps to forming a new business in Florida**

1. You will need to think up a name for your new company. A good name should be unique, yet tells what kind of business you are doing.
2. Make a choice on what type of company you want to form. Do you want to:
   - File a DBA (fictitious name) to create a sole proprietorship or partnership?
   - Incorporate as a corporation or LLC (Limited Liability Company)?
3. Whatever you choose, you need to register your company with the state, county and obtain a bank account for the company. You are required to do these steps even if you have an online business or an at home business. For example, if you are doing booth sales regularly at a flea market or selling beauty products in an at home party setting you will need to take these steps.

### *Choosing a DBA Start a Business*

1. **Register with the State:** With a DBA/fictitious name you will be able to register the name with the state to conduct business with this name for the entire state. A lot of very small businesses choose this path, or those who are not sure if the company is going to fly and want to start small and work up to incorporating later.
2. **What to Consider:** If you choose the DBA as your filing, then name you choose can be used by another company. So the name is not to you alone in Florida. The other thing to consider is that if you file a DBA, there is no limited liability. What this may mean to you is that if someone sued the company, your personal assets would be available in a lawsuit. If this is not a concern then a DBA would be fine.
3. **Legal Notice and Business License:** Once you have the DBA filed with the state, then you will need to do a Legal Notice in a local newspaper, then obtain a business license with your county. A business license/occupational license or business tax receipt is required by most counties in Florida to have the legal ability to do have a business in that county. Check with your local tax collectors office to see what they require.

### *Choosing to Incorporate a Business*

1. **Select a Name:** If you choose to create a Corporation or LLC in Florida the name you choose must be unique. No other company can have the exact same name, so be creative and unique in the naming of your new business.
2. **How to Incorporate a Business?** The first step to incorporating your business is choosing if you want to have an LLC or a corporation. Your accountant, tax preparer or bookkeeper may the best person to go to help you make this choice. An attorney is also an excellent choice for guidance. The formation of a company is an important decision so having this kind of assistance is very helpful in doing it right the first time.
3. **Articles of Incorporation:** Once you have chosen the type, you would then file the Articles with the Florida Department of State to legally create the entity. You will need a company name, principal address (which must be a physical Florida address) and a mailing address for the company which can be a PO Box if you would like. You will also need the names and addresses of all the owners in the company as the state requires this information. An email address is also necessary to file with the state.
4. **EIN Filing:** Your next step would be obtaining an EIN or Federal Employer Identification Number from the IRS. This is a unique tax ID for your new legal entity and needs to be used with any transactions for the company. Some people choose not to obtain an EIN for the LLC if it is a single member. This means they will have to use their Social Security number instead for all business transactions. All corporations have to obtain and use an EIN.
5. **Business License:** The next step is the business license or occupational license with the county. A business license/occupational license or business tax receipt is required by most counties in Florida to have the legal ability to do have a business in that county. Check with your local tax collectors office to see what they require.

6. **Bank Account:** The last step would be a bank account for the new company. You are required to have a bank for the LLC or corporation. All monies coming in and going out must go through the company bank account.

Once you have all these steps in place, either for a DBA/Fictitious name or if you want in incorporate as an LLC or a corporation then you are ready to begin your business and are legal in the state of Florida. More: http://www.stateofflorida.com/corporations.aspx

## GENERAL REQUIREMENTS FOR "TYPE OF BUSINESS"

| | |
|---|---|
| Corporation: | **Articles of Incorporation**. Send a copy of the articles of incorporation signed by the original organizers. Include all amendments or name changes with the original articles. **Certificate of Good Standing** from the Louisiana Secretary of State |
| | |
| | |
| General Partnership: | **Partnership Agreement**. You must provide a copy of the partnership agreement which includes the names of the partners and the date of |
| | |
| Limited Liability Corporation: (LLC) | **Articles of Organization**. You must provide a copy of the articles or organization which lists the MEMBERS (not managers or managing members) and gives the date of organization. |
| | |
| Limited Liability Partnership: (LLP) | **Partnership Agreement**. You must provide a copy of the partnership agreement which includes the names of the partners and the date of organization. **Certificate of Good Standing** from the Louisiana Secretary of State |
| | |
| Sole Proprietorship: | General documentation |

## FIDUCIARY RESPONSIBILITIES OF OFFICERS AND DIRECTORS

### *Fiduciary duties explained*

Fiduciary duties include;

- confidentiality
- disclosure of facts-in full
- acting truthfully
- acting fairly
- no deceit
- no deception
- explanation in full all real estate concepts in full to a principal (client)
- Informing clients towards making a fully informed rent, lease, purchase, sale, borrow, or lend decision.

Common infractions regarding breach of fiduciary duty are;

**Commingling**- mixing of funds with other accounts-

**False Promise**- Usually involves a lack of performance promised for a future date. Example: Saying ,"Property values will go up by 20 percent in this neighborhood by next year", when in fact they only rise by five percent.

**Misrepresentation**- Usually arise from the failure to disclose a certain fact (usually negative fact) about the construction or existence of a deficiency on a building or property. Can also be a failure to truthfully explain the ability by license category to perform work. Example: A construction licensee claims they are licensed to do plumbing work.

**Secret Profit**- Happens when a company manager receives any profit other than the contracted amount, and hides monies from partners, shareholders, or tax authorities.

### Ethics and Responsibility

Business ethics are complicated. They involve the relationships between investors, employees, enterprises, etc. Unethical situations occur when one party benefits over others, which is common in international business. In large organizations, ethics officers are appointed to create policies and handle conflicts. The policies created should be written and explained orally. There should also be clear procedures for policy violations. Code of ethics govern employee behavior. Professional ethics address interpersonal relationships, and professional conduct addresses professional relationships.

Social responsibility in corporations or corporate social responsibility **(CSR)** considers the impact of an organization on communities, the environment, shareholders, employees, and customers. CSR is voluntary and goes beyond legal compliance. CRS typically works by giving aid or supporting the community in some way.

## OPEN VS. CLOSED CORPORATIONS

### *Closed Corporation:*

A close corporation is a corporation whose ownership interests, i.e.the shares of the corporation, are not available for exchange on any public market. Shares of a close corporation may still be exchanged in private transactions, if such transactions are allowed. While the corporation may thus change hands, there is not much liquidity in the corporation. In close companies, the directors, officers, and majority shareholders are obliged to proceed with complete fairness in any transaction that affects the other shareholders. A privately held company is called a "close" company because its shares are "closely held". In other words, they are held under the total control of the shareholder, without the ease of exchange provided by a public market.

### *Open Corporation:*

An open corporation is a corporation whose ownership shares are available for exchange on a public market. The market on which the shares are traded may be an organized market such as the New York Stock Exchange (NYSE), the American Stock Exchange (AMEX), or the NASDAQ electronic marketplace (which is technically not an exchange, but serves a similar function). Alternatively, the shares might be exchanged in private, so-called "over-the-counter" (OTC) transactions. These transactions involve the shares of companies that are not listed on an exchange, but whose shares are still available for public trading.

## INSURANCE TYPES AND LIMITATIONS

See PowerPoint 1 - 'Insurance and Risk Management' for more info on insurance

### *General*

Insurance is a necessary part of risk management to provide protection in cases of accident or theft.

- **Property Insurance** – protects in cases of damage to business and personal property
- **Builder's Risk Insurance** – protects the supplies of the jobsite and the building if damaged during construction. It does not cover equipment and tools; an equipment floater policy is required for this.
- **CGL** – Commercial general liability protects the business in the event of employee injury and property damage.
- **Business owner policies** – such as professional liability insurance (PLI), protect owners by combining liability and property coverage.
- **Key man insurance** – protects specific individuals.
- **Umbrella insurance** – provides extra coverage beyond auto and general liability.
- **Claims Made** – a policy that covers claim made during the policy period.

- **Occurrence Policy –** the general liability for contractors.

### *State Law*

State law requires contractors have coverage for workers' compensation insurance for any companies with employees. The benefits provided are medical, temporary disability, permanent disability, vocational rehabilitation, job displacement, and death benefits.

Insurance required for Florida General, Residential, and Building contractors

Minimum amounts required for General Liability insurance for General, Residential, and Building contractors are **$300,000 for bodily injury and $50,000 for property damage.**

All contractors are required to carry Worker's Compensation Insurance OR Exemption Certificate.

## UNDERWRITING REQUIREMENTS FOR BONDING

### *Surety Bonds: The Basics*

### *What is a Surety Bond?*

A surety bond ensures contract completion in the event of contractor default. A project owner (called an obligee) seeks a contractor (called a principal) to fulfill a contract. The contractor obtains a surety bond from a surety company. If the contractor defaults, the surety company is obligated to find another contractor to complete the contract or compensate the project owner for the financial loss incurred.

There are four types of surety bonds:

1. **Bid Bond:** Ensures the bidder on a contract will enter into the contract and furnish the required payment and performance bonds if awarded the contract.
2. **Payment Bond:** Ensures suppliers and subcontractors are paid for work performed under the contract.
3. **Performance Bond:** Ensures the contract will be completed in accordance with the terms and conditions of the contract.
4. **Ancillary Bond:** Ensures requirements integral to the contract, but not directly performance related, are performed.

A surety bond is an agreement between three parties. As the business owner, you are called the principal. You are the one responsible for seeking the bond. The person or group you do business with is called the obligee.

In between you and who you are contracting with is the surety bonding company. The company works with the principal to assess its capacity to manage projects or comply with regulations and provides financial reassurance to the obligee. If you fail to complete a project, your company is ultimately responsible for paying the surety company for the amount it pays to the obligee.

### *Steps to obtaining a bond:*

**Step #1: Contact Surety Company**

If you would like to get a surety bond in Florida, you should begin by contacting a surety bond agent. An agent will work with you to do a preliminary examination of your financial and organizational health. The agent can connect you with a company that offers the Florida surety bond that you need.

**Step #2: Work with an Underwriter**

After you've connected with a surety bonding company, you'll work closely with that company to ensure that your financial house is in order.

The underwriter (risk evaluator) for the company will ask for your financial and credit history and will look at other financial elements such as your ability to access credit for the project or manage the project should things go awry.

The underwriter will also work with you to examine your organizational structure, history of project management, and references.

**Step #3: Get Approve for Bond and Pay**

After you're approved for a Florida surety bond, all that's left to do is pay for it and file it with the obligee.

After your bond has been filed, you need to continue to do your due diligence. If you fail to follow the rules and regulations of your industry or you are not following through on a project, a bonding company may not continue to support your bond application.

Surety bonding is different from insurance: If your project does not succeed, you're financially responsible for repaying the surety company for any compensation they provide to your clients.

### *Federal Contracts and the Small Business Association*

### *When do I need a surety bond?*

Any Federal construction contract valued at $150,000 or more requires a surety bond when bidding or as a condition of contract award. Most state and municipal governments as well as private entities have similar requirements. Many service contracts, and occasionally supply contracts, also require surety bonds.

## INSURANCE

### *General*

Depending on the type of operation that is being insured, rates and coverage limits may vary.

- General Liability Insurance
- Product Liability Insurance
- Professional Liability Insurance
- Property Insurance.
- Workman's Compensation Insurance
- Commercial Auto Insurance
- Umbrella Policies

### *For Small Business Owners*

See- The PPT. Risk Management and Insurance

1. **General Liability Insurance:** Every business, even if home-based, needs to have liability insurance. The policy provides both defense and damages if you, your employees or your products or services cause or are alleged to have caused Bodily Injury or Property Damage to a third party.
2. **Property Insurance**: If you own your building or have business personal property, including office equipment, computers, inventory or tools you should consider purchasing a policy that will protect you if you have a fire, vandalism, theft, smoke damage etc. You may also want to consider business interruption/loss of earning insurance as part of the policy to protect your earnings if the business is unable to operate.
3. **Business owner's policy (BOP):** A business owner policy packages all required coverage a business owner would need. Often, BOP's will include business interruption insurance, property insurance, vehicle coverage, liability insurance, and crime insurance . Based on your company's specific needs, you can alter what is included in a BOP. Typically, a business owner will save money by choosing a BOP because the bundle of services often costs less than the total cost of all the individual coverage's.
4. **Commercial Auto Insurance:** Commercial auto insurance protects a company's vehicles. You can protect vehicles that carry employees, products or equipment. With commercial auto insurance you can insure your work cars, SUVs, vans and trucks from damage and collisions. If you do not have company vehicles, but employees drive their own cars on company business you should have non-owned auto liability to protect the company in case the employee does not have insurance or has inadequate coverage. Many times the non-owned can be added to the BOP policy.

5. **Worker's Compensation:** Worker's compensation provides insurance to employees who are injured on the job. This type of insurance provides wage replacement and medical benefits to those who are injured while working. In exchange for these benefits, the employee gives up his rights to sue his employer for the incident. As a business owner, it is very important to have worker's compensation insurance because it protects yourself and your company from legal complications. State laws will vary, but all require you to have workers compensation if you have W2 employees. Penalties for non-compliance can be very stiff.
6. **Professional Liability Insurance:** this type of insurance is also known as **Errors and Omissions Insurance**. The policy provides defense and damages for failure to or improperly rendering professional services. Your general liability policy does not provide this protection, so it is important to understand the difference. Professional liability insurance is applicable for any professional firm including lawyers, accountants, consultants, notaries, real estate agents, insurance agents, hair salons and technology providers to name a few..
7. **Data Breach**: If the business stores sensitive or non-public information about employees or clients on their computers, servers or in paper files they are responsible for protecting that information. If a breach occurs either electronically or from a paper file a Data Breach policy will provide protection against the loss.
8. **Home as the Business's prime location-office, and/or operations:** Many people who work out of their homes assume that their homeowner's insurance will cover them against property and liability losses. But in reality, a typical homeowner's policy is not sufficient to cover business equipment and liability. In fact, many homeowner insurance policies limit the amount paid for the loss of electronic equipment to $2,500, and will not cover the business's liability if a client trips and falls on the property. Additional protection is required, although it may be possible to add a rider to the homeowner's policy for business equipment and liability.
9. Small business owners seeking insurance protection should first identify their company's main areas of exposure to risk. A risk analysis survey or questionnaire, available through many insurance companies and agents, can be a useful tool in this process. Next, the business owner can evaluate the probability of each risk and determine the potential severity of the loss associated with it.
10. Armed with this information, the owner can decide which risks insuring against and the amount of coverage needed. According to the Small Business Administration, the most common types of risks encountered by small businesses involve: property losses; legal liability for property, products, or services; the injury, illness, disability, or death of key employees; and the interruption of business operations and income due to the occurrence of these other losses. Each category of loss can be managed with a corresponding type of insurance.

**PROPERTY** The types of property losses that can befall a small business include theft, physical damage, and loss of use. Losses from theft can result from the criminal activity of outsiders, as in the case of burglary, or from the illegal activities of employees, including fraud, embezzlement, and forgery.

Physical damage can occur due to fire, severe weather, accidents, or vandalism. In analyzing the risk of physical property damage, it is important for the small business owner to consider the potential for damage to the contents of a building as well as to the structure itself.

For example, a manufacturing company might lose expensive raw materials in a fire, a retail store might lose valuable inventory in a flood, and any type of business could lose important records to computer vandalism.

Although loss of use of property usually results from another covered event, in some instances it can occur without actual physical damage to the property. For example, an office building may be closed for several days due to a gas leak, or a restaurant may be shut down by a health inspector for unsanitary practices.

In insuring against property losses, experts recommend that small business owners purchase a comprehensive policy that will cover them against all risks, rather than just the ones specifically mentioned in the policy. Comprehensive property insurance policies help small business owners avoid gaps in coverage and the expense of duplicating coverage.

In addition, they usually allow for speedier settlements of claims. Still, additional insurance may be needed to adequately cover a specific calamity that is particularly likely in the business's geographic area—such as a hurricane in Florida or an earthquake in California. Experts also recommend that business owners purchase a policy that covers the full replacement cost of materials and equipment in order to protect them against inflation.

Small businesses may be able to improve their property insurance rates by implementing a variety of safety measures and programs. For example, installing locks, alarm systems, sprinkler systems, and smoke vents may help lower premiums. In addition, some companies can improve their rates by joining a highly protected risk (HPR) classification that is preferred by insurers. The HPR designation is based on stringent property protection programs and involves routine compliance checks.

**LEGAL LIABILITY** A small business's legal liability usually comes in two forms: general liability and product liability. General liability covers business-related injuries to employees, customers, or vendors, on the company premises or off, that occur due to the company's negligence.

Product liability covers problems that occur due to defective merchandise or inadequately performed services. In both the manufacturing and retail sectors, a company is legally responsible for knowing if a product is defective.

This responsibility lasts long after the product leaves the company's control. Indeed, a company that bases its legal defense for a faulty product on the fact that it met safety standards at the time it was sold may still be vulnerable to crippling financial judgments or penalties. Even in the service sector, the service provider may be held liable under certain circumstances—for example, if a repair later causes an injury, or if a poorly prepared tax return leads to an IRS audit.

Whether the determination of the company's liability results from a court decision, a legal statute, or a violation of the terms of a contract, litigation can be time-consuming and expensive. Basic liability insurance is available to protect small businesses against the costs associated with these and other sources of liability.

A comprehensive general liability policy, which is recommended for nearly every sort of business, covers accidents and injuries that may occur on the company's premises, or off the premises when they involve a company employee. Such policies generally cover the medical expenses, attorney fees, and court fees associated with the liability.

These policies do not, however, cover product liability or automobile accidents. A separate policy can cover product liability, though producers of some types of products—such as children's toys or food products—may find it difficult or expensive to obtain coverage.

**KEY PERSON LOSS** Small businesses often depend on a few key people (owners, partners, managers, etc.) to keep operations running smoothly. Even though it is unpleasant to think about the possibility of a key employee becoming disabled or dying, it is important to prepare so that the business may survive and the tax implications may be minimized.

In the case of a partnership, the business is formally dissolved when one partner dies. In the case of a corporation, the death of a major stockholder can throw the business into disarray. In the absence of a specific agreement, the person's estate or heirs may choose to vote the shares or sell them. This uncertainty could undermine the company's management, impair its credit, cause the flight of customers, and damage employee morale.

Small businesses can protect themselves against the loss of a key person in a number of ways. One is to institute a buy-sell agreement, which gives the surviving partner(s) or stockholders the right to purchase the deceased person's portion of the business. Another way a business can protect itself is by purchasing a key person insurance policy.

This type of insurance can provide an ill or disabled person with a source of income, and can facilitate financial arrangements so that the business can continue operations in his or her absence. Partnership insurance basically involves each partner acting as beneficiary of a life insurance policy taken on the other partner.

In this way, the surviving partner is protected against a financial loss when the business ends. Similarly, corporate plans can ensure the continuity of the business under the same management, and possibly fund a repurchase of stock, if a major stockholder dies.

**Health Insurance for Small Business** In recent years, many health insurance providers have begun offering affordable plans for small businesses. In some states, businesses are required to provide health insurance if they employ more than five workers.

The type of coverage a business needs depends upon its work force. For example, a company with a work force consisting primarily of married people with dependent children will need more comprehensive coverage than a company with a mostly unmarried, childless work force.

Many insurance companies offer computer models that enable small businesses to determine the most economical insurance plan for them. Another option that can reduce premiums is pooling insurance with other small businesses through trade associations, chambers of commerce, and other organizations.

The two basic health insurance options are fee for-service arrangements and managed care plans. In a fee-for-service arrangement, employees can go to the hospital or doctor of their choice. The plan reimburses costs at a set rate—for example, the insurance company might pay 80 percent and the company or employee might pay 20 percent—for all services rendered.

This type of plan declined in popularity during the 1990s in favor of managed care plans. These plans, the most common of which are run by Health Maintenance Organizations (HMOs) and Preferred Provider Organizations (PPOs), require participants to use an approved network of doctors and hospitals. They pay the health care providers a predetermined price for each covered service.

The employee may have a deductible and a small co-pay amount. It is important to note that a company that employs more than twenty people and provides group health insurance to its employees is obliged to offer an employee who leaves the company the option to continue that coverage for a certain period of time at his or her own expense under the terms of the Consolidated Omnibus Budget Reconciliation Act (COBRA).

### *Types of Commercial Insurance*

In the U.S. all small businesses that employ workers are required by law to have some insurance coverage, such as workers' compensation, unemployment insurance, and in some states, disability insurance. If your business uses a car or truck, your state may also require you to purchase commercial auto insurance.

However, there are many additional types of insurance beyond this basic minimum. General liability insurance is a broad umbrella policy that covers a business against injuries, accidents and claims of negligence. Product liability insurance covers against financial loss from claims of injurious product defects, while professional liability covers service businesses against claims of negligence, malpractice and errors.

Commercial property insurance covers the loss of your business property from fire, vandalism or severe weather, according to the U.S. Small Business Administration. These policies can be purchased separately or as part of a bundle called a business owner's policy.

**Directors and Officers Insurance:** this type of insurance protects the directors and officers of a company against their actions that affect the profitability or operations of the company. If a director or officer of your company, as a direct result of their actions on the job, finds him or herself in a legal situation, this type of insurance can cover costs or damages lost as a result of a lawsuit.

## WORKERS' COMPENSATION

A special category of liability coverage pertains to workers' compensation. This type of insurance is mandatory in most states and provides medical and disability coverage for all job related injuries to employees, whether they occur on company property or not.

A few states provide workers' compensation through state-run funds, and companies simply pay a mandatory premium per employee, depending on their line of business. Other states allow private insurers to compete for companies' workers' compensation dollars. Another option available to some businesses is self-insurance, in which the company creates a special reserve fund to use in case a workers' compensation claim is filed against it.

In effect, these companies assume the risk themselves rather than transferring it to an insurer. A company's workers' compensation rates depend on its line of business and accident record. The best way to reduce rates is to reduce the risk of employee injuries by improving safety standards.

**COMPANY VEHICLE** Company vehicles must be insured, just like vehicles that are intended for personal use. Automobile insurance is usually handled separately from other property and liability coverage. Experts recommend that business owners be sure to list all employees on the insurance policies for company vehicles. In order to determine needed coverage and obtain the most favorable rates, small businesses can consult an insurance watchdog agency.

**LIFE AND HEALTH** Some experts claim that since the most valuable asset in many businesses is the employees, ensuring employee welfare is a vital form of coverage. Group life and health insurance are common methods companies use to provide for employee welfare. This type of coverage falls under the category of employee benefits, along with disability and retirement income.

Specialized plans are available to provide survivors with income upon an employee's death. Other plans can protect the firm against financial losses due to the death or disability of a key employee. It is important to note, however, that when the company is named as beneficiary of a life insurance policy taken on an employee, the cost is not tax deductible for the business.

**BUSINESS INTERRUPTION** Though property, liability, and other types of insurance can provide businesses with protection against specific risks, most policies do not cover the indirect costs associated with losses. When a small business suffers a loss, as in the case of property damage in a fire, it may be forced to shut down for some time or move to a temporary location.

A typical property damage policy will cover the cost to repair or replace buildings and equipment, but it will not cover the loss of income the business is likely to experience during its downtime. The business thus may be forced to tap cash reserves in order to pay expenses that continue—such as taxes, salaries, loan payments, etc.—even when the company has no income.

In addition, the company may face extra expenses in a crisis, such as employee overtime or rent on a temporary location. Business interruption insurance (also known as business income protection, profit protection, or out-of-business coverage) provides a company with the difference between its normal income and its income during a forced shutdown. The prior year's records or tax returns are usually used to determine the payment amount.

**BUSINESS OPPORTUNITY PLANS** A wide variety of specialized insurance packages that cover a custom combination of risks are available to small businesses. One popular option is a Business Opportunity Plan or BOP, which acts as a starting point for many small businesses that require insurance.

A BOP provides basic property coverage for computers and other office equipment, plus liability protection for work-related accidents. In some cases, a BOP might also include business interruption coverage that will maintain the company's income stream for up to a year if a catastrophe disrupts business.

Many BOPs also offer optional coverage against power failures and mechanical breakdowns, liability for workplace practices (including discrimination, sexual harassment, and compliance with the Americans with Disabilities Act), professional liability, and other risks.

**E-COMMERCEINSURANCE** In recent years, the Internet has emerged as a major business tool for companies large and small. This has led some insurers to introduce policies that protect businesses in the event that their Internet presence is disrupted by hackers or other problems. Hacker attacks, known as "denial of service" among insurance professionals, are a particular cause of concern for companies that rely on Internet sales.

Read more: http://www.referenceforbusiness.com/small/Bo-Co/Business-Insurance.html#ixzz4M2nhnjIi

## DISADVANTAGES OF INSURANCE

### *Expense*

Although business insurance may offer you a hedge against disaster and help you sleep more soundly, it rarely comes cheap. The expense of business insurance is its main disadvantage for small-business owners, who seldom have a lot of cash to devote to "what ifs." You should shop around to get the best possible commercial insurance rates, but be careful to check out an unfamiliar company to be sure it's reputable. You may also choose a policy with a higher deductible to cut your monthly payments, but if you do, prudence demands that you set the deductible amount aside in case you suddenly have to come up with it. You must also weigh the coverage a cheaper policy affords. In some cases, the skimpy coverage may not justify the expense.

### *Advantages*

Some insurance coverage, such as health insurance, is a necessity in a world where one serious illness can cause you to lose your home. If a fire or other disaster strikes, commercial insurance can be the difference between staying in business or going bankrupt. Depending on the policy, it can replace lost income and money, restore damaged or destroyed property, or provide a shield against a lawsuit. Commercial credit risk insurance can also reduce the risk of doing business, because it covers you against customer bankruptcy, refusal of delivery or other non-payment.

## COSTS IN GENERAL

### *Cost Measurement*

Costing has basic approaches:

- **Standard –** comes from the act of dividing the fixed cost by the produced items to find a variable cost, which allows the fixed costs to be disregarded. Direct cost and indirect cost are terms that may be used in place of fixed and variable.
- **Activity based –** (ABC) focuses on activities. The activities are divided among employees' time to equal 100%, which allows you to determine what percentage of payment is spent on each task. A baseline must be established before the ABC may be done.
- **Life-cycle cost –** (LCC) used mainly in engineering projects and is the cost of a product over its lifetime.
- **Throughput accounting –** technically a costing alternative. It requires the following three measures: Throughput (money that the system gains from sold product), Inventory (what is invested in items to be sold), and Operating expenses (funds used to convert to throughput).

**Cost behavior** examines how cost behaves when multiple units are made. This requires understanding the total cost and cost per unit. The total fixed cost does not change, but the total variable cost increases with the higher production. Overhead falls under the total cost heading.

The assumptions necessary for cost behavior requires the following assumptions: 1) the units produced are the same as the units sold; 2) the behavior is linear; 3) it will occur in relevant range, which is the range that is true of cost behavior.

**Fixed costs** are inverse to productions and sales. Fixed costs are either committed or discretionary. Discretionary costs may be altered with increased or limited spending. Committed costs are difficult to change.

**Step costs** are short-term and step up when sale activities rise. **Mixed costs** do not change proportionally, and they include both variable and fixed costs.

Transferring the mixed costs to fixed costs will make it possible to predict future costs. A linear equation is used when the fixed costs and variables are known. A linear equation is:

$$Y = mx + b$$

- Using a subjective judgment to estimate variable and fixed cost is an **account analysis**.
- **Scatter graphs** visually portray the different costs at different level to estimate fixed and variable costs.
- The variable and fixed portions of the mixed cost is estimated using the **high low method,** which tracks the highest and lowest activity.
- **Regression** requires the use spreadsheet software and is used to determine the variable and fixed portions of the mixed cost.
- Extra funds added to the estimate make up the **cost contingency**, which is usually requires the use of statistical analysis. Predetermined guidelines, expert judgment, parametric modeling, and simulation analysis can estimate contingency.

## FICA

http://www.bizfilings.com/toolkit/sbg/tax-info/payroll-taxes/employers-responsibility-fica-payroll-taxes.aspx

Employers' Responsibility for FICA Payroll Taxes

An employer's federal payroll tax responsibilities include withholding from an employee's compensation and paying an employer's contribution for Social Security and Medicare taxes under the Federal Insurance Contributions Act (FICA).

Employers have numerous payroll tax withholding and payment obligations. Of the utmost importance is the proper payment of what are commonly known as FICA taxes. FICA taxes are somewhat unique in that there is required withholding from an employee's wages as well as an employer's portion of the taxes that must be paid.

The Federal Insurance Contributions Act (FICA) is the federal law that requires you to withhold three separate taxes from the wages you pay your employees. FICA is comprised of:

- a 6.2 percent Social Security tax;
- a 1.45 percent Medicare tax (the "regular" Medicare tax); and
- beginning in 2013, a 0.9 percent Medicare surtax when the employee earns over $200,000.

You must withhold these amounts from an employee's wages.

The law also requires you to pay the **employer's portion** of two of these taxes:

- a 6.2 percent Social Security tax; and
- a 1.45 percent Medicare tax (the "regular" Medicare tax).

As you can see, the employer's portion for the Social security tax and the regular Medicare tax is the same amount that you're required to withhold from your employees' wages. (Different rules apply for employees who receive tips.)

- There is no employer portion for the 0.9 percent Medicare surtax on high-earning employees.

In other words, you withhold a 6.2 percent Social Security tax from your employee's wages and you pay an additional 6.2 percent as your employer share of the tax;

(6.2 employee portion + 6.2 employer portion = 12.4 percent total).

Also, you withhold a 1.45 percent Medicare tax from your employee's wages and you pay an additional 1.45 percent as your employer share;

(1.45 employee portion + 1.45 employer portion = 2.9 percent total).

The total of all four portions is 15.3 percent;

(6.2 percent employee portion of Social Security + 6.2 percent employer portion of Social Security + 1.45 percent employee portion of Medicare + 1.45 percent employer portion of Medicare = 15.3 percent).

Unlike the other FICA taxes, the 0.9 percent Medicare surtax is imposed on the **employee portion** only. There is no employer match for the Medicare surtax (also called the Additional Medicare Tax). You withhold this 0.9 percent tax from employee wages and you do not pay an employer's portion. Also, unlike the other FICA taxes, you withhold the 0.9 percent Medicare surtax only to the extent that wages paid to an employee exceed $200,000 in a calendar year. You begin withholding the surtax in the pay period in which you pay wages in excess of this $200,000 "floor" to an employee and you continue to withhold it each pay period until the end of the calendar year.

### *Wage Caps and Floors*

The Social Security tax (also called OASDI) is subject to a dollar limit, which is adjusted annually for inflation. However, there is **no** annual dollar limit for the 1.45 percent Medicare tax. Unlike the other FICA taxes, the 0.9 percent Medicare surtax is not withheld unless wages paid to an employee exceed $200,000.

***Social Security wage cap.*** For 2013, your obligation to withhold and to pay the Social Security tax for an employee ends once you've paid that employee total wages of $113,700. (For 2014, the amount is $117,000.)

***Medicare wages.*** As there is no ceiling on the 1.45 percent portions of the Medicare tax, you must continue to withhold and to pay the Medicare tax regardless of how much you pay an employee.

***Medicare surtax wage floor.*** You withhold the 0.9 percent Medicare surtax only to the extent you pay an employee wages in excess of $200,000 in a calendar year. You do not begin withholding the Medicare surtax until the pay period in which you pay wages in excess of $200,000 to an employee. There is no employer share: you withhold the 0.9 percent surtax from employee wages.

**Example** Trevor, your employee, received $170,000 in wages from you through November 30, 2013. On December 1, 2013, you pay Trevor a $50,000 bonus. Prior to December 1, you were not required to withhold the Medicare tax surcharge. On December 1, you are required to withhold Additional Medicare Tax on $20,000 of the $50,000 bonus. You may not withhold Additional Medicare Tax on the other $30,000. You must also withhold the additional 0.9 percent Medicare tax on any other wages paid to Trevor in December 2013.

### *Calculating the Withholding and Employer's Portion Amounts*

You simply multiply an employee's gross wage payment by the applicable tax rate to determine how much you must withhold and how much you must pay in Social Security and regular Medicare taxes.

The Social Security and regular Medicare taxes owed are unaffected by the number of withholding exemptions an employee may have claimed for income tax withholding purposes.

Calculating the Medicare Surtax Withholding Amount

Unlike the 6.2 percent Social Security tax and the 1.45 percent Medicare tax, the 0.9 percent surcharge is imposed only on the employee. You withhold the surtax from employee wages, but there is never a matching payment required by the employer.

The employer's and employee's obligations with respect to the Medicare surtax are different. In some cases, there may be a "mismatch" between the amounts you are obligated to withhold and the amount of your employee's surtax liability.

From the **employee's** perspective, the 0.9 percent Medicare surtax is imposed on wages, compensation and self-employment earnings above a threshold amount that is based on the employee's filing status. Once the threshold is reached, the tax applies to all wages that are currently subject to Medicare tax, to the Railroad Retirement Tax Act or to the Self-Employment Compensation Act.

The threshold amounts are as follows:

| Filing Status | Threshold Amount |
|---|---|
| Married filing jointly - COMBINED INCOME | $250,000 |
| Married filing separately | $125,000 |
| Single, Head of Household, Qualifying Widow(er) | $200,000 |

From the **employer's** perspective, the obligation to withhold the 0.9 percent Medicare surtax is triggered without regard to whether the employee will, in fact, be liable for the tax. You must begin withholding the Medicare surtax as soon as wages and compensation that you pay to an individual employee exceeds $200,000 in the calendar year. (Any taxable fringe benefits are included in this computation, but nontaxable fringe benefits are not.)

The obligation to withhold applies only to amounts in excess of $200,000. However, once you are obligated to begin withholding the Medicare surtax, you continue to withhold it each pay period until the end of the calendar year.

In making this determination, you do not consider wages paid by other employers or earnings of the individual's spouse. Even if your employee is married and the couple's combined income will not exceed the **employee's $250,000 filing threshold**, you still must withhold the additional tax once the **employer's $200,000 withholding threshold** is reached. Also, the "ignore the spouse's earnings" rule applies even if both spouses work for the same company.

### Tip

If you have tipped employees, provide taxable fringe benefits, operate your business through more than one entity, or any other non-standard compensation arrangements, you should read the IRS Questions and Answers for the Additional Medicare Tax.

***"Mismatch" between employer's withholding obligation and employee's tax liability.*** The fact that your employer withholding is triggered at $200,000 per employee per employer, while your employee's tax liability threshold is based on filing status and combined earnings, can create over- or under-withholding issues.

**Example 1** Richard, your employee, earns $220,000 from you during 2013. He is married, but his wife does not have any earned income. You must start withholding the additional 0.9 percent Medicare tax when Richard's earnings exceed $200,000. Richard will be over-withheld because the couple's combined income is beneath the married, filing jointly threshold of $250,000.

**Example 2** Hannah, your employee, earns $130,000 from you during 2013. Hannah's husband Samuel earns $100,000 from one employer and $60,000 from another employer during 2013. Their combined earnings are $290,000, which is $40,000 over the married, filing jointly threshold. However, none of their employers are required to withhold the 0.9 percent surtax because neither spouse earned over $200,000 from any one employer.

To the extent the employer does not withhold the 0.9 percent Medicare surtax, the employee must pay the tax. Employees who anticipate being under-withheld for the Medicare surtax can make estimated payments or they can request additional income tax withholding on Form W-4. The employee can then apply the additional income tax withheld against Medicare surtax liability on his or her Form 1040, U.S. Individual Income Tax Return.

## FEDERAL UNEMPLOYMENT (FUTA)

https://www.irs.gov/individuals/international-taxpayers/federal-unemployment-tax

### *Federal Unemployment Tax*

The Federal Unemployment Tax Act (FUTA), with state unemployment systems, provides for payments of unemployment compensation to workers who have lost their jobs. Most employers pay both a Federal and a state unemployment tax. A list of state unemployment tax agencies, including addresses and phone numbers, is available in Publication 926, Household Employer's Tax Guide. Only the employer pays FUTA tax; it is not deducted from the employee's wages. For more information, refer to the Instructions for Form 940.

U.S. Citizens and Resident Aliens Employed Abroad - FUTA

Aliens Employed in the U.S. - FUTA

Persons Employed in U.S. Possessions - FUTA

Persons Employed by a Foreign Employer - FUTA

Persons Employed by a Foreign Government or International Organization - FUTA

Tax Withholding on Foreign Persons

### *The following are calculations taken from the 2015 instructions for form 940 and are only excerpts. For the full form see:*

https://www.irs.gov/pub/irs-pdf/i940.pdf

**Who Must File Form 940?**

Except as noted below, if you answer "Yes" to either one of these questions, you must file Form 940.

Did you pay wages of $1,500 or more to employees in any calendar quarter during 2014 or 2015?

Did you have one or more employees for at least some part of a day in any 20 or more different weeks in 2014 or 20 or more different weeks in 2015? Count all full-time, part-time, and temporary employees. However, if your business is a partnership, don't count its partners.

If your business was sold or transferred during the year, each employer who answered "Yes" to at least one question above must file Form 940. However, don't include any wages paid by the predecessor employer on your Form 940 unless you are a successor employer. For details, see *Successor employer* under *Type of Return*.

If you aren't liable for FUTA tax for 2015 because you made no payments to employees in 2015, check box *c* in the top right corner of the form. Then go to Part 7, sign the form, and file it with the IRS.

If you won't be liable for filing Form 940 in the future because your business has closed or because you stopped paying wages, check box *d* in the top right corner of the form. See *Final: Business closed or stopped paying wages* under *Type of Return* for more information.

When Must You File Form 940?

The due date for filing Form 940 for 2015 is February 1, 2016.

However, if you deposited all your FUTA tax when it was due,

you may file Form 940 by February 10, 2016.

**When Must You File Form 940?** The due date for filing Form 940 for 2015 is February 1, 2016. However, if you deposited all your FUTA tax when it was due, you may file Form 940 by February 10, 2016.

If we receive your return after the due date, we will treat your return as filed on time if the envelope containing your return is properly addressed, contains sufficient postage, and is postmarked by the U.S. Postal Service on or before the due date or sent by an IRS-designated private delivery service on or before the due date. However, if you don't follow these guidelines, we will consider your return filed when it is actually received. For a list of IRS-designated private delivery services, see Pub. 15.

**When Must You Deposit Your FUTA Tax?** Although Form 940 covers a calendar year, you may have to deposit your FUTA tax before you file your return. If your FUTA tax is more than $500 for the calendar year, you must deposit at least one quarterly payment.

You must determine when to deposit your tax based on the amount of your quarterly tax liability. If your FUTA tax is $500 or less in a quarter, carry it over to the next quarter. Continue carrying your tax liability over until your cumulative tax is more than $500. At that point, you must deposit your tax for the quarter. Deposit your FUTA tax by the last day of the month after the end of the quarter. If your tax for the next quarter is $500 or less, you aren't required to deposit your tax again until the cumulative amount is more than $500.

**Fourth quarter liabilities.** If your FUTA tax for the fourth quarter (plus any undeposited amounts from earlier quarters) is more than $500, deposit the entire amount by February 1, 2016. If it is $500 or less, you can either deposit the amount or pay it with your Form 940 by February 1, 2016.

**In years when there are credit reduction states, you must include liabilities owed for credit reduction with your fourth quarter deposit.**

## When To Deposit Your FUTA Tax

| If your undeposited FUTA tax is more than $500 on . . .* | Deposit your tax by . . . |
|---|---|
| March 31 | April 30 |
| June 30 | July 31 |
| September 30 | October 31 |
| December 31 | January 31 |

*Also, see the instructions for line 16.

**TIP** *If any deposit due date falls on a Saturday, Sunday, or legal holiday, you may deposit on the next business day. See* Timeliness of federal tax deposits, *later.*

# How Do You Figure Your FUTA Tax Liability for Each Quarter?

You owe FUTA tax on the first $7,000 you pay to each employee during the calendar year after subtracting any payments exempt from FUTA tax. The FUTA tax is 6.0% (.060) for 2015. Most employers receive a maximum credit of up to 5.4% (.054) against this FUTA tax. Every quarter, you must figure how much of the first $7,000 of each employee's annual wages you paid during that quarter.

## Figure Your Tax Liability

Before you can figure the amount to deposit, figure your FUTA tax liability for the quarter. To figure your tax liability, add the first $7,000 of each employee's annual wages you paid during the quarter for FUTA wages paid and multiply that amount by .006.

The tax rates are based on your receiving the maximum credit against FUTA taxes. You are entitled to the maximum credit if you paid all state unemployment tax by the due date of your Form 940 or if you weren't required to pay state unemployment tax during the calendar year due to your state experience rate.

***Example.*** During the first quarter, you had three employees: Employees A, B, and C. You paid $11,000 to Employee A, $2,000 to Employee B, and $4,000 to Employee C. None of the payments made were exempt from FUTA tax.

To figure your liability for the first quarter, add the first $7,000 of each employee's wages subject to FUTA tax:

| | |
|---|---|
| $7,000 | Employee A's wages subject to FUTA tax |
| 2,000 | Employee B's wages subject to FUTA tax |
| + 4,000 | Employee C's wages subject to FUTA tax |
| $13,000 | Total wages subject to FUTA tax for the first quarter |

| | |
|---|---|
| $13,000 | Total wages subject to FUTA tax for the first quarter |
| x .006 | Tax rate (based on maximum credit of 5.4%) |
| $78 | Your liability for the first quarter |

In this example, you don't have to make a deposit because your liability is $500 or less for the first quarter. However, you must carry this liability over to the second quarter.

If any wages subject to FUTA tax aren't subject to state unemployment tax, you may be liable for FUTA tax at the maximum rate of 6.0%. For instance, in certain states, wages paid to corporate officers, certain payments of sick pay by unions, and certain fringe benefits are excluded from state unemployment tax.

***Example.*** Employee A and Employee B are corporate officers whose wages are excluded from state unemployment tax in your state. Employee C's wages aren't excluded from state unemployment tax. During the first quarter, you paid $11,000 to Employee A, $2,000 to Employee B, and $4,000 to Employee C.

| | |
|---|---|
| $ 9,000 | Total FUTA wages for Employees A and B in first quarter |
| x .060 | Tax rate |
| $540 | Your liability for the first quarter for Employees A and B |

| | |
|---|---|
| $4,000 | Total FUTA wages subject to state unemployment tax |
| x .006 | Tax rate (based on maximum credit of 5.4%) |
| $24 | Your liability for the first quarter for Employee C |

| | |
|---|---|
| $540 | Your liability for the first quarter for Employees A and B |
| + 24 | Your liability for first quarter for Employee C |
| $564 | Your liability for the first quarter for Employees A, B, and C |

In this example, you must deposit $564 by April 30 because your liability for the first quarter is more than $500.

## JOB COMPLETION SCHEDULES

See Job completion schedules in Guide to Accounting

| Task Name | Start | End | Duration (days) |
|---|---|---|---|
| Start date | 9/21/2014 | 9/30/2014 | 9 |
| Demo Prep | 10/1/2014 | 10/6/2014 | 5 |
| Demolition | 10/6/2014 | 10/24/2014 | 18 |
| Excavation | 10/25/2014 | 10/29/2014 | 4 |
| Concrete | 11/1/2014 | 11/13/2014 | 12 |
| Pre backfill | 11/13/2014 | 11/15/2014 | 2 |
| Framing | 10/25/2014 | 12/5/2014 | 41 |
| Roof | 11/19/2014 | 12/10/2014 | 21 |
| Plumbing | 10/29/2014 | 12/9/2014 | 41 |
| Windows | 11/22/2014 | 12/15/2014 | 23 |
| HVAC | 11/29/2014 | 12/20/2014 | 21 |
| Electrical | 12/10/2014 | 12/22/2014 | 12 |
| A/V | 12/10/2014 | 12/15/2014 | 5 |
| House wrap | 12/27/2014 | 12/30/2014 | 3 |
| Insulation | 12/3/2014 | 12/21/2014 | 18 |
| Drywall | 1/3/2015 | 1/23/2015 | 20 |
| Exterior stone | 1/3/2015 | 1/17/2015 | 14 |
| Exterior case work | 1/4/2015 | 1/13/2015 | 9 |
| Laundry/furnace room flooring | 2/16/2015 | 3/11/2015 | 23 |
| Hardwoods | 1/19/2015 | 3/10/2015 | 50 |
| Tile | 2/3/2015 | 2/14/2015 | 11 |

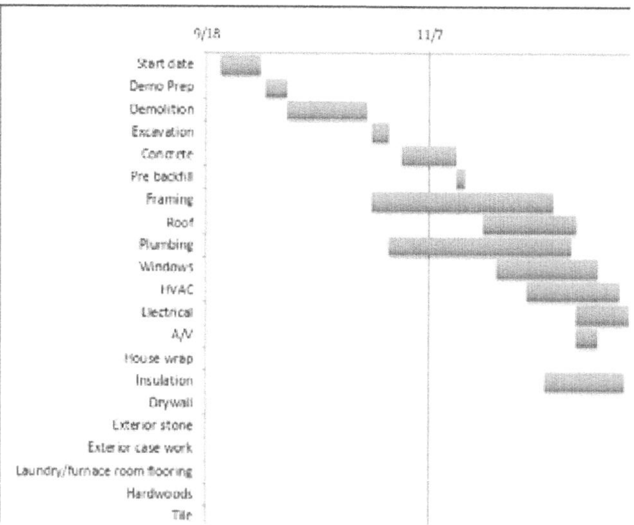


The draw schedule is a detailed payment plan for a construction project. If a bank is financing the project, the draw schedule determines when the bank will disburse funds to you and the contractor.

The goal is to make progress payments to the contractor as work is completed. You don't want to pay for materials that have not been delivered or work that is not complete. It's not your job to provide working capital for the contractor. (If you are an owner-builder, the draw schedule will determine when the bank releases money to you to pay for materials and subcontractors.)

Draw schedules are typically proposed by the contractor and may be further negotiated between the contractor, the bank, and yourself. If a bank is involved, they may want to use their own standardized draw schedule. But in any case, the bank's appraiser will make sure the draw schedule is reasonable based on his Knowledge of construction costs. If you are paying cash, you will need to do your own independent estimate (or hire an estimator or appraiser to review the draw schedule), or trust that the contractor's proposed payment schedule it is reasonable.

The number of payments in the draw schedule will depend on the size of the project and the preferences of the builder or bank. A draw schedule of five to seven payments is common for a new house.

Most draw schedules link payments with milestones in the project, such as completion of the foundation and completion of the rough framing. Sometimes, the draws are more generally based on the percent complete of the total job. In either case, the payment should be roughly equal to the value of the work completed. These line-item values have been determined by the owner or builder in their detailed estimate, and are summarized in budget breakdown called a *schedule of values*. This cost breakdown will also become your project budget. If you are working with a lender, contact them first to see if they have a specific format to follow.

## SCHEDULE OF VALUES

To avoid conflicts over payment, it's important that the draw schedule closely reflect the actual value of work completed. The schedule of values can be highly detailed or pretty basic, depending on the type and size of project and the financing arrangements. In either case, a good draw schedule is based on an accurate, detailed estimate, and the resulting schedule of values:

See FLA XTRA 2 9 JOB COMP SCHED New Home Schedule of Values.

Sample Schedule of Values for a 2000 sq. ft. Custom Home

| | **Cost** | % of total |
|---|---|---|
| Plans and specs | $2,000 | 1 |
| Permits, fees, inspections | 4,000 | 2 |
| Impact fee | 3,000 | 1.5 |
| Clear lot, rough grade | 1,500 | 1 |
| Survey | 1,000 | 0.5 |
| Water hookup and fees | 3000 | 1.5 |
| Sewer hookup and fees | 3000 | 1.5 |
| Well, pump, hookup, and water treatment | NA | |
| Septic system and hookup | NA | |
| Excavation and backfill | 4,000 | 2 |
| Foundation and flatwork | 12,000 | 6 |
| Rough Framing | 31,000 | 15 |
| Windows | 6,000 | 3 |
| Exterior doors and hardware | 2,000 | 1 |
| Roofing | 5,000 | 2.5 |
| Siding and ext. trim | 10,000 | 5 |
| Gutters and downspouts | 1,000 | 0.5 |
| Plumbing rough-in | 9,000 | 4.5 |
| Electrical rough-in | 8,000 | 4 |
| HVAC | 8,000 | 4 |
| Insulation | 3,000 | 1.5 |
| Drywall | 10,000 | 5 |
| Stairs | 3,000 | 1.5 |
| Interior trim | 7,000 | 3.5 |
| Interior doors | 2,000 | 1 |

| | | |
|---|---|---|
| Painting interior/exterior | 7,000 | 3.5 |
| Cabinets and countertops | 12,000 | 6 |
| Appliances | NA | |
| Lighting Fixtures | 2,000 | 1 |
| Plumbing Fixtures | 4,000 | 2 |
| Floor coverings: wood, tile, carpet, vinyl | 12,000 | 6 |
| Garage doors and opener | 2,000 | 1 |
| Porch, wood deck, or patio | 5,500 | 3 |
| Driveway and walkways | 6,000 | 3 |
| Landscaping | 6,000 | 3 |
| Other | 5,000 | 2.5 |
| TOTAL CONSTRUCTION COST | $200,000 | |

- Note: Add $30,000 to $40,000 (15% to 20%) for contractor's overhead and profit, plus an additional $6,000 (3%) for construction financing, and an additional 5% for sales and marketing, if purchased from a developer.

The sample above is based on a typical, small custom home. The numbers, of course, will vary enormously, depending on a wide variety of factors, including the size and quality of the home, the materials selected, and the location. But the numbers in this sample are typical for an average new home, and will give you a sense of where the money goes, and where you may be able to cut if your house comes in over budget and you need to make cuts.

If the estimate was done by you, the owner, the numbers will represent your actual cost for materials and labor. If your contractor does the estimate, these numbers will be as much as 20% to 25% higher, accounting for the contractor's overhead and profit.

### *THE PAYMENT SCHEDULE*

Banks distribute money for a project in several payments as the work progresses. While procedures vary a bit from lender to lender, all follow the general principal that the bank does not want to pay for work that has not been completed. (Nor should you if you are funding the project with your own cash!)

A typical draw schedule for a new home has five to seven payments, but some may disburse money as frequently as once a week. Most draw schedules link payments to the "substantial completion" of a phase of work such as the foundation or rough framing. Some correspond more generally to the percent of completion of the entire project, a more difficult number to track, leaving greater room for disagreement. A bank draw schedule is generally more complex than a cash job. Compare the draw schedule in Fannie Mae's model Construction Loan Agreement to the samples below from owner-financed projects.

Sample Draw Schedule: Small Remodeling Project
(owner-financed)

| | Work Completed | Amount |
|---|---|---|
| Draw 1 | Demolition | 3,000 |
| Draw 2 | Framing, wiring and plumbing rough-in, insulation. | $6,000 |
| Draw 3 | Drywall, windows, cabinets. | 6,000 |
| Draw 4 | Patch exterior, painting, flooring, fixtures, cleanup. | 5,000 |

Sample Draw Schedule: Custom Home or Addition(owner financed)

| | Work Completed | Amount |
|---|---|---|
| Draw 1 Foundation | Plans and specifications, permits, excavation, footings, foundation. | $37,500 (15%) |
| Draw 2 Rough Framing | Wall and roof framed and sheathed. Subflooring, interior partitions. | $37,500 (15%) |

| | | |
|---|---|---|
| Draw 3 Dry In | Asphalt shingle roofing, wood siding, windows, exterior doors. | $37,500 (15%) |
| Draw 4 Rough In | Rough HVAC, electrical, plumbing. Set tubs and shower. Insulation. Flatwork. | $30,000 (12%) |
| Draw 5 Trim Out | Drywall, interior doors, cabinets, countertops, interior trim, finish flooring. | $50,000 (20%) |
| Draw **Substantial Completion** | Exterior trim, gutters, water and sewer hookups, finish plumbing and electric, carpeting, garage doors. | $45,000 (18%) |
| Draw 7 Retainage | Substantial Completion | $12,500 (5%) |

**Payment for work completed.** The contractor, naturally, is in a rush to get paid for work completed and would like to be a little ahead to have some working capital. You and the bank, on the other hand, only want to pay for materials delivered and work completed. It's not your job, or the bank's, to provide the contractor with working capital. However, some jobs do require more money than normal upfront, for example, to for costly special-order items such as SIPs (structural insulated panels).

Simply put, the contractor is afraid of not getting paid for work completed or materials he has purchased and the owner (and bank) is afraid of paying ahead of time for work that may never be done or done incorrectly.

A good draw schedule strikes a reasonable balance between the builder's need to get paid on time and the owner's and bank's need to pay only for work completed. The key is to have a payment plan that based on an accurate budget, fair to all parties, and easy to follow. In that case, there should be few problems with payments.

**Front-loading.** Some builders like to front-load the payment schedule to improve their cash flow and to act as a buffer in case, for any reason, the owner withholds the final check. They may ask for a large down payment, or simply fatten the early draws to stay ahead of their expenses. Another ploy is to link payments to the beginning, not the completion, of a phase of work. This is risky for you since many things can be started without any being completed.

For example, if $20,000 is due at the start of Rough-In, it doesn't mean that the siding has been installed even though it was paid for in the previous draw. This benefits the contractor, but can leave the owner far ahead on payments. Banks will not approved this type of payment schedule and neither should you if you are paying cash.

## *DISBURSING THE FUNDS*

The most common approach is to make payments contingent on substantial completion of key phases of construction, such as the foundation or rough frame. Banks send an inspector to approve each payment and charge an inspection fee of $50 to $100. If no bank is involved, you (or your construction manager) will want to stop by to confirm that the reported progress is being made.

"Substantial completion" means that the payment request if valid even if a few 2x4s are missing from an otherwise complete frame. The contractor should not request a payment before it is due, and you should not nitpick a few loose ends. An exception is the final check, which should not be released until everything is complete and correct.

**Title companies**. Some bankers use a title company to conduct the inspections and disperse funds. This adds more fees and delays payments, so discuss the pros and cons of this procedure with your lender, as you may be able to opt out of using a title company and handle the disbursements yourself.

**Lien wavers.** Assuming the inspection passes, the proper documentation is supplied, and the general contractor signs a lien waver, the funds will be wired to the builder's account, minus the 5% to 10% held back for retainage. The bank may require other lien wavers, for example, from key subcontractors, or the largest supplier, before the last check is released. Even without a lender involved, you will want to get lien wavers from the general contractor and main suppliers, at least before cutting the final check.

**Change orders.** It is in the best interests of all parties to keep the work on schedule, pass all inspections, and avoid changes to the plan. Some banks will not pay for change orders, which can be a good thing as it motivates the builder to make sure nothing essential is left out of his bid. If the owners decide to add a $3,000 jetted tub or to upgrade from carpet to hardwood floors, they will have to come up with the cash out of pocket.

**Final payment**. Generally, progress payments are made directly from the lender to the contractor, while the final check is made jointly payable to the owner and contractor after all work is complete and certificate of occupancy (CO) has been issued. The joint check, requiring both endorsements to cash, gives you, the owner, some leverage to get the contractor to take care of any punch list items, or other loose ends before handing over the final check.

**Conflicts over payment.** While most projects with a reputable builder proceed pretty smoothly, occasionally bad things happen. A contractor can skip town or go bankrupt, a sub can show up drunk or not at all, an innovative building system may not work out as planned, or the new super-duper paint specified for the project peeled off the new wood siding for some reason.

## MEDIATION AND ARBITRATION PROCESSES

http://buildingadvisor.com/project-management/finance/draw-schedules/

**Mediation** Mediation is an informal and non-binding process oriented toward working out an agreeable compromise. Things said in the session are confidential and cannot be used against you in court. It's best to work with a mediator with experience in residential construction. A contract can call for mediation first, and specify that if that fails, the dispute goes to binding arbitration or civil court. While mediation often fails to reach its goal, it may be worth a try as it is quick and inexpensive, compared to the alternatives.

**Binding arbitration vs. litigation** Arbitration is the method of dispute resolution specified in most residential construction contracts. In general, this is faster and less expensive than civil litigation. However, it can still take several months and cost thousands of dollars in legal fees. A lawsuit, by contrast, will usually drag on for one to two years or more and cost tens of thousands of dollars. Most people are represented by a lawyer in an arbitration hearing. The decision of the arbitrator is binding and the right to appeal is very limited. Often arbitrators have expertise in construction and they are more likely to split the difference than a judge and jury. It's important that the contract clause regarding arbitration be consistent with state law. Some arbitration clauses specify that the proceedings will be administered by the American Arbitration Association, a good source of information on the process. An arbitration clause may state that:

Any claim or dispute arising out of or relating to this contract, or breach thereof, shall be decided by binding arbitration in accordance with state law, and judgement on the award rendered by the arbitrator(s) may be entered into any court having jurisdiction thereof.

**Small claims court** Each state has its own procedures and dollar limits for small claims court – ranging from $2,500 to $15,000 in a couple of states. For many states, the maximum amount of damages ranges from $5,000 to $10,000. In general, the parties represent themselves in small claims court in a fairly informal hearing. They may get a little coaching from a lawyer in how best to prepare for the hearing, but paying a lawyer to represent you would not be worth it for the amount of money involved. Also the proceedings are informal, making it very feasible to represent yourself. In most states, you can appeal a judgement in small claims court under certain conditions within 30 days of the original hearing.

**Collecting the money** Even if you win a case in arbitration or court, you still have to collect the money. If the other party does not pay up, you may need to have your lawyer pursue collection actions such as garnishing wages or a bank account. What if the contractor has declared bankruptcy by then, or started a new company under another name, or moved to another state or just wants to be difficult? Yet more reasons to try to resolve things peacefully.

**Bottom line** Arbitration or litigation should always be your last resort. As is often said, the only people who really benefit from most lawsuits are the lawyers. Most experts recommend arbitration over civil litigation in residential construction disputes. Either way, your contract should contain a disputes clause describing how disputes should be handled if all else fails.

# MAINTAIN OSHA/SAFETY RECORDS

*Document/record retainage requirements*

| | |
|---|---|
| • Part Number: | 1904 |
| • Part Title: | Recording and Reporting Occupational Injuries and Illness |
| • Subpart: | D |
| • Subpart Title: | Other OSHA injury and Illness Recordkeeping Requirements |
| • Standard Number: | 1904.33 |
| • Title: | Retention and updating. |
| | |
| • GPO Source: | e-CFR |

1904.33(a)

***Basic requirement.*** You must save the OSHA 300 Log, the privacy case list (if one exists), the annual summary, and the OSHA 301 Incident Report forms for five (5) years following the end of the calendar year that these records cover.

1904.33(b)

***Implementation.***

1904.33(b)(1)

***Do I have to update the OSHA 300 Log during the five-year storage period?*** Yes, during the storage period, you must update your stored OSHA 300 Logs to include newly discovered recordable injuries or illnesses and to show any changes that have occurred in the classification of previously recorded injuries and illnesses. If the description or outcome of a case changes, you must remove or line out the original entry and enter the new information.

1904.33(b)(2)

***Do I have to update the annual summary?*** No, you are not required to update the annual summary, but you may do so if you wish.

1904.33(b)(3)

***Do I have to update the OSHA 301 Incident Reports?*** No, you are not required to update the OSHA 301 Incident Reports, but you may do so if you wish.

[66 FR 6131, Jan. 19, 2001]

https://www.shrm.org/resourcesandtools/hr-topics/risk-management/pages/osha-document-retention-requirements.aspx

Employers can also be unsure of how long to retain certain documents required under OSHA. Some OSHA regulations require a specific retention period for documents. Other OSHA regulations, however, do not (although it is often advisable to retain certain documents even if retention is not technically required).

**Categories of Documents** The following list sets out the typical OSHA standards and the General Duty Clause that may require an employer to create, retain and produce certain documents during the course of an inspection, if requested by the OSHA compliance officer. Obviously, whether the employer is required to have certain of these programs or others will be dependent upon the nature of the work activities at the site. This list is focused on the standards that are applicable to employers in general industry and not construction, although some general industry standards are substantially similar and also applicable to the construction industry. There are many hazards that are common to each industry but the regulatory obligations frequently differ. For those employers in the construction industries, it will be necessary to reference the existing regulations addressing hazards in that industry when responding to an OSHA document request.

During the inspection, the employer should request the compliance officer to make the document request in writing (it can be handwritten) so that there is no confusion over what documents are being requested and so that the employer is not cited for failure to produce a document it did not believe was requested by the compliance officer. The employer's onsite representative should review this request with management and decide which documents will be produced to the compliance officer. It is important to remember that the employer has no duty to produce certain documents (e.g., post-accident investigations, insurance audits, consultant reports, employee personnel information) because no regulation requires such production. It is important to note that any documents produced can be utilized to issue citations, thus, the employer should not produce any documents unless required by law.

**Control of Hazardous Energy – Lockout/Tagout (LOTO)** The regulation requires the employer to develop procedures to protect employees who service or maintain its machines against unexpected energization or startup of equipment or release of stored energy. The employer must train its "authorized" employees how to perform LOTO with these procedures, as well as "affected" employees who may be exposed to the equipment. The rule requires the onsite employer and outside employer to inform each other of their respective lockout or tagout procedures.

**Document retention:** The LOTO standard requires employers to certify that periodic inspections have been performed at least annually. Accordingly, employers should retain certifications for one year, or until a new certification is created. It is also advisable that employers retain employee LOTO training records for the duration of employment.

**Occupational Noise Exposure** The standard requires the employer to provide a hearing conservation program (education, annual audiograms, hearing protection) for employees who are exposed to noise levels equal to or exceeding an 8-hour time-weighted average of 85 decibels on the A scale. The employer must conduct a noise survey to determine those jobs which may require employees to be included in the program. Employees who suffer hearing loss at certain frequencies must be included on the OSHA 300 Log. The employer must develop a written program and administer it.

**Document retention:** Employers must retain noise exposure measurement records for two years. Employers must also retain audiometric test records for the duration of the affected employee's employment.

**Personal Protective Equipment (PPE)** The employer must conduct an initial certified hazard assessment of the workplace to determine if hazards are present which require personal protective equipment for eyes, face, head and extremities to protect against injury. The employer must provide each employee with the necessary PPE, train the employee in the use of PPE and enforce its use. The employer must pay for the PPE with limited exceptions.

A second certification is required to confirm that the PPE was provided, the employee received training in how to utilize it and that the employee "understood" the training.

**Document retention:** Employers should retain the written certifications of a hazard assessment and employee training for the duration of employment for all employees exposed to identified hazards. It is also advisable for employers to retain employee PPE training records for the duration of employment.

**Hazard Communication (Employee Right to Know)** The regulation requires the employer to develop a written hazard communication program to protect employees against any hazardous chemical which presents a physical or health hazard. The employer is required to conduct an assessment to determine which hazardous chemicals may be present, to inform employees of the presence of the hazardous chemicals, and train employees on how to read a safety data sheet (SDS) for each hazardous chemical.

Employees are entitled to access to the SDSs and to obtain copies.

**Document retention:** Employers must retain SDSs for the duration of employment plus 30 years for all employees exposed to the chemical in question, unless there is some other record of the identity of the substance or chemical, where it was used and when it was used. The employer must also be sure it has a copy of all SDSs for all chemicals that are currently in use. It is also advisable for employers to retain employee hazard communication training records for the duration of employment.

**Process Safety Management (PSM)** This standard requires employers who utilize certain toxic, reactive, flammable or explosive chemicals in certain quantities, to develop a written fourteen (14) part PSM program. The PSM program addresses all aspects of work around the covered "process" that utilizes the chemicals.

The regulations requires training of contractor employees who perform certain work around the covered process concerning the hazards and elements of the PSM program.

**Document retention:** Employers must retain process hazard analyses (PHAs) for the life of the covered process. In addition, the employer must prepare a written record that each employee who is involved in the operation of the process was trained and understood the training. These verification records should be retained for the length of the employee's employment. We recommend that employers also retain all process safety information (PSI) used for developing, maintaining, auditing, and otherwise managing all processes for the life of the processes. Any incident investigations conducted under the PSM standard must be retained for five years. Additionally, employers must retain the two most recent compliance audit reports conducted under the PSM standard.

**Emergency Action Plans (EAPs)** The rule requires the employer to develop an emergency action plan to protect employees against the hazards of fires or other emergencies. The EAP must include provisions for reporting a fire or other emergency, evacuation procedures and the alarm system. The employer must train each employee.

**Document retention:** There are no specific document retention requirements, aside from the requirement that employers develop and maintain a written EAP. If the employer has ten or fewer employees, the plan does not have to be in writing.

**Fire Extinguishers** Employers required to provide fire extinguishers must mount, locate and identify them so that they are readily accessible to employees.

If employees are expected to use the fire extinguishers, the employer must provide training upon initial employment and at least annually thereafter. The employer must develop an educational program if it expects the employees to use the fire extinguishers. Many employers specifically prohibit employees from using the fire extinguishers to avoid this training obligation. If the employer permits the employees to use the fire extinguishers, the educational program and training should be in writing and maintained for the length of employment.

**Permit-Required Confined Spaces** Employers are required to identify all confined spaces within the workplace that employees or outside contractors may be required to enter and contain a hazardous atmosphere, engulfment hazard, an internal configuration that could trap or asphyxiate an entrant or other serious safety or health hazard. The employer must develop a written program and procedures for employees who enter the confined spaces. Only trained and authorized employees can enter the space.

The standard requires the host-employer to provide certain information to other contractors who will have their employees enter the space.

**Document retention:** Employers must retain each canceled entry permit for at least one year and review them within one year after each entry. It is also advisable to retain employee confined space training records for the duration of employment.

**Bloodborne Pathogens** This regulation requires an employer to develop a written program to protect employees at the workplace who are reasonably expected to have occupational exposure to bloodborne pathogens, i.e., bloodborne diseases. The employer is required to assess all jobs to determine if there is such exposure and if so, to train employees in the hazards, provide PPE and to develop procedures for medical evaluation and treatment if an employee has actual exposure.

**Document retention:** Employers must retain employee exposure records for the duration of employment plus 30 years. Training records must be retained for three years from the date on which the training occurred, although it is advisable to retain training records for the duration of employment.

**Respiratory Protection** The standard requires the employer to conduct an assessment of the workplace to determine if there are harmful dusts, fumes, mists, sprays or vapors which may create a respiratory health hazard. If there are such hazards, the employer is required to develop a written respiratory protection program, to evaluate employees to determine if they are physically capable of wearing a respirator, to provide such respiratory protection at the employer's cost, and train employees how to wear and maintain respiratory protection. The employer must enforce use of the respiratory protection.

**Document retention:** Employers must retain records of employee medical evaluations for the duration of employment plus 30 years. Employers must also retain fit-test records for respirator users until the next fit test is administered.

**Electrical Safety (Safety-Related Work Practices)** The rules require an employer who will permit its employees to perform work on or in the vicinity of exposed energized parts (which cannot be locked out and tagged out) to provide extensive training in the hazards of working or in the vicinity of live electrical equipment, protective clothing and insulated tools and devices. The employer must designate employees as "authorized" in order to perform such work or "unqualified" in which case such employees cannot perform such work. The employer may be required to conduct an electrical exposure hazard survey of electrical equipment under NFPA 70E in order to determine what PPE should be used, what training is necessary, and to otherwise be in compliance with OSHA safety requirements.

**Document retention:** OSHA's electrical safety standards do not have any specific record retention requirements, however it is advisable to retain employee training records under these standards for the duration of employment. If an employer conducts an electrical exposure hazard survey, the employer should retain it for as long as the hazard exists.

**Access to Employee Exposure and Medical Records** Employers are required to inform employees of their right to have access to all records maintained by the employer that reflect an employee's exposure to any toxic substance or harmful physical agent (e.g., chemicals, dusts, vapors, noise, mold, etc.) or any medical records which the employer maintains on an employee, except for certain exceptions. Employees are entitled to have access and to obtain a copy at the employer's expense.

**Document retention:** Employers must retain employee exposure records for the duration of employment plus 30 years. If the employer maintains certain employee medical records, the employer must retain them for the duration of employment plus 30 years.

**Powered Industrial Trucks** The regulation requires an employer to develop a written program to train all employees who will be required and authorized to operate powered industrial trucks (including forklifts, manlifts, etc.) as to the hazards of such equipment and to certify their training after they receive classroom-type training and are actually observed operating the equipment under the physical conditions at the workplace, such as aisles, ramps, etc. The employee must be retrained and recertified every three years, at minimum, or after an accident or "near miss" which resulted from an unsafe act.

**Document retention:** The powered industrial truck standard does not specify how long training certifications must be retained after the initial certification or the certification required every three years or after a near miss. It is advisable that employers retain the training certifications for the duration of employment for each employee.

**OSHA 300 Log of Work-Related Fatalities, Injuries and Illnesses** The OSHA 300 Log must be maintained by employers unless there is an exemption, based on the NAICS code or the size of the employer. The employer is required to record on the log, within seven calendar days, each fatality, injury or illness that is recordable under OSHA definitions. The host employer is required to enter into its log the injuries or illnesses of outside employees at the worksite under certain conditions, for example, temporary employees who are under the direction and control of the host employer.

The OSHA 300 Log must be maintained and certified by the employer on an annual basis. For each entry on the log, there must be an OSHA 301 Incident Report form, or its equivalent, which can be the employer's First Report of Injury or Illness form required by the state worker's compensation law. An annual summary must be prepared and posted using the 300A annual summary form or an equivalent. In order to comply with OSHA's recordkeeping requirements, it is critical that employees are trained from their initial employment that they must immediately report any occupational injury or illness to determine if it is recordable.

**Document retention:** The OSHA 300 Log, the annual summary, and the OSHA Incident Report forms must be retained by employers for five years following the end of the calendar year that these records cover. The OSHA 300 Log must be maintained on an "establishment basis" based on NAICS codes. It is possible that employers may have some "establishments" where a log must be maintained, and others where maintaining a log is not necessary.

**General Duty Clause** Section 5(a)(1) of the Occupational Safety and Health Act requires an employer to identify "recognized hazards likely to cause serious injury or death" to an employee, which hazards may not be regulated by a specific OSHA regulation, and to take "feasible" actions to abate or correct such hazards. This duty can be based upon the "recognition" of the hazard in the employer's own, existing programs, or within the employer's industry. Some examples of this legal obligation may cover ergonomics, heat illness, workplace violence and combustible dust.

**Document retention:** While there are no specific standards for "recognized hazards" covered under the General Duty Clause, and thus no specific record retention requirements, it is advisable for employers to retain any training records it has developed addressing any "recognized hazards" for the duration of employment, including the written policy, training records and documents that evidence discipline for violation of the policy. Remember that certain documents related to General Duty Clause obligations may also fall under exposure/medical recordkeeping requirements.

**Disciplinary Records** There is no regulation that requires an employer to maintain written records of employee discipline for violations of the employer's safety and health policies. If, however, the employer wants to credibly assert the "unavoidable employee misconduct" defense to avoid liability for OSHA citations, the employer is highly recommended to maintain written records of discipline indicating the nature of the violation, the date, the name of the employee who committed the violation and the name of the supervisor who imposed the discipline.

This same documentation can be useful in the event that the employer has to defend an employment discrimination or wrongful termination action by being able to prove that the action was based on a legitimate nondiscriminatory reason such as violation of safety and health policies.

**Conclusion** In addition to the summary of OSHA-related documents discussed above, there are numerous other OSHA regulations that may have document retention requirements. If an employer is subject to any of these regulations, the regulations must be reviewed and appropriate document retention procedures must be developed.

Remember that it is critical that an employer control the flow of information during the inspection, including the information contained in documents. By avoiding production of documentary evidence that is not required by law, the employer reduces the potential for regulatory citations. It is also critical that employers understand what documents they are required to create and retain. Even when an OSHA standard does not specify how long certain records must be retained, it is advisable to consider retaining such records for a significant length of time. For example, many OSHA standards require employee training, but do not necessarily require documentation of training or retention of training documents. Nonetheless, it is advisable to prepare and retain training documents for the duration of employment because training documents are often indispensable in asserting certain defenses to citations.

## TERMS AND ABBREVIATIONS ON INVOICES

Here's the meaning behind common invoice, bill and contract acronyms:

**Ad Valorem** – a term from Latin means "according to value"; usually refers to a tax, duty, or charge based on the cargo's value.

**Ad Valorem Duty** – Duty and taxes which are calculated on the basis of value.

**Agency** - The right given by an individual, body or firm to another person or company to act on its behalf. Agency appointments are normally given for a stated period of time or indefinitely by means of a written contract or letter of intent.

**Air Waybill –** The forwarding agreement or carrying agreement between shipper and air carrier and is issued only in nonnegotiable form.

**Bill of Lading (B/L)** – A document that establishes the terms of a contract between a shipper and a transport company. It serves as a document of title, a contract of carriage and a receipt for goods.

**Bill of Sight** – A form of provisional entry for goods which the importer is not possession of full information

**Bond** – A binding agreement that is presented to Customs by an importer, guaranteeing the performance or nonperformance of a specified act

**Bonded Warehouse** – A warehouse authorized by Customs authorities for storage of goods on which payment of duties is deferred until the goods are removed

**Broker** - An intermediary who negotiates terms for charters, insurance, sales and purchase of ships and/or generation of cargo. Not normally the owner of a ship or of the cargo being negotiated.

**Canalization** - the principle of the Customs Departments control of imported and exported goods, where all goods and persons entering or leaving a country must do so through a Customs controlled channel.

**Cargo** - General meaning of merchandise transported on a ship.

**Cargo Declaration** – See Manifest

**Carnet** – An international Customs document which may be used, in lieu of national Customs documents and as security for import duties and taxes, to cover the temporary admission of goods (for display, demonstration or similar purposes) and, where appropriate, the transit of goods.

**Certificate of Origin** – An international business document that certifies the country from which a consignment of goods originates.

**C/O stands for Care/Of.** C/O can be used on invoices, bills, and contract terms. It alludes to who needs to be addressed in the document. For example, if an invoice is for a company, you can put C/O to have it sent to a specific person like the head of the accounting department.

**CFO stands for Cancel Former Order.** To CFO is to cancel out an order that was previously placed and/or billed for.

**COD stands for Cash on Delivery.** COD is a billing term that requires payment when an item is delivered.

**CR stands for Credit.** A credit in billing terms can refer to the decreasing an expense account or increasing a capital, liability, or revenue account. A credit in invoicing terms can be the same or it can refer to an agreement where goods and services are exchanged against a promise to pay.

**DFI stands for Discount for Invoice.** A DFI is a way for businesses to draw loans from outstanding invoices. They do not have to relinquish administrative control of the invoices but will make payments with interest and fees to an invoice discounting company.

**DR stands for Debit.** A DR stands for money owed. It's a billing term that is used often.

**ETA stands for Estimated Time of Arrival.** ETA is a term that is often used in contracts to state when a project is due.

**Free Alongside (FAS)** – The seller must deliver the goods to a pier and place them within reach of the ship's loading equipment. See Terms of Sale

**Free on Board (FOB)** – The term used when the buyer of the goods being shipped assumes ownership, responsibility, and financial risk when the cargo is on board the ship

**Free Zone** – An area considered as being outside the territorial boundaries and the goods brought therein are not considered as imports and do not face import duties

**Freight Forwarder** – A carrier that collects small shipments from shippers, consolidates the small shipments and uses a basic mode to transport these consolidated shipments to a destination where the freight forwarder delivers the shipment to the consignee

**Full Container Load (F.C.L.) –** The maximum permissible weight for the value of the cargo carried in a container.

**Gift Allowance** – This is the dutiable value or specified quantities of personal items such as new clothing, footwear, and articles for personal hygiene and grooming that travelers are permitted to bring into the country in their accompanied baggage or to buy them at an inwards duty free shop, free from duties and taxes; does not include commercial items.

**Gross Weight** – Entire weight of goods, packaging and freight car or container, ready for shipment

**Home** – Local or domestic; as opposite of foreign (as used in Warehousing below)

**Importer** – The party who makes (or on whose behalf an agent or broker makes) an import declaration, and who is liable for the payment of liable duties on the imported goods; also known as consignee in the shipping documents and/or as the buyer in the exporter's invoice

**Indicator** – Any abnormality or inconsistency in information or physical appearance which could create a reasonable suspicion in the mind of a Customs Officer.

**Inter alia –** among other things

*In Bond*

FOC stands for Free of Charge. FOC on an invoice, bill or contract refers to something not requiring payment. It's known as a freebie.

I/O stands for Invoice/Order. An I/O is something that businesses and ICs use to request payment and to keep track of products sold and services rendered.

IC stands for Independent Contractor. An IC is a person that is hired by a company not as a paid employee but as someone who performs a service for them for a specific amount of time.

NDA stands for Non-Disclosure Agreement. A NDA is typically used in contracts with IC, vendors, and other businesses. It prevents sensitive information from being shared with others. It's essentially how businesses keep their operations secretive.

**Net Weight** – Weight of the goods alone without any immediate wrappings

**Over Carried Goods** – cargo not landed that was manifested to do so and was on board the aircraft or vessel when it was last in port in the Federation

**Over Landed Goods** – cargo landed in excess of the quantity that which has been invoiced, valued or declared

**Origin of Goods** – the "economic" nationality of goods in international trade. It is necessary to determine the origin of goods as any duties and/or equivalent charges or any customs restrictions or obligations applicable to them will depend on their origin.

**Packing List** – Itemized list of commodities with marks/numbers but no cost values indicated.

**POP stands for Point of Purchase.** POP is a place where sales are made. It is referred to in many contracts.

**Pro Forma Invoice** – A provisional invoice provided by a supplier prior to the shipment of merchandise, informing the buyer of the supplier's commitment to supply the kinds and quantities of goods to be sent, their value, and specifications (weight, size, etc.)

**Prohibited Goods** – Any goods, the import or export of which is subject to any ban under the Customs Act or any other law for the time being in force

**Racking** – The process of packing performed in a warehouse, under Customs supervision, by which packages may be repacked into smaller or larger packages

**Reefer Container** – Refrigerated container

**Refund of Duty** –Amounts found to be overpaid as duties that may be refunded by Customs to the relevant party within one year on application made by the importer, done on a "G Form"

**Registered Baggage** – this is baggage which, once registered in the departure airport, is neither accessible to the traveller during the flight nor at the stopover if there is one. This luggage is carried in the baggage hold of the plane

**Repacking** – The process by which an importer can change the contents of packages under the supervision of Customs by making full packages out of packages that are not full.

**Restricted Goods** – any goods the import or export of which is subject to any controls or regulations under the Customs Act or any other law for the time being in force

TAX stands for Tax and Expenditures. Tax is tacked onto bills and invoices. You'll see it on both. It's based on a percentage rate.

## SALVAGE RESALE VALUES

**Salvage value** is the estimated **resale value** of an asset at the end of its useful life. **Salvage value** is subtracted from the cost of a fixed asset to determine the amount of the asset cost that will be depreciated. Thus, **salvage value** is used as a component of the depreciation calculation.

Salvage value is the estimated resale value of an asset at the end of its useful life. Salvage value is subtracted from the cost of a fixed asset to determine the amount of the asset cost that will be depreciated. Thus, salvage value is used as a component of the depreciation calculation.

For example, ABC Company buys an asset for $100,000, and estimates that its salvage value will be $10,000 in five years, when it plans to dispose of the asset. This means that ABC will depreciate $90,000 of the asset cost over five years, leaving $10,000 of the cost remaining at the end of that time. ABC expects to then sell the asset for $10,000, which will eliminate the asset from ABC's accounting records.

If it is too difficult to determine a salvage value, or if the salvage value is expected to be minimal, then it is not necessary to include a salvage value in depreciation calculations. Instead, simply depreciate the entire cost of the fixed asset over its useful life. Any proceeds from the eventual disposition of the asset would then be recorded as a gain.

The salvage value concept can be used in a fraudulent manner to estimate a high salvage value for certain assets, which results in the under-reporting of depreciation and therefore of higher profits than would normally be the case.

Salvage value is not discounted to its present value.

### *Similar Terms*

Salvage value is also known as *residual value.*

## ACCOUNTING

A construction project requires a basic understanding of accounting principles.

### *Terms to Remember:*

- **Source documents –** are documents that are related to a project such as receipts, invoices, time cards, etc.
- **Financial statements – i**ncludes cash flow statement, balance sheet, and income statement.
- **Asset –** any money or items owned by the business
- **Balance sheet –** includes the equity, assets, and liabilities.
- **Fixed asset –** tangible assets such as land and buildings.
- **Current asset –** cash or assets that can become cash within a year.
- **Liability –** all obligations and/or debts.
- **Current liability –** debts that need to be paid within a year.
- **Long term liability –** debt that needs to be paid after a year.
- **Income statement –** called the profit and loss statement (PNL) shows expenses and revenues.
- **Cash basis accounting –** that cash and payments are not accounted until they are received and paid.
- A**ccrual accounting –** must be used in business over $5 million. The money is counted when orders are made, deliveries occur, or services occur.

## FORMULAS:

**Equity:** assets – liability

**Net working capital:** current assets – current liability

**Net income:** revenue – expenses

**Debt ratio:** liabilities/assets

**Annual depreciation:** depreciation amount / years of depreciation

**Depreciation amount:** cost – value of salvage

**Gross profit:** income - cost of goods

**Liquidity ratio:** current assets/current liability

**Cost-volume profit:** sales revenue – variable costs – fixed costs = profit

## ACCOUNTING PRINCIPLES

### *Accounting*

A construction project requires a basic understanding of accounting principles.

### *Terms to Remember:*

- **Source documents –** are documents that are related to a project such as receipts, invoices, time cards, etc.
- **Financial statements –** includes cash flow statement, balance sheet, and income statement.

- **Asset** – any money or items owned by the business
- **Balance sheet** – includes the equity, assets, and liabilities.
- **Fixed asset** – tangible assets such as land and buildings.
- **Current asset** – cash or assets that can become cash within a year.
- **Liability** – all obligations and/or debts.
- **Current liability** – debts that need to be paid within a year.
- **Long term liability** – debt that needs to be paid after a year.
- **Income statement** – called the profit and loss statement (PNL) shows expenses and revenues.
- **Cash basis accounting** – that cash and payments are not accounted until they are received and paid.
- **Accrual accounting** – must be used in business over $5 million. The money is counted when orders are made, deliveries occur, or services occur.

*Formulas:*

**Equity** = assets – liability

**Net working capital** = current assets – current liability

**Net income** = revenue – expenses

**Debt Ratio** = liabilities/assets

**Annual depreciation** = depreciation amount / years of depreciation

**Depreciation amount** = cost – value of salvage

**Gross profit** = income - cost of goods

**Liquidity ratio** = current assets/current liability

## PRINCIPALS, STANDARDS, AND ACCOUNTING PRACTICES

The International Financial Reporting Standards (IFRS) was adopted by the International Accounting Standards Board in 1989. They are principle based standards that used to be called the International Accounting Standards (IAS). The International Accounting Standards Board (IASB) is based in London but has 9 members of the board for other nations that create global accounting standards.

Accounting in the United States focuses on standards based accounting. The generally accepted accounting principals (GAAP) outlines the principals and concerns are involved in accounting preparation. Principals involved in the GAAP are:

- **Accrual** – funds are recorded when earned and expenses when incurred.
- **Historical cost** – outlays that are needed to buy an acquisition along with the assets, principle, natural resources, and intangibles based on the acquisition cost.
- **Consistency** – the same method of preparation is used in different periods, and changes must be explained in notations.
- **Prudence**
- **Materiality**
- **Matching**
- **Going concern concept** – this assumes that the company will continue to move forward.
- **Conservative principle** – requires that the assets not be overstated and the liabilities nit be understated.
- **Separate legal entity** – requires personal and business accounts to remain separate from personal accounts.

The Securities and Exchange Commission (SEC) oversees the Financial Accounting Standards Board (FASB), which establishes accounting standards called the Statements of Financial Accounting Standards (SFAS).

Foreign registrants that do not use GAAP statements must reconcile the information using Form 2 from the SEC.

Trial balances are schedules in which one column is lists debits and the other credits. **Credit balance**s include liabilities, equity, and revenue. **Debit balances** include assets and expenses. They may be prepared before entries are adjusted and after they are adjusted. Typically, the transactions in a single period are collected and placed in the general ledger.

Adjusted trial balance – acts as an internal document; it is the list of titles and balances that remain the ledger once the entries have been adjusted.

Post-closing trial – the balance that is left after the temporary accounts are closed. The closing entries for the accounts are prepared so that the balance is zero.

Adjusting entries are completed before the financial statements are prepared, but closing entries are done the last day of the period and are completed after the financial statements.

The accounting equation shows how the equity, liabilities, and assets interact;

Assets = Liabilities + Equity of the Owner

## BOOKKEEPING

Bookkeeping may be single entry or double entry. **Single entry** is usually used in sole proprietorships. This method defines each transaction as either an expense or deposit. **Double entry** creates a debit and credit entry for each transaction, and each property class would have its own account. Debits (dr) increase assets and credits (cr) decrease them. Any imbalance between debits and credits indicate an error was made.

- A debit balance means that the debit total is greater than the credit total.
- A credit balance means that the debit total is greater than the credit total.
- When using journals, the debit accounts would be listed first.

Journals and ledgers are not the same. Journals are used to record each transaction fully. The general journal is the most common. The entries are representative of different transaction, but a transaction is only recorded one time and they comply with the guidelines of debit and credit.

Ledgers have all of the business accounts that are divided into separate sections. Transactions in journals are transferred to the ledger, and each account is numbered:

- Assets – 100
- Liability – 200
- Net assets – 300
- Revenues – 400
- Expenses – 500

The left side of the ledger's pages contains the transaction title, date, posting reference, and debit. The right side contains the transaction title, date, posting reference, and credit.

Regardless of the account used, bank reconciliation is necessary. The statement is compared to the records to find errors. Book reconciliation is done with credit memos, debit memos, and errors. Book reconciling, on the other hand, is done with outstanding checks, errors, and deposits in transit.

It is necessary to retain source documents for auditors and tax purposes. These include invoices, timesheets, payments, etc.

*Terms to Remember:*

- **Overdraft** – removal of funds creates a negative balance, and it is subject to fees and interest.
- **Loans** – may be structured or unstructured.
- **Secured loan** – the borrower provides collateral
- **Unsecured loan** – the borrower does not provide collateral in secured assets.

## PAYMENTS RECEIVED AND SENT

Payment requests are typically submitted each month. The first step to requesting payment is discovering the schedule of values, which finds and allocates values to different aspects of the project. The schedule is a list with specific amounts.

Construction agreements for payment used by third-tier subcontracts and suppliers are joint check agreements and are typically made between a general contractor, subcontractor, and supplier. The general contractor, who may pay third parties, typically issues the checks.

*Terms to remember:*

- **Retention/retainage** – a portion of the payment to contractors/subcontractors that held back to ensure completion. This is outlined in the contract and is typically 5% throughout the project. It may also be 10% until the project is half finished.
- **Back-charge** – amount of money deducted from subcontractor's payment to cover costs that the subcontract should have paid.
- **Unconditional lien release** – issued when all payments are received and the lien rights are given up.
- **Conditional lien release** – a release that is conditional upon payment and given with a payment request.
- **Cost codes** – will vary by state and structure, and they allow the costs and estimates to be compared.

When the project manager requests money or time that the owner disagrees with, a contract claim is implemented due to a breach of contract. A breach of contract is resolved in one of the following ways:

- **Mediation** – a method of resolving a dispute that uses a neutral third party in settlements.
- **Litigation** – a legal action or lawsuit that is long and costly.
- **Arbitration** – uses a neutral third party to decide the case rather than pursuing litigation.

Arbitration in the construction industry is governed by the American Arbitrations' Construction. When claims are under $50,000, they are fast tracked and heard within 60 days. Any dispute involving a claim that is $1,000,000 or more will require a complex arbitration process.

## RECORDKEEPING

Important-Employee training records require written certification that is signed and dated by the employee. The employer is responsible for maintaining the records.

Keep all records of employment taxes for at least 4 years. These should be available for IRS review. Your records should include the following information.

- Your EIN.
- Amounts and dates of all wage, annuity, and pension payments.
- Amounts of tips reported to you by your employees.
- Records of allocated tips.

- The fair market value of in-kind wages paid.
- Names, addresses, social security numbers, and occupations of employees and recipients.
- Any employee copies of Forms W-2 and W-2c returned to you as undeliverable.
- Dates of employment for each employee.
- Periods for which employees and recipients were paid while absent due to sickness or injury and the amount and weekly rate of payments you or third party payors made to them.
- Copies of employees' and recipients' income tax withholding allowance certificates (Forms W-4, W-4P, W-4(SP), W-4S, and W-4V).
- Dates and amounts of tax deposits you made and acknowledgment numbers for deposits made by EFTPS.
- Copies of returns filed and confirmation numbers.
- Records of fringe benefits and expense reimbursements provided to your employees, including substantiation.

## EMPLOYMENT/LABOR LAWS

### *Labor Laws*

**Policies** The commitment of management requires the organization to have policies, procedures, disciplinary actions, and procedures at an organizational level. These and other communications must be easy to understand. The rules should be posted in writing, and training should be offered to employees and supervisors.

Employers are required to follow the stricter standards for employees, and state laws are often stricter than federal laws. Agreements between employees and employers may not violate these rules. Some employees are exempt from the following protections:

overtime premiums, minimum wage, reporting time pay, record requirements, equipment and uniforms, meal periods, meals and lodging, and rest periods.

A daily log or daily report is used to track the day's events, but is should never include personal comments. The daily job diary includes information about all of the work done that day and is managed by the Superintendent. It must be written in ink and dated before it is stored in a hard covered binder.

### *Screening/Interviews*

Interview questions should not allude to illegal topics: age, sex, race, disability, etc. The policies and procedures can be outlined in an employee handbook, which includes:

- Equal opportunity statement
- At will employment statement
- Harassment policies
- Taking leaves
- Technology and communication policies

**Labor Laws** The **American with Disabilities Act (ADA)** makes it illegal to use tests that screen disabilities unless the test is job related such as carrying a specific weight. The Age Discrimination Employment Act (ADEA) make it illegal to deny employment or discriminate because of age.

Employees need to be reported to the state directory once they are hired. The company must follow the Fair Labor Standards Act and other labor laws. For example, each violation of the child labor laws is $11,000. Violations of the FLSA are $10,000. The FLSA ensures that employees receive the minimum wage $7.25 and an overtime rate of 1 ½ past 40 hours a week. A workweek is 168 hours. The FSLA does not require vacation days, but it does require employers to record the day and hour when the workweek begins. The time that a non-exempt employee leaves does not need to be recorded, but the exempt employee does need to be recorded.

**FSLA** The FLSA does not apply to business that have under $500,000 unless they are hospitals, medical institutions, schools for the gifted or disabled, preschools, higher education, elementary education, secondary education, government agencies (federal, local, and state).

Other FSLA stipulations include the youth wage, which is the $4.25 for employees under the age of 20. The rate lasts the first 90 days, and it is illegal to displace other employees for youths. When tips are considered wages, a base pay of $2.13 per hour is necessary. Rates per piece are allowed when the amount equals the minimum wage. Additionally, the FSLA must be visibly posted in English, and employment records need to be kept.

When hiring specialty contractors, the project managers must evaluate them using criteria that are standardized. In most projects, the subcontractors will be responsible for 75% to 85% of the work because they cost less, are specialized, and limit personal risk. Subcontractors need to have their own certificates of insurance.

## OVERTIME

Overtime is 1 ½ the rate of pay for 8 to 12 hours on the sixth and seventh day are worked. When over 12 hours are worked on any day, double the pay rate. The rate should also be doubled when 8 hours are worked on the seventh day. Overtime is based on the hourly rate of pay. This must be calculated for salaried individuals by breaking down the yearly pay to month, week, day, and hour. Two pay rates require using the weighted average to discover overtime. The commission rate is the regular rate used to calculate overtime. Bonuses that are not discretionary are calculated into overtime, but discretionary bonuses are not. Employer must pay overtime that is and is not authorized. Overtime is not payable to executives, administrative employees, and salespeople who spend over half the time making outside sales.

**Acts** The Wage and Hour Division also enforces the **Contract Work Hours and Safety Standards Act.** The act governs federally funded service contracts and assisted construction contracts that are worth more than $100,000. It guarantees that mechanics and laborers are paid pay time and a half for working over 40 hours a week.

In 1978, the **Civil Service Reform Act (CSRA)** forbids discrimination in federal personnel acts based on color, race, national origin, sex, religion, disability, and age. Marital status, political affiliation, and other limited factors may not affect performance. The EEOC does not enforce the EEOC.

Employers who hire employees that are nonimmigrant employees to take specialty positions are bound by the **Immigration and Nationality Act**, which is enforced by the ETA. The H-1B nonimmigrant visa classification is required, and no employees may be displaced within 90 days of nonimmigrant hiring. These employees need to be paid the actual wage or the local wage. (The higher rate must be paid.) Additionally, the same benefits must be offered.

**The False Claims Act (FCA)** discovers fraud in government programs.

**Government bureaus, offices** The **(EEOC) US Equal Employment Opportunity Commission** prohibits discrimination based on color, race, sex, age, disability, and national origin. In 1991, the Civil Rights Act created other protections and added compensation to the EEOC.

**The National Labor Relations Board (NLRB)** protects employees in their right to organize and develop unions. It is a federal agency that protects the employees from dangerous labor practices.

**Unions and Labor Relationships** The goals of management and labor are at odds. Management is focused on cost, profitability, and productivity. Labor and their representatives focus on benefits, wok conditions, and pay.

Unions represent the interest of employees. Unions vary between states, and they should be understood. They have the power of collective bargaining, which includes wages, work conditions, and hours of the collective. Unions are protected by law, and employees are more likely to develop union interests later in their careers. National unions such as the Service Employees International Union are affiliated with the local unions, which handle situations in the workplace. National unions are under the labor federations, which lobby the government and provide employee training.

Unions have the exclusive right of negotiation when they are exclusive representatives. Wages are based on union negotiations rather than merit. Representation or unionization occurs after an election campaign where most employees choose a representative for collective bargaining. Unions may or may not be voluntarily recognized by both employees and employers. If the election is adversarial, union negotiations will be difficult.

Unions are known to improve the working conditions, hours, and wages of employees, but may reduce shareholder returns. Bargaining may be integrative (an engagement that focuses on cooperation) or distributive (an engagement that focuses on winning). After negotiations, a collective bargaining agreement (CBA) is reached. The CBA will outline the conditions, rights, and obligations of the different parties, etc. Management rights are not limited by CBAs in any form.

## BREAKS AND HOURS

Employees must have at least one full day off in a full week. If an employee needs to work 7 days in a row, the day off must be made up in the same month. This is not necessary if an employee works fewer than 30 hours during this period.

Any workday that is longer than 5 hours requires a 30-minute lunch break. Another 30-minute break is necessary if an employee works 10 hours or more. Employees who are allowed to leave for breaks are not paid for the breaks, but breaks are paid if employees are not allowed to leave. An additional hour of pay is required if breaks cannot be taken.

Every 4 hours of work require a paid 10-minute rest period, which is separate from lunch breaks. This should be taken half-way through the work day when the shift is at least 3 ½ hours long. Breaks must be provided for breastfeeding mothers, but they do not have to be paid.

Employers must provide break areas for employees who are required to stay at work. Employers are not required to pay for transportation unless it is work related, but they are required to pay for time necessary to prepare for work.

Leaves must be honored for volunteer firefighters, peace offers, rescue personnel, etc. They must be reinstated and provided with lost wages. Employers who fail to do so may be found guilty of misdemeanors.

Sick leave is a benefit that accrues over time. Employees who have sick leave cannot be denied its use. Employees may use the amount of sick leave that accrues in 6 months.

Employees may take 8 hours a month and 40 hours a year to participate in daycare or school activities when advanced notice is given. This applies to companies with 25 employees or more.

Employer with 15 employees or more must give paid leave to employees who give bone marrow or organs. Bone marrow requires 5 days of leave, and 30 days are necessary for organ donation. This does not include FMLA or CFRA.

Employers do not have to offer paid vacation. Vacation that accrues must be paid in the final paycheck if unused. Employers may not deduct advanced vacation pay. Forfeiting vacation is not legal, but employers are allowed to restrict the when it can be taken and who receives it as a benefit.

## HIRING NEW EMPLOYEES

**Eligibility for employment.** You must verify that each new employee is legally eligible to work in the United States. This includes completing the U.S. Citizenship and Immigration Services (USCIS) Form I-9, Employment Eligibility Verification. You can get Form I-9 from USCIS offices or by calling 1-800-870-3676. For more information, visit the USCIS website at *www.uscis.gov*, or call 1-800-375-5283 or 1-800-767-1833 (TDD).

**New hire reporting.** You are required to report any new employee to a designated state new hire registry. A new employee is an employee who hasn't previously been employed by you or was previously employed by you but has been separated from such prior employment for at least 60 consecutive days.

Many states accept a copy of Form W-4 with employer information added. Visit the Office of Child Support Enforcement website at *www.acf.hhs.gov/programs/cse/newhire* for more information.

**W-4 request.** Ask each new employee to complete the 2016 Form W-4. See section 9.

**Name and social security number (SSN).** Record each new employee's name and SSN from his or her social security card. Any employee without a social secur-ity card should apply for one.

**Income tax withholding.** Withhold federal income tax from each wage payment or supplemental unemployment compensation plan benefit payment according to the em-ployee's Form W-4 and the correct withholding table. If you have nonresident alien employees, see *Withholding income taxes on the wages of nonresident alien employ-ees* in section 9.

Withhold from periodic **pension and annuity payments** as if the recipient is married claiming three with-holding allowances, unless he or she has provided Form W-4P, Withholding Certificate for Pension or Annuity Pay-ments, either electing no withholding or giving a different number of allowances, marital status, or an additional amount to be withheld. Don't withhold on direct rollovers from qualified plans or governmental section 457(b) plans. See section 9 and Pub. 15-A, Employer's Supplemental Tax Guide. Pub. 15-A includes information about with-holding on pensions and annuities.

Following table from IRS https://www.irs.gov/pub/irs-pdf/p15.pdf

# DISCRIMINATION LAWS

### *Harassment and Discrimination*

Discrimination complaints must be made with a year of the complaint to the Labor Commissioner.

Harassment and discrimination must be considered before terminations. Employees who claim illegal termination due to discrimination must have a threshold or *prima facie*. If this occurs, the employer needs to provide a legitimate reason for termination, which the employee may prove to be a pretext.

In the event of age discrimination accusations, the following occurs;

- Determine if there is a nondiscriminatory cause for terminations.
- Discover if the investigation is impartial and adequate.
- Be sure that the discharge was in good faith.
- The but-for factor proves that age is the factor in the action.
- The cat's paw theory considers discrimination of those in authority. The individual who has authority over the decision maker influences the decision.

A hostile work environment is created by sexual harassment. The employer is responsible for the actions of employees and nonemployees. Claims of retaliation require the employee to prove the employer's responsibility. The connection between the events and the termination must be established with timing. Title VII guarantees the employees the right to be safe from retaliation in discrimination filings. Whistle blower protection is only provided if the information is reported beyond the organization.

# SAFETY HAZARDS

There are three federal laws that protect the health and safety of employees:

- Metallic and Nonmetallic Mines Safety Act (1966)
- Federal Coal Mine Health and Safety Act of 1969
- Occupational Safety and Health Act of 1970

Almost all employers are required to follow OSHA regulations.

### *Safety*

Safety engineers have the responsibility to protect the work environment, employees, and property. This is done by predicting the conditions and policies that present hazards; developing programs that address hazards; monitoring control programs; and writing safety plans and statements for the future.

Safety plans have their own safety life cycles that move through the phases:

- Initiation
- Safety requirement specifications
- Covering design
- Safety feature development
- Decommissioning

Employers are responsible for providing a safe workspace, and a safe space is sure to increase morale and profits. Any employer with more than 10 employees must provide a written emergency plan outlined in **OSHA**. (see- Manage Administrative Duties-Develop a Safety Program)

The enforcement of OSHA regulations is done by the industrial hygienists (IH), and they make up more than 40% of the OSHA compliance officers. They play a role in developing standards and provide support to regional and national offices. The IH role also includes:

- Aid in field procedures
- Interpret OSHA standards
- Identify and analyze hazards and stressors
- Find measures to control hazardous conditions

### *Health and safety programs have the following elements:*

- The commitment and involvement of both management and employees
- Continual analysis of the worksite
- Control and prevent hazards and exposure
- Hazard trainings for supervisors, managers, and employees.

In the event that 3 or more employees are hospitalized, OSHA needs to be notified within 8 hours.

### *Violations:*

- Willful violations have $5,000 fines at minimum, but they do not exceed $70,000.
- Citations for a serious violation have $7,000 fines at minimum, but they do not exceed $70,000.
- Failure to fix violations carries a $7,000 fine per day.
- Violation of Section 6 state plans that result in death is a $10,000 fine and/or 6 months in prison. A repeat of this will result in a $20,000 fine and/or a year in prison.
- Making a false statement results in a $10,000 fine and/or 6 months in prison.

OSHA inspections may be programmed or unprogrammed. Programmed inspections occur in areas with high rate of injury. The main risks associated with construction are vehicle sediment, open burning of debris becoming uncontrolled, dust, CFCs, and combustion gases.

## TRAINING AND REPORTING REQUIREMENTS

**OSHA Standards/ 29 CFR Part 1926** Employers are not responsible for CPR certification, but must provide other safety training. They are also responsible for medical care and first aid services. First aid kits need to be weatherproof and hold individually sealed package. Employers are responsible for the checking the contents weekly.

OSHA Forms 300, 300A, and 301 are injury and illness logs, and they must be kept a minimum of 5 years from the incident. Form 301 addresses individual injuries while form 300 outlines and describes the case. Material Safety Data Sheets (MSDS) should be kept on file for every chemical used and consulted if an employee is exposed to a harmful substance. An MSDS must include: 1) the name 2) the ingredients and health information 3) Safe handling and use 4) contact information for the manufacturer or importer. When an MSDS is amended, the label must be amended on the worksite. All employees should be trained in the use of MSDS.

In the event that 3 or more employees are hospitalized, OSHA needs to be notified within 8 hours.

### *Violations:*

- Willful violations have $5,000 fines at minimum, but they do not exceed $70,000.
- Citations for a serious violation have $7,000 fines at minimum, but they do not exceed $70,000.
- Failure to fix violations carries a $7,000 fine per day.

- Violation of Section 6 state plans that result in death is a $10,000 fine and/or 6 months in prison. A repeat of this will result in a $20,000 fine and/or a year in prison.
- Making a false statement results in a $10,000 fine and/or 6 months in prison.

OSHA inspections may be programmed or un-programmed. Programmed inspections occur in areas with high rate of injury. The main risks associated with construction are vehicle sediment, open burning of debris becoming uncontrolled, dust, CFCs, and combustion gases.

A daily safety log or daily report is used to track the day's events, but is should never include personal comments. The daily job diary includes information about all of the work done that day and is managed by the Superintendent. It must be written in ink and dated before it is stored in a hard covered binder.

### *OSHA Standard Rules*

Among the standards that impose similar requirements on all industry sectors are those for access to medical and exposure records, personal protective equipment, and hazard communication.

- **Access to Medical and Exposure Records**: This standard requires that employers grant employees access to any of their medical records maintained by the employer and to any records the employer maintains on the employees' exposure to toxic substances.
- **Personal Protective Equipment:** This standard, included separately in the standards for each industry segment (except agriculture), requires that employers provide employees, at no cost to employees, with personal protective equipment designed to protect them against certain hazards. This can range from protective helmets to prevent head injuries in construction and cargo handling work, to eye protection, hearing protection, hard-toed shoes, special goggles (for welders, for example) and gauntlets for iron workers.
- **Hazard Communication**: This standard requires that manufacturers and importers of hazardous materials conduct a hazard evaluation of the products they manufacture or import. If the product is found to be hazardous under the terms of the standard, containers of the material must be appropriately labeled and the first shipment of the material to a new customer must be accompanied by a material safety data sheet (MSDS). Employers, using the MSDSs they receive, must train their employees to recognize and avoid the hazards the materials present.

In general, all employers (except those in the construction industry) should be aware that any hazard not covered by an industry-specific standard may be covered by a general industry standard; in addition, all employers must keep their workplaces free of recognized hazards that may cause death or serious physical harm to employees, even if OSHA does not have a specific standard or requirement addressing the hazard. This coverage becomes important in the enforcement aspects of OSHA's work.

Other types of requirements are imposed by regulation rather than by a standard. OSHA regulations cover such items as recordkeeping, reporting and posting.

**Recordkeeping:** Every employer covered by OSHA who has more than 10 employees, except for certain low-hazard industries such as retail, finance, insurance, real estate, and some service industries, must maintain OSHA-specified records of job-related injuries and illnesses. There are two such records, the OSHA Form 200 and the OSHA Form 101.

The OSHA Form 200 is an injury/illness log, with a separate line entry for each recordable injury or illness (essentially those work-related deaths, injuries and illnesses other than minor injuries that require only first aid treatment and that do not involve medical treatment, loss of consciousness, restriction of work or motion, or transfer to another job). A summary section of the OSHA Form 200, which includes the total of the previous year's injury and illness experience, must be posted in the workplace for the entire month of February each year.

The OSHA Form 101 is an individual incident report that provides added detail about each individual recordable injury or illness. A suitable insurance or workers' compensation form that provides the same details may be substituted for the OSHA Form 101.

Unless an employer has been selected in a particular year to be part of a national survey of workplace injuries and illnesses conducted by the Department of Labor's **Bureau of Labor Statistics (BLS)** , employers with ten or fewer employees or employers in traditionally low-hazard industries are exempt from maintaining these records; all employers selected for the BLS survey must maintain the records. Employers so selected will be notified before the end of the year to begin keeping records during the coming year, and technical assistance on completing these forms is available from the state offices which select these employers for the survey.

Industries designated as traditionally low hazard include: automobile dealers; apparel and accessory stores; furniture and home furnishing stores; eating and drinking places; finance, insurance, and real estate industries; and service industries, such as personal and business services, legal, educational, social and cultural services and membership organizations.

**Reporting**: In addition to the reporting requirements described above, each employer, regardless of number of employees or industry category, must report to the nearest OSHA office within 8 hours of any accident that results in one or more fatalities or hospitalization of three or more employees. Such accidents are often investigated by OSHA to determine what caused the accident and whether violations of standards contributed to the event.

**Employee and Employer Rights and Responsibilities** Employees are granted several important rights by the OSH Act. Among them are the right to: complain to OSHA about safety and health conditions in their workplace and have their identity kept confidential from the employer, contest the time period OSHA allows for correcting standards violations, and participate in OSHA workplace inspections.

**Are all employees covered by the OSH Act?** The OSH Act covers all employees <u>except workers who are self-employed and public employees in state and local governments.</u>

In states with OSHA-approved state plans, public employees in state and local governments are covered by their state's OSHA-approved plan. Federal employees are covered under the OSH Act's federal employee occupational safety and health programs, see 29 CFR Part 1960. United States Postal Service employees, however, are subject to the same OSH Act coverage provisions as are private sector employers.

The OSH Act does not apply to particular working conditions addressed by regulations or standards affecting occupational safety or health that are issued by federal agencies, other than OSHA, or by a state atomic energy agency. Other federal agencies that have issued requirements affecting job safety or health include the Mine Safety and Health Administration and some agencies of the Department of Transportation.

**What are your responsibilities as an employer?** If you are an employer covered by the OSH Act, you must provide your employees with jobs and a place of employment free from recognized hazards that are causing, or are likely to cause, death or serious physical harm. Among other actions, you must also comply with the OSHA statutory requirements, standards, and regulations that, in part, require you to do the following:

- Provide well-maintained tools and equipment, including appropriate personal protective equipment;
- Provide medical examinations;
- Provide training required by OSHA standards;
- Report to OSHA within 8 hours accidents that result in fatalities;
- Report to OSHA within 8 hours accidents that result in the hospitalization of three or more employees;
- Keep records of work-related accidents, injuries, illnesses.and their causes.and post annual summaries for the required period of time. A number of specific industries in the retail, service, finance, insurance, and real estate sectors that are classified as low-hazard are exempt from most requirements of the regulation, as are small businesses with 10 or fewer employees (see 29 CFR Part 1904);
- Post prominently the OSHA poster (OSHA 3165) informing employees of their rights and responsibilities;
- Provide employees access to their medical and exposure records;
- Do not discriminate against employees who exercise their rights under the OSH Act;
- Post OSHA citations and abatement verification notices at or near the worksite;
- Abate cited violations within the prescribed period; and
- Respond to survey requests for data from the Bureau of Labor Statistics, OSHA, or a designee of either agency.

**What are your rights as an employer?**

When working with OSHA, you may do the following:

- Request identification from OSHA compliance officers;
- Request an inspection warrant;

- Be advised by compliance officers of the reason for an inspection;
- Have an opening and closing conference with compliance officers;
- Accompany compliance officers on inspections;
- Request an informal conference after an inspection;
- File a Notice of Contest to citations, proposed penalties, or both;
- Apply for a variance from a standard's requirements under certain circumstances;
- Be assured of the confidentiality of trade secrets; and
- Submit a written request to the National Institute for Occupational Safety and Health for information on potentially toxic substances in your workplace.

**What are your responsibilities as an employee?**

To help prevent exposure to workplace safety and health hazards, you must comply with all OSHA requirements that apply to your actions and conduct.

**Employee Rights**

to do the following:

- Review employer-provided OSHA standards, regulations and requirements;
- Request information from your employer on emergency procedures;
- Receive adequate safety and health training when required by OSHA standards related to toxic substances and any such procedures set forth in any emergency action plan required by an OSHA standard;
- Ask the OSHA Area Director to investigate hazardous conditions or violations of standards in your workplace;
- Have your name withheld from your employer if you file a complaint with OSHA ;
- Be advised of OSHA actions regarding your complaint, and have an informal review of any decision not to inspect or to issue a citation;
- Have your employee representative accompany the OSHA compliance officer on inspections;
- Observe any monitoring or measuring of toxic substances or harmful physical agents and review any related monitoring or medical records;
- Review at a reasonable time the Log of Work-Related Injuries and Illnesses (OSHA 300) if your employer is required to maintain it;
- Request a closing discussion following an inspection;
- Object to the abatement period set in a citation issued to your employer; and
- Seek safe and healthful working conditions without your employer retaliating against you.

**Anti-Discrimination Provisions**

Private sector employees who exercise their rights under OSHA can be protected against employer reprisal, as described in **Section 11(c) of the OSH Act**. Employees must notify OSHA within 30 days of the time they learned of the alleged discriminatory action. This notification is followed by an OSHA investigation. If OSHA agrees that discrimination has occurred, the employer will be asked to restore any lost benefits to the affected employee. If necessary, OSHA can take the employer to court. In such cases, the worker pays no legal fees.

Read more at http://www.ehso.com/oshaoverview.php#jVCTuFET6bbrR6SP.99

## TAXES

**Federal Taxes** The Internal Revenue Service (IRS) administers federal payroll taxes, including social security, Medicare, federal unemployment insurance and federal income tax withholding.

**Backup withholding.** You generally must withhold 28% of certain taxable payments if the payee fails to furnish you with his or her correct taxpayer identification number (TIN). This withholding is referred to as "backup withholding."

Payments subject to backup withholding include interest, dividends, patronage dividends, rents, royalties, com-missions, nonemployee compensation, payments made in settlement of payment card or third-party network transactions, and certain other payments you make in the course of your trade or business. In addition, transactions by brokers and barter exchanges and certain payments made by fishing boat operators are subject to backup withholding.

*Backup withholding doesn't apply to wages, pensions, annuities, IRAs (including simplified em-ployee pension (SEP) and SIMPLE retirement plans), section 404(k) distributions from an employee stock ownership plan (ESOP), medical savings accounts (MSAs), health savings accounts (HSAs), long-term-care benefits, or real estate transactions.*

You can use Form W-9 or Formulario W-9(SP) to re-quest payees to furnish a TIN. Form W-9 or Formulario W-9 (SP) must be used when payees must certify that the number furnished is correct, or when payees must certify that they aren't subject to backup withholding or are ex-empt from backup withholding. The Instructions for the Requester of Form W-9 or Formulario W-9(SP) includes a list of types of payees who are exempt from backup with-holding. For more information, see Pub. 1281, Backup Withholding for Missing and Incorrect Name/TIN(s).8

## UNEMPLOYMENT INSURANCE TAXES

### *Base period*

A "base period" is used as the basis for an unemployment claim and consists of the wages paid to the claimant by any employer during the time period established as the base period. "Base Period" means the first four of the last five completed calendar quarters immediately preceding the first day of an individual's benefit year. If a claimant's benefit year begins anytime within the third quarter of 2009, the base period would be established as follows:

Example:
2009-3 = current quarter = does not count
2009-2 = lag quarter = does not count
2009-1 = in base period
2008-4 = in base period
2008-3 = in base period
2008-2 = in base period

The day a claim is established, a base period is determined and remains in effect until one year passes and the claim period expires. If a subsequent claim is filed, a new base period is determined using different calendar quarters. Base period quarters used for a previous claim are not used again as the basis of a new claim. An employee's wages with your company would be used in the base period of any future claim as long as there were wages reported by your company in any of the quarters considered.

# BUSINESS & FINANCE QUICK GUIDE EXAM

1. Which of the following is a goal of enterprise risk management

a. defining which risks the program will manage

b. deciding how to petition the Department of Homeland Security for financial help

c. refining the business plan for risk management

A. defining which risks the program will manage Explanation: ERM is Enterprise Risk Management which helps define which risks the program will manage, what risk management processes will be required, and how risk management efforts will be coordinated across the firm.

2. ________ risk involves a chance of either profit or loss

a. Insurable

b. Insurable

c. Speculative Explanation:

Speculative risk can result in either profit or loss. A firm takes on speculative risk, for example, by buying new machinery that may or may not do what they expect it to do.

3. In designing an addition to his successful bed and breakfast, Harold realized that water sprinklers and smoke detectors were now required by state regulations. His existing structure already had sprinklers and detectors because he felt that this was an effective strategy to:

a. self-insure against the risk of fire loss

b. minimize the speculative risk of a fire.

c. reduce the risk of a fire loss

d. avoid the risk of a fire loss

The type of risk that concerns most businesspeople is pure risk. This type of risk threatens the very existence of some form.

4. Amusement parks often have a minimum height restriction on some of their most thrilling rides. This risk management strategy is done in an effort to

a. minimize the speculative risk associated with an injury.

b. reduce the risk associated with a potential accident

c. self-insure against a speculative accident.

Reducing pure risk or any kind of risk is a goal that companies try to reach. They do this by reducing the risk, avoiding the risk, self-insuring against the risk, or buying insurance against the risk.

5. One guideline to determine that a risk is generally insurable is:

a. the loss is measurable.

b. the loss is due to a price change.

c. the loss is speculative

D. it is due to operational issues such as a strike

Not all risks are insurable. Examples of things that cannot be insured include political risks such as losses from war, and some personal risks such as loss of a job.

6. __________ insurance provides benefits to the survivors of workers who die as a result of work-related injuries.

a. Product liability

b. Professional liability

c. Workers' compensation

d. Malpractice

Workers compensation insurance guarantees payment of wages, medical care, and rehabilitation services to employees who are injured on the job. Employers in every state in the country are required to provide this insurance.

7. Risk management today means the evaluation of:

a. worldwide risks such as global warming

b. worldwide issues such as disease

c. political risks in South America

d. All of the above

Today, risk management goes way beyond the protection of individuals, businesses, and organizations from known risks. It means the evaluation of worldwide risks with many unknowns including climate change. It prioritizes these risks so that international funds can be spent where they can do the most good.

8. During execution of a project, an identified risk event occurs that results in additional cost and time? The project had provisions for contingency and management reserves. How should these be accounted for?

a. Contingency reserves

b. Residual risks

c. Management reserves

d. Secondary risks

Contingency reserves Reserves are meant for making provisions in cost and schedule, to accommodate for consequences of risk events. Provisions for 'unknown unknowns' are in management reserves while those for 'known unknowns' are accommodated in contingency reserves. Management reserves are at the discretion of senior management while the contingency reserves are at the project manager's discretion. Residual and secondary risks are remaining unmitigated risks and resultant risks of mitigation, respectively. These are not reserves. In this case, the risk event is one of the identified risks and therefore, 'contingency reserve' is the one where the cost and schedule impact would be accommodated in.

9. An organization is certified to a stringent environmental standard and uses that as the key differentiator with its competitors. Alternative identification during scope planning for a particular project has thrown up an expeditious approach to achieve a project need, but this involves a risk of environmental contamination. The team evaluates that the likelihood of the risk is very low. What should the project team do?

a. Drop the alternative approach

b. Work out a mitigation plan

c. Procure an insurance against the risk

d. Plan all precautions to avoid the risk

Drop the alternative approach. The organization's reputation being at stake, the threshold for such a risk would be very low. The best option would be to drop the approach - that is, complete avoidance of the risk.

10. Which one of the following is an example of the cost of nonconformance to quality?

a. Prevention costs

b. Destructive testing loss

c. Appraisal costs

d. Liabilities

The cost of nonconformance to quality defines the costs of poor quality. It's the monies, time, reputation, energy, and other negative aspects that come of poor quality execution. Liabilities is an example of external failure costs; all other answers are part of the cost of conformance to quality. Note that destructive testing loss is an appraisal cost to test the quality.

For more information see PMBOK 8.1.2.2.

11. Gary is managing a construction project for his organization. In the project his team has identified some dangerous activities that they should not do. Gary agrees and hires a vendor to complete these tasks in the project. What type of risk response has Gary used?

a. Mitigation

b. Transference

c. Avoidance

d. Exploit

When a project manager, such as Gary, hires someone else or an organization to manage the risk he's using the risk response of transference. You can remember this as Gary is transferring the risk to some other party. Mitigation is a risk response to reduce the probability and/or impact of a risk event. Avoidance are actions to avoid the risk altogether. Exploit is used for a positive risk to take advantage of a positive risk outcomes, such as selling a byproduct or crashing a project to finish early and receive a bonus.

12. A contractual action that authorizes commencement of work prior to the establishment of a final definitive price but less than the "not to exceed' price is known as a(n):

a. Undefined contractual action

b. Letter contract/Letter of Intent (LOI)

c. Constructive change

d. Request for Bid

13. Which of the following is not a viable acquisition method?

a. Request for Information (RFI)

b. Invitation for sealed bids

c. Negotiating a price through bargaining

d. Purchase order

14. When using an Invitation for Bids (IFBs) acquisition method, you should typically do all of the following except:

a. Create a clear and concise description of the product or service required

b. Establish the price that you wish to pay

c. Open the bid to all potential qualified vendors

d. Prepare procedures for evaluating the bids received

15. In which of the following circumstance(s) would you most likely procure the goods or services instead of producing them in-house?

a. Your company has excess capacity and your company can produce the goods or services

b. Your company has no excess capacity and cannot produce the goods or services

c. There are many reliable vendors for the goods or services that you are attempting to procure but the vendors cannot achieve your level of quality

d. Your company has skills in a critical area that require development

16. Which of the following contract types has the highest risk to the seller?

a. Firm Fixed Price (FFP)

b. Time and Materials (T&M)

c. Cost Plus Fixed Fee (CPFF)

d. Cost Reimbursable

17. In which type of contract arrangement is the buyer at the greatest risk of absorbing excessive cost overruns?

a. Cost Plus Percentage of Cost

b. Firm Fixed Price

c. Time and Materials

d. Fixed Price Incentive Firm Target

18. You are the Project Manager responsible for the completion of a global project. Project teams will be located in several countries around the world although contract execution will be driven by a single contract. As the buyer's Project Manager, you should accomplish the following during procurement planning:

a. Establish evaluation criteria to ensure all project teams can communicate

b. Issue an RFI to determine potential sources in the other countries

c. Choose the type of contract to use considering the various countries' legal requirements

d. Document in the statement of work how the country project teams will report progress

19. Which of the following conditions is not required for a contract to be regarded as a legal and binding document?

a. Mutual agreement
b. Fixed monetary value
c. Contract capacity
d. Legal purpose in a form provided by law

20. Contract close-out is similar to the project's administrative closure in that both involve:

a. Negotiation
b. Planning and execution
c. Product verification and administrative close-out activities
d. Cost-benefit analyses

21. The Statement of Work (SOW) document is:

a. A non-binding document used to determine the responsibilities of the seller
b. A definition of the contracted work used only for government contracts
c. A narrative description of the work to be accomplished and/or the resource skills required
d. A listing of contract deliverables

22. Which of the following does not affect a seller's ability to perform the contracted activities after the contract is signed?

a. A poor definition of contract deliverables
b. The extent of project subcontracting
c. The complexity of the contracted effort
d. The contract type

23. A Bid Bond is ______________________

a. Required by Auctioneers
b. A very small bond
c. Bond that accompanies a construction proposal

24. Surety Consent (to accompany bid) ______________________

a. Promises to provide the related Performance and Payment Bond
b. Agrees to all conditions in the related contract
c. Agrees that bond claims will be paid within 30 days

25. Bid Bond Percentage is ____________________

a. Ratio of successful bid proposals
b. Portion of bid bonds used in one calendar year
c. Determines the dollar value of the bid bond

26. Performance Bond

a. Always makes reference to a written contract
b. May not be cancelled by the surety
c. Both a. and b.

27. The Balance of Contract Amount means;

a. The point at which a contract becomes profitable
b. The unpaid portion of the contract
c. Relationship between labor and material costs

28. A Payment Bond is ______________________

a. Used to guarantee loans and leases
b. Guarantees payment of proper union wages
c. Guarantees suppliers of labor and material will be paid

29. What is a 'Third Tier Sub'

a. A class of subcontractors not covered by the Payment Bond
b. Subs that do not bid
c. Low quality subcontractors

30. What is meant by Subdivision Bonds?

a. Similar to Sub-multiplication and Sub-addition bonds
b. Similar to Site Bonds
c. Similar to subcontractor bonds

31. What is meant by a 'Penal Sum'

a. Dollar value of a bond
b. A source of retribution, a penalty
c. When two bonds are added together

32. What are 'Site Bonds'

a. Guarantees improved site conditions
b. Guarantees the construction of public improvements
c. Guarantees a construction contract

33. What is meant by a 'Single Job Limit'

a. The largest job a contractor ever performed
b. The largest job a contractor is interested in undertaking
c. The largest job a surety is willing to bond

34. What is 'Work on Hand'?

a. Remaining "cost to complete" for open projects

b. Underbillings

c. Costs relating to labor performed by hand

35. What is meant by "Full" Indemnity

a. The indemnity of the applicant company including all of its assets

b. The indemnity of the applicant company, all owners and spouses, plus other owned/controlled companies

c. Indemnity equal to the full value of the bond amount in question

36. Who should attend a bidder conference?

a. All prospective sellers and buyers

b. The selected seller and the buyer

c. The selected seller and the project manager

d. All buyers

Bidder conferences are part of the procurement process and should be attended by all prospective sellers and buyers. The bidder conference is an opportunity to review the statement of work for clarifications so all bidders have the same information to create a bid or proposal for the buyer. For more information see PMBOK 12.2.2.1.

37. The development and application of employees' skills and energies to accomplish the goals and objectives of the organization is called:

a. human resource management.

b. human resource planning.

c. selection.

d. recruiting.

38. The first step in the human resource planning process is:

a. preparing a job analysis.

b. forecasting future human resource needs.

c. assessing future demand.

d. assessing future supply.

39. Human resource planning techniques include the use of some or all of the following:

a. human resource inventories.

b. action plans.

c. control and evaluation.

d. all of the above.

40. Which term describes the process of gathering, analyzing and synthesizing information about the jobs that are being done and any new jobs that are envisioned?

a. job description.

b. job analysis.

c. job specification.

d. human resource inventory.

41. The first step in a typical job analysis is to examine the overall organization. The next step is:

a. collect data on jobs.

b. prepare job description.

c. prepare job specification.

d. select jobs to be analyzed.

42. A job _________ is a written statement of the job's activities, the equipment required for it, and the working conditions in which it exists.

a. analysis.

b. specification.

c. design.

d. description.

43. Which of the following is a written statement of the skills, knowledge, abilities, and other characteristics needed to perform a job effectively?

a. job design.

b. job specification.

c. job analysis.

d. job description.

44. Job ___________ is the process of describing jobs and arranging their interrelationships.

a. design.

b. specification.

c. analysis.

d. description.

45. Increasing the number and variety of tasks assigned to a job is called:

a. job rotation.

b. job enlargement.

c. job enrichment.

d. A & C.

46. Which of the following is not a core dimension of a job?

a. skill variety.

b. task identity.

c. task significance.

d. high internal work motivation.

All of the following are sources of internal recruiting except:

a. job posting.

b. employee recommendations.

c. advertisements.

d. transfers.

48. An individualized outline of training, experience and possibly education designed to facilitate an employee's growth and enhance opportunities for advancement is called:

a. job description.

b. career development plan.

c. assessment sheet.

d. interview form.

49. A formal, systematic appraisal of the qualitative and quantitative aspects of an employee's performance is called:

a. performance evaluation.

b. performance appraisal.

c. performance analysis.

d. orientation.

50. Which of the following is not a personal benefit?

a. sick leave.

b. flex benefit.

c. sales bonus.

d. dental plan.

51. ______________ is a percentage on the volume of sales.

a. profit sharing.

b. piecework.

c. commission.

d. bonus.

52. Which of the following provides the foundation for team development?

a. Motivation

b. Organizational development

c. Conflict management

d. Individual development

53. According to the Design Build Institute of America (DBIA), what is the most common project delivery method used in the United States today?

a. Design-bid-build

b. Design-build

c. Engineering, procurement, construction

d. At-risk construction management

Design-bid-build. Although various project delivery alternatives have come into greater use in recent years, especially in the case of design-build, the traditional design-bid-build method is still the dominant delivery method preferred by owners. The DBIA predicts design-build will surpass design-bid-build as the dominant method sometime before 2020.

54. What project delivery method typically involves design being 100 percent complete?

a. Design-bid-build

b. Design-build

c. Public/private partnerships

d. At-risk construction management

Design-bid-build. In design-bid-build, the owner of a project first contracts with a DP or DP team. The DP performs and completes the design plans and specifications. The 100 percent completed plans and specifications are then advertised by the owner for bid. GCs compete for the construction contract, and once awarded, the GC will construct the project according to the 100 percent completed plans and specifications.

55. Who is ultimately responsible for design errors on a construction project?

a. Contractor

b. Owner

c. Design professional (DP)

d. All of the above

While it is natural to want to choose the DP or the contractor (in the design-build delivery method), it's the owner who ultimately retains responsibility for damages associated with design errors. Of course, the owner may attempt to shift the risk via proper selection of design firm/team, contract language, insurance, and so forth, but if any or all of these techniques fail, they retain the ultimate responsibility.

56. When construction begins before the design is 100 percent complete, it is commonly referred to as

a. fast-tracking.
b. fast-balling.
c. fast-talking.
d. fast-designing.
e. engineering, procurement, construction.

Fast-tracking. It can sometimes sound like fast-talking, but the answer is fast-tracking.

57. What type of construction specifications present contractors with a higher degree of professional liability risk?

a. Design specifications
b. Prescriptive specifications
c. Performance specifications
d. Lean specifications

Performance specifications. Performance-based specifications focus on outcomes or results rather than on the construction process. Conversely, design or prescriptive specifications are detailed and outline exactly how the contractor must construct a project. When performance specifications are applied, the contractor is free to use his/her expertise, experience, and knowledge to determine what products, equipment, materials, or process is best suited to provide the required outcome. This can expose contractors to professional liability risk.

58. Under the construction manager at risk (CMR) delivery method, which of the following entities holds the primary contract for design of the project with the DP?

a. Owner
b. General contractor (GC)
c. Finance company
d. Agency construction manager

In the CMR project delivery method, the owner typically still holds two contracts. One contract is with the design DP, and the second is with the CMR, who then holds contracts with the subcontractors and is responsible for the performance of the construction work and typically under a guaranteed maximum price.

59. Which of the following project delivery methods involves a multiparty agreement where the common procurement option in selecting the team is qualifications based?

a. At-risk construction management
b. Design build
c. Public/private partnerships
d. Integrated project delivery (IPD)

The selection process for all answers listed is qualifications based, but the key phrase with IPD is "multiparty agreement." There are several variations of the definition of IPD, but the simplest is—a collaborative process or delivery method that joins the owner, architect, and contractor (and, in some cases, other entities such as major subcontractors, suppliers, and engineering firms) under a single contract so that the risk and responsibility are collectively managed and appropriately shared.

60. Contractors perform a variety of services that expose their organizations to professional liability. One type of service provided by a subcontractor that involves supplementing the engineer of record's design by providing supporting engineering services either in house or subcontracted is often referred to as

a. bridging services.

b. systems engineering.

c. design assist.

d. construction means and methods.

Design assist. Design assist is a collaborative team-oriented technique that draws upon the specialty expertise of certain subcontractors by engaging them early in the design phase to optimize project cost, value, and constructability efficiency.

61. The legal doctrine that holds one entity (the GC) liable/accountable for the negligent actions of another entity (the subcontractor), even though the first entity was not directly responsible for the resulting harm or damages, is generally referred to as

a. vicarious liability.

b. nothing important in our lines of insurance.

c. strict liability.

d. prudent person defense.

e. Spearin doctrine.

Vicarious liability. If there are still GCs that hold design-build contracts (or may have specialty subcontractors who hold contracts with engineering firms) and don't think they can be liable for the design just because they didn't design, they need to better understand this concept.

62. Techniques created/used/applied by contractors to assist them in constructing the permanent structure/project are typically referred to as what?

a. Construction principles and services

b. Construction means and methods

c. Prescriptive specifications

d. IPD

e. All of the above

Construction means and methods. It's important to understand there is professional liability risk associated with means and methods. Whether it's a GC hiring an engineer to design a tower crane base, falsework, or scaffolding system (to name a few), contractors are exposed to various professional risks not insured through the commercial general liability policy, especially the economic damages associated with such errors in services.

63. Is a motor vehicle an asset or a liability?

Answer- Asset

64. Is inventory an asset or a liability?

Answer- Asset

65. Are accounts receivable an asset or a liability?

Answer- Asset

66. Which account is debited if a customer pays 300 by check, Accounts receivable or Cash

Answer- Cash

67. A business is started with 5,000 cash from the owner paid into the bank account. Which account is credited, Cash or Capital

Answer- Capital

68. Faulty equipment for 200 is returned to the supplier. Assuming the equipment has not yet been depreciated, which account is the credit entry made to Fixed assets or Accounts payable?

Answer- Fixed assets

69. 100 .00 cash is taken from the bank account of the business and placed into petty cash, which account is credited Petty cash or Cash?

Answer-Cash

70. A supplier is paid 500 by check, is the cash account debited or credited?

Answer-Credited

71. A loan principal repayment of 400 is made using a direct transfer from the bank, do you debit or credit the loan account?

Answer-Debit

72. Is a bank loan an asset or a liability?

Answer-Liability

73. What occurs when bids are revealed to create more competition?

a. Bid rigging
b. Bid package
c. Bid shopping
d. None of the above

Bid shopping and bid rigging are questionable activities in most states. Bid shopping occurs when bids are revealed to create more competition.

74. What benefit does an S Corporation provide?

a. Prevent double taxation

b. Direct control

c. No shareholders

d. Limit liability

The S Corporation has a distinct advantage over the C Corporation. It provides many of the advantages of corporation without the double taxation rate.

75. How many weeks are employees entitled to under the Family Medical Leave Act?

a. 8 weeks

b. 6 weeks

c. 24 weeks

d. 12 weeks

3. B. Onsite

Employees have the right to inspect their records. This means that the records should be stored onsite so that they can be accessed when necessary.

76. Federal unemployment tax must be paid after an employee works _______.

a. 7 weeks

b. 20 weeks

c. 1 week

d. 10 weeks

The employer is responsible for paying federal unemployment tax. The tax must be paid on an employee after he or she has worked a total of 20 weeks.

77. What is the debt ratio?

a. liabilities/assets

b. assets/liabilities

c. income – cost of goods

d. profit – expenses

The debt ratio determines the leverage that a company has. The formula for finding the debt ratio is liabilities/assets.

78. A contractor's license is necessary if the residential project is valued over ________.

a. $10,000

b. $50,000

c. $25,000

d. $30,000

There are five divisions in the California Labor Code. They are Department of Industrial Relations, Employment Regulation Service, Employment Relations, Workers' Compensation and Insurance, and Safety and Employment

79. When is a contract considered accepted?

a. Oral acceptance

b. After negotiations

c. When signed

d. All of the above

Contracts need to be valid in order to be honored. A contract is considered to be fully accepted when they are signed.

80. What is the most accurate method of estimate?

a. Unit price

b. Bid/Design

c. Selection

d. Quantity Take-off Method

The Quantity Take-off Method and the unit price method are both methods of estimate. The Quantity Take-off Method is the most accurate.

81. Projects worth how much require bonds under the Miller Act?

a. $100,000

b. $110,000

c. $25,000

d. $50,000

The Miller Act governs federal contracts. Projects valued at $100,000 or more fall under the Miller Act.

82. Assets/Liability is which ratio?

a. Debt

b. Income

c. Capital

d. Liquidity

Ratios are used for different purposes. The liquidity ratio is assets/liabilities.

83. Contracts that must be in writing to be valid include contracts:

a. For the sale of real property

b. Which cannot be performed within 1 year

c. To pay the debt of another

d. All of the above

See Statute of Frauds

84. What should be included in a contract when it is important that it be performed by a certain deadline?

a. A sentence saying that there are no exceptions to any stated deadlines.

b. The word "rush" in bold type

c. "Time is of the essence"

d. There is no need to include anything but the date by which it must be performed.

See time is of the essence

85. When signing a check, or other negotiable instrument, a person may not:

a. Sign in pencil.

b. Use any name other than his or her own.

c. Sign with an X or other symbol.

d. A person signing a check may do all of the above.

See signature

86. What is the Statute of Frauds?

a. A statute that requires certain contracts to be in writing and signed by the parties

b. Any statute that lists the elements of fraud

c. A statute that says fraudulent contracts are voidable

d. The statute that says fraudulent contracts are void

See Statute of Frauds

87. The 4 elements of a contract are:

a. offer, acceptance, consideration, competency

b. agreement, competency, consideration, legality

c. offer, acceptance, consideration, legality

d. agreement, consideration, competency, performance

See Elements of a Contract. *While many will include offer and acceptance, or meeting of the minds/mutuality as elements of a contract, agreement means that there has been an offer and an acceptance and that the parties both agree to the same thing, or have a meeting of the minds.

88. The parole evidence rule:

a. Is a rule that says prior negotiations are not admissible as evidence that a party who wishes to settle a lawsuit

b. Is a rule that prevents a written contract from being altered by any prior or future oral agreements

c. Has nothing to do with contracts

d. None of the above

See Parole Evidence Rule

89. Under which of the following circumstance may a party fail to perform under a contract, without being held liable for breach of contract?

a. After the other party has breached the contract

b. If the subject of the contract is destroyed

c. If performance has been made impossible by the other party

d. All of the above

See Impossibility and Repudiation

90. Contracts of a minor, which may not be avoided include:

a. business contracts

b. contracts for necessaries

c. student loans

d. all of the above

See Contracts with Minors are Voidable and Contracts of Minors

91. On Monday, Joe agrees to sell his boat to Mike for $7,000. The two will meet on the dock the following day at noon to complete the transaction. Monday night brings a big storm, which destroys the boat. Mike informs Joe that will no longer be purchasing the boat, and Joe sues. What is Mike's defense for backing out of the sale once an oral contract had been made?

a. Quasi contract

b. Estoppel

c. Act of God

d. None of the above

See Act of God

92. XYZ gas company ("XYZ") discovers that there is being gas consumed at an address that has no account and no record of a meter. The last record of an account at the address was 14 years ago. John Doe ("Mr. Doe") is living at the address. XYZ sues Mr. Doe and wins. XYZ's cause(s) of action was:

a. bilateral contract

b. quasi contract

c. unjust enrichment

d. both b and c

See Brooklyn Union Gas Co. v. Diggs, 2003 WL 42106 (N.Y.)

### *True – False*

93. Kmart runs an ad in your local paper listing a sale price of a printer as $39 and its regular price as $89. You go to Kmart and try to purchase the printer, but Kmart refuses to give you the sale price, and wants $89 for the printer. You sue Kmart.

True or False? You win the claim against Kmart based on unfair advertising practices.

False - See Geismar v. Abraham & Strauss, 439 N.Y.S.2d, 1005 (N.Y.Dist. Ct.) An ad is not an offer, but an invitation to negotiate.

94. ABC electric company ("ABC") contracts with the state department of corrections ("DOC") to provide electricity to a tract of land. The land is not a part of the city, so ABC is the legal provider of electricity. The DOC then asks the city to annex the land. The city annexes the land, making it a part of the city, for which the city is the legal provider of electricity. The DOC now gets its electricity from the city. ABC sues to enforce the contract.

True or False? The DOC is discharged from the contract by operation of law, as it would be illegal for it to obtain electricity from ABC, when the land is part of the city.

False - See Farmers' Elec. V. Missouri Dept. of Corrections, 977 S.W.2d 266 (Mo.) A party may now put itself in the position of being unable to perform a contract and then use the inability as an excuse to not perform.

95. Alice sells a wedding ring to Bob. Bob writes Alice a bad check for $1,000. Before Alice discovers that Bob's check is bad, Bob sells the ring to Charlie.

True of False? Charlie is now the legal owner of the ring and Alice has no claim against him.

False - See Farmers' Elec. V. Missouri Dept. of Corrections, 977 S.W.2d 266 (Mo.) A party may now put itself in the position of being unable to perform a contract and then use the inability as an excuse to not perform.

96. Nancy is a real estate agent. She shows a house to Sally, who puts a deposit on the property, but never signs the agreement to purchase the home. Nancy sues Sally for the commission she should have earned on the sale, had Sally went through with it.

True of False? Sally is liable to Nancy for the commission because she made a deposit, which was a promise to pay.

False – See the Statute of Frauds

97. Mr. Smith purchased a life insurance policy, from ABC Life ("ABC"), naming his wife as beneficiary, and then stopped paying the premiums shortly thereafter. In June, ABC mailed Mr. Smith an offer to reinstate the policy. On June 12, the documents required to reinstate the policy were properly mailed. On June 13, Mr. Smith was shot and killed. ABC refused to pay the claim and Mrs. Smith sued.

True of False? ABC is liable to Mrs. Smith for the amount of the policy.

True – See Bruegger v. National Old Line Insurance, Co., 387 F. Supp. 1177 (D. Wyo.) Mr. Smith's acceptance of the offer was effective when it was properly mailed, on June 12.

## *Uniform Commercial Code*

98. In a contract for the sale of goods, the offer may include any terms the offeror wishes; the offeree must accept on exactly those terms or reject the deal.

True
False

99. Sellers can be bound by written warranties but not by oral statements.

True
False

100. Under strict liability, an injured consumer could potentially recover damages from the product's manufacturer and the retailer who sold the goods.

True
False

101. A contract for the sale of $300 worth of decorative stone must be in writing to be enforceable.

True
False

102. Which one of the following transactions is not governed by Article 2 of the UCC?

a. Purchasing an automobile for $35,000
b. Leasing an automobile worth $35,000
c. Purchasing a stereo worth $501
d. Purchasing a stereo worth $499

103. To record depreciation for a delivery van the entry would be

a. debit Delivery Equipment and credit Accumulated Depreciation-Delivery Equipment
b. debit Accumulated Depreciation-Delivery Equipment and credit Delivery Equipment
c. debit Accumulated Depreciation-Delivery Equipment and credit Depreciation Expense-Delivery Equipment
d. debit Depreciation Expense-Delivery Equipment and credit Accumulated Depreciation-Delivery Equipment

104. Accumulated Depreciation is

a. an asset account

b. a liability account

c. a contra asset account

d. n expense account

105. The adjustment for depreciation is recorded

a. on the adjustment section of the work sheet

b. on the trial balance section of the work sheet

c. on the adjusted trial balance section of the work sheet

d. on the income statement section of the work sheet

106. Depreciation expense is closed to

a. Retained Earnings

b. Accumulated Depreciation

c. Plant Assets

d. Income Summary

107. Depreciation expense is recorded on the

a. balance sheet

b. income statement

c. Owners Capital section

d. both the balance sheet and the income statement

108. After the work sheet is completed and the financial statements are prepared, adjustments for depreciation are recorded

a. on the work sheet

b. on the income statement

c. in the general journal

d. in the general ledger

109. When is an employee allowed to view their own personnel file?

a. never

b. when they have a court order

c. whenever they wish

d. during employee evaluations

110. As required by the immigration reform act, all employees hired on or after November 7, 1986 must complete Form ______ to verify their employment eligibility status.

a. I-9

b. W-4

c. US- 99

d.N-14

111. By law, a "hard laborer" may not be younger than ______ years old.

a. 14

b. 15

c. 16

d. 17

112. Ms. Gomez applies for a job. Of the following, the only reason an employer may lawfully deny her employment is:

a. she is over 50 years of age

b. she is Hispanic and everyone else is African-American or Caucasian.

c. lifing is involved and she is a woman

d. she has no work experience or Social Security number

113. A contractor has had a problem with employees stealing tools and equipment from job sites. When conducting job interviews, may the contractor ask prospective employees about their arrest records?

a. It is legal to ask prospective employees about arrests not leading to convictions.

b. It is not legal to ask prospective employees about arrests not leading to convictions.

c. It is legal for a private employer to ask about arrests not leading to convictions, but it would not be legal for city or county agencies to ask about such arrests.

d. It is legal for a private employer to ask about arrests leading to convictions, but it would not be legal for a federal, state, or local public agency to do so.

114. Who must sign a joint control addendum to a home improvement contract?

a. contractor only

b. owner and contractor

c. owner, contractor and Notary Public

d. owner, contractor, and joint control officer

115. A contractor entered into a home improvement contract for more than $500 with Mrs. Swenson to remodel her kitchen and bathroom. The contract calls for a down payment before work is to begin. According to the Business and Professions Code, how much may the contractor accept from Mrs. Swenson as down payment for the work?

a. The contractor may accept as much as Mrs. Swenson agrees to pay.

b. The down payment is limited to $1,000 or 10% of the total price, whichever is less.

c. The contractor may require enough of a down payment to cover the total cost of materials, but not labor costs.

d. Nothing. The contractor must wait until the work is completed to accept any payment.

116. When should you let an attorney see a construction contract?

a. Before you let your client see the contract.

b. After the contract is prepared, but before you sign it.

c. After the building permit is obtained.

d. After the contract is signed by you and your client.

117. If a sales presentation is made in Spanish, the home solicitation contract:

a. must be in Spanish

b. may be in English if the writing is plain and simple

c. must be co-signed by an English-speaking person if the contract is in English

d. must be translated into English and notarized

118. A contractor and a homeowner sign a home solicitation contract. If the owner lawfully cancels the contract, how long does the contractor have to pick up unused materials that were delivered to the owner's property?

a. within 24 hours after cancellation

b. within 10 days after cancellation

c. within 20 days after cancellation

d. It's too late. If the materials are delivered to the property before a notice of cancellation is received, the materials become the property of the owner

119. Of the following, which is best for determining the number of hours required for different phases of a project and for making sure the job is on schedule?

a. bar graph and chart

b. cash analysis chart

c. review plans

d. critical path method

120. Who is responsible for checking the site before the building inspector arrives?

a. contractor

b. owner

c. foreperson

d. architect

121. Who would be held responsible if a contractor completes a project according to plans and later discovers that there is a building code violation?

a. contractor

b. architect

c. both the contractor and the architect

d. owner

122. After a job is completed, the owner decides to have additional work done. How should the contractor proceed?

a. Write a new contract and ask the owner to sign it.

b. Make an oral agreement with the owner.

c. Do the additional work for free.

d. Get the owner to sign a change order.

123. You have been awarded a job. It requires two days for site preparation and one day for clean-up. The contract involves two seaparate tasks - one lasting seven days and the other 10 days. If the two tasks can be done simultaneously, for how many days do you schedule the job?

a. 7 days

b. 13 days

c. 15 days

d. 20 days.

124. For which of the following would you not obtain a short-term loan?

a. wages

b. bid bond

c. job materials

d. office rent

125. As part of the safety training process, contractors' supervisors are required to conduct "toolbox" or "tailgate" safety meetings. How often must these meetings be held?

a. daily

b. at least once every ten working days

c. at least once a month

d. at least once a quarter

126. OSHA must investigate a complaint charging a serious violation of health or safety standards within:

a. one working day

b. two working days

c. three working days

d. five calendar days

127. Every employer of ______ or more full- or part-time employees must keep written health and safety records for ______ years.

a. 1 ..... 3

b. 7 ..... 4

c. 10 .... 3

d. 11 .... 5

128. If required safety devices are missing from tools, what should an employee do?

a. Notify the contractor, who is responsible for safety.

b. Notify the property owner, who is responsible for safety.

c. Safety devices are the employee's responsibility.

d. Call OSHA

129. The liability of the owner(s) extends not only to the company assets, but to the personal assets of the owner(s) as well in a:

a. limited liability corporation.

b. sole proprietorship.

c. corporation.

d. subchapter S corporation.

130. In a limited partnership, which partner is active in the management of the firm and has unlimited liability to its creditors?

a. Limited

b. General

c. Contributing

d. Silent

131. The form of business which is considered separate and apart from its owners and continues to exist upon the death of one of its owners is a:

a. sole proprietorship.

b. limited partnership.

c. general partnership.

d. corporation.

132. Which of the following is required to have a contractor's license?

a. A property owner who is making home improvements on his own residence.

b. A person donating labor and service for the construction of a church building.

c. A person who submits a bid in the amount of $50,000 or more to repair 25 miles of a highway.

d. A farmer building a barn for his own use which will cost $80,000.

133. From the time the Board receives the contractor's license application to the time the license is issued, out of state applicants have a mandatory waiting period of:

a. 15 days.

b. 30 days.

c. 45 days.

d. 60 days.

134. Which type of license below requires a four hour course in "Unfair Trade Practices and Consumer Protection Law"?

a. Residential License.

b. Building Construction License.

c. Mold Remediation License.

d. Hazardous Waste Treatment or Removal License.

135. According to the Fair Labor Standards Act, a period of 168 hours during seven consecutive 24-hour periods, beginning on any day of the week and any hour of the day is:

a. an employment agreement.

b. a wage garnishment law agreement.

c. a contract work hour.

d. a work week.

136. An employee earns $10 per hour. He worked 38 hours from Monday to Friday. On Saturday, he worked eight hours. Overtime is paid at the rate of 1-1/2 times the regular rate; therefore, his total compensation for the hours worked on Saturday is

a. $80

b. $90

c. $110

d. $120

137. What is a common tax related term for a business that is owned and operated by a single entity?

a. Partnership

b. Limited Liability Corporation

c. Tax Shelter

d. Sole Proprietorship

138. The Internal Revenue Service requires employers to retain all records of employment taxes for a period of at least how many years after the date the tax to which they relate becomes due?

a. 2

b. 4

c. 5

d. 6

139. Given: An employee's final wages are paid on April 30. The employee requests a Wage and Tax Statement (Form W-2) from the employer on that date. The employer must provide the employee his W-2 no later than:

a. May 30 of the same year.

b. December 31 of the same year.

c. January 1 of the following year.

d. January 31 of the following year.

140. A contractor is reconciling the March, 1988 bank statement to the Cash in Bank balance shown on the balance sheet. He determines that:

(1) The bank statement shows an ending balance of cash in the bank of $20,665.

(2) Outstanding checks as of March 31 total $5,630.

(3) The bank erroneously charged the Company's account for a check in the amount of $300 on March 21.

(4) The bank statement reflects a $15 service charge which has not been entered in the company's accounting records.

(5) A deposit in the amount of $1,500 made on March 29 was not posted by the bank until April 1. After completing the reconciliation, the contractor finds that the Cash in Bank balance shown on the March 31 balance sheet should be:

a. $16,835.

b. $17,200.

c. $20,665.

d. $22,165.

141. A contractor estimates the following direct costs on a job:

Materials $20,000

Materials' sales tax 6%

Labor $10,000

Overhead markup 50% of labor costs

Contingencies $1,000

Profit markup 10% of total costs

Assume that all costs to be considered are shown above.

142. The total bid on the project should be between:

a. $36,000 and $38,000

b. $38,000 and $40,000

c. $40,000 and $42,000

d. $42,000 and $44,000

143. When a contractor will provide the financing, permitting, and land for the owner of a project, this is called a:

a. Traditional Contract.

b. Turnkey Project.

c. Phased Contract.

d. Fast-track Project.

144. The retainage is paid the contractor:

a. at the midway point of the project.

b. when the project is substantially completed.

c. when the project is finished.

d. when the lien period has expired and no lien has been filed.

145. A periodic payment or cost reimbursement made to the contractor during the construction period is a:

a. retention release.
b. progress payment.
c. borrowed fund.
d. final payment.

146. Theft of office equipment would be covered under which type of policy below?

a. Comprehensive General Liability.
b. Director's and Officer's Liability.
c. Professional Liability.
d. Property Insurance.

147. A lien is best defined as:

a. a legal interest one person has in the property of another.
b. a legal claim against real property for payment of fees owed for the improvement of that property.
c. the title to real property held in trust until claims are settled.
d. a right which prevents an individual from occupying his own home until all improvements have been paid for.

148. OSHA requires employers to post an annual summary of occupational injuries and illnesses. This summary shall be posted no later than:

a. December 1
b. January 1
c. February l
d. une 1

149. The Occupational Safety and Health Act requires which employers to have an emergency action plan in place in writing for their employees?

a. All employers.
b. Only employers with 10 or more employees.
c. Only employers doing business with the federal government.

150. The initial responsibility of a business plan is to help to develop a ......... business strategy.

a. strict
b. hidden
c. regional
d. solid

151. First, you should describe your products and services and discuss the market that you are;

a. goaling

b. aiming

c. targeting

d. goading

152. If you wish to interest investors, you need to emphasize the company's profit

a. potential

b. chance

c. taking

d. deal

153. You should be particularly careful to adequately ......... the risks in the business.

a. launch

b. bare

c. disclose

d. unleash

154. You should examine customer ......... and the benefits of your products and services.

a. pockets

b. files

c. needs

d. returns

155. ......... the strong and weak points of any firms in competition with yours and look for marketplace opportunities.

a. Equate

b. Evaluate

c. Erase

d. Eliminate

156. If you can find a particular market ......... to focus on, you should investigate this further.

a. location

b. corner

c. industry

d. niche

157. It may also be possible for you to ......... your products differently in the marketplace to attract new customers.

a. position
b. set
c. spread
d. situate

158. It is not a good idea to exaggerate sales projections, and it is just as poor an idea to ......... operating costs.

a. overtake
b. undertake
c. overestimate
d. underestimate

159. If you forecast conservatively, you will be more likely to maintain an extra ......... of cash.

a. denomination
b. currency
c. pillar
d. cushion

160. While reviewing the progress, the project manager assesses that an activity has been missed out from the implementation plan. A milestone, scheduled to be achieved within another week, would be missed with the current implementation plan.

Which of the following is the next best action for the project manager in this situation?

a. Report the error and the expected delay
b. Omit the status update on the milestone
c. Report the error and the planned recovery actions
d. Assess alternatives to meet the milestone

161. An organization has recently started outsourcing work to a low cost, high value engineering center located in a different country. Which of the following should the project manager ensure for the team as a proactive measure?

a. A training course on the laws of the country
b. A course on linguistic differences
c. An exposure to the cultural differences
d. A communication management plan

162. Who should be involved in the creation of lessons learned, at closure of project? (choose the BEST answer)

a. Stakeholders
b. Project team
c. Management of the performing organization
d. Project office

163. Which of the following is a common format for performance reporting?

a. Pareto diagrams

b. Bar charts

c. Responsibility assignment matrices

d. Control charts

164. Once the project is complete, the complete set of project records should be put in which of the following?

a. Project archives

b. Database

c. Storage room

d. Project report

165. What should a project manager do or follow to ensure clear boundaries for project completion?

a. Scope verification

b. Completing a scope statement

c. scope definition

d. Risk management plan

166. What should be done by the project manager to ensure that all work in the project is included?

a. Create a contingency plan

b. Create a risk management plan

c. Create a WBS

d. Create a scope statement

167. What process is a project manager doing when she defines and documents the stakeholders' needs to meet the project objectives?

a. Collect requirements

b. Quality assurance

c. Quality control

d. Scope verification

50081252R00143

Made in the USA
Columbia, SC
31 January 2019